IMAGES
of America

DILLON AND SILVERTHORNE

AF807691

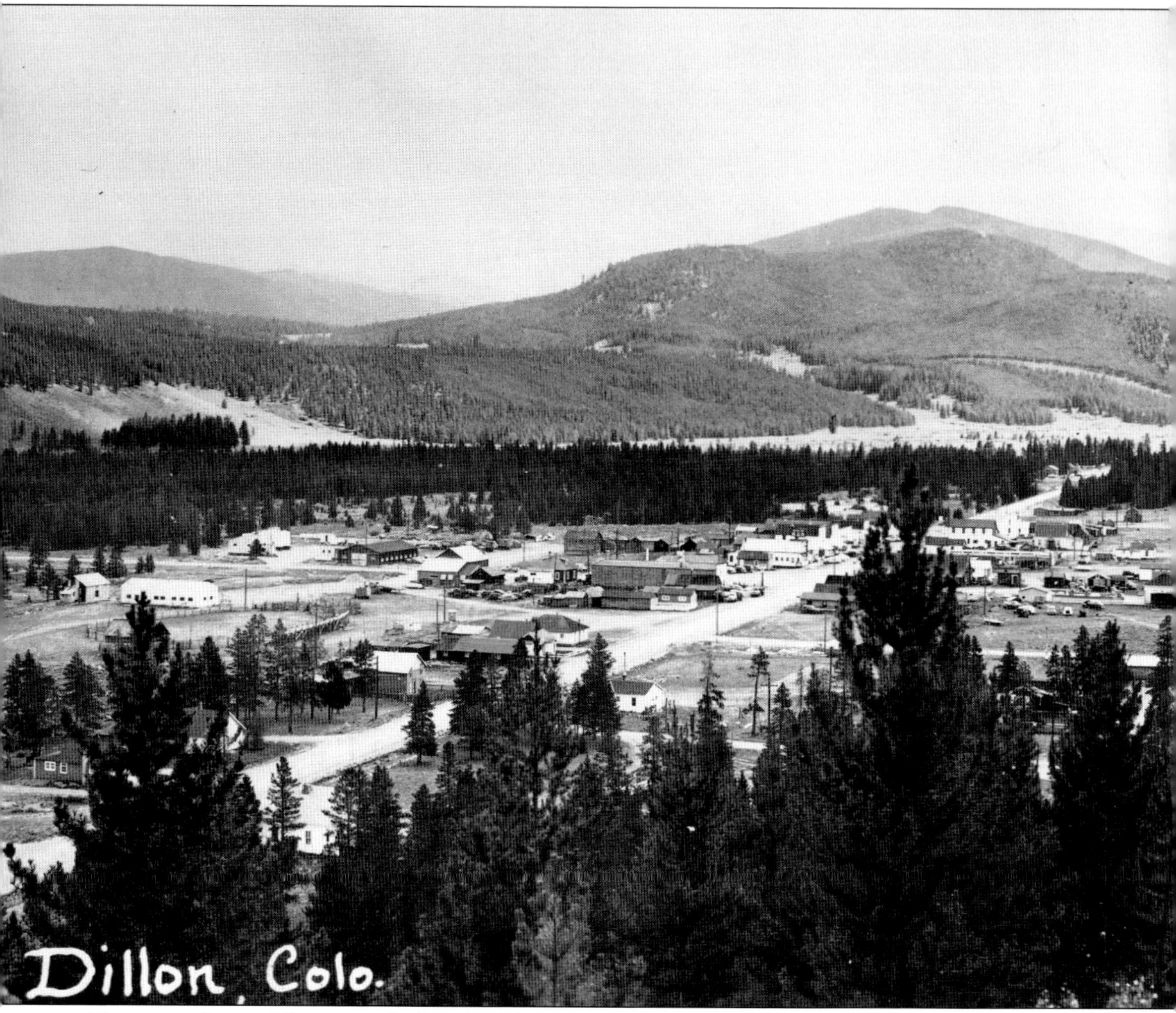

FOREVER GONE. The one-of-a-kind, old town of Dillon, Colorado, is depicted here, before it became the bottom of the material for Dillon Reservoir. This photograph was taken sometime before 1960. The view is looking south near the site of the west dam abutment.

ON THE COVER: Roberts Tunnel is seen here with its access shaft, displaying construction workers, mucking car, tracks, drilling equipment, steel arch supports, lighting, and ventilation equipment. (Courtesy of Denver Water.)

IMAGES
of America

DILLON AND SILVERTHORNE

Roy Goodliffe, Ph.D

ARCADIA
PUBLISHING

Copyright © 2009 by Roy Goodliffe, Ph.D.
ISBN 978-0-7385-7016-7

Published by Arcadia Publishing
Charleston SC, Chicago IL, Portsmouth NH, San Francisco CA

Printed in the United States of America

Library of Congress Control Number: 2009922886

For all general information contact Arcadia Publishing at:
Telephone 843-853-2070
Fax 843-853-0044
E-mail sales@arcadiapublishing.com
For customer service and orders:
Toll-Free 1-888-313-2665

Visit us on the Internet at www.arcadiapublishing.com

This book is dedicated to all who contributed to the construction of Dillon Dam and the new town of Silverthorne. Also praises must go to Denver Water and Summit Historical Society.

Contents

Acknowledgments

I'm forever indebted to Denver Water's Duncan O. McCollum, manager of records and documents, and Jackie Shumaker. These two wonderful individuals donated enormous amounts of time to recovering the images and placing them in the correct photographic image format acceptable to Arcadia Publishing. Unless otherwise noted, the photographs within these pages came from Denver Water.

In addition, Jerry Roberts, acquisitions editor at Arcadia, was responsible for constant follow-up to make sure everything necessary was accomplished with correct publishing style and technique. Thank you, Jerry.

Finally David Spencer ("Spense") must be acknowledged. He contributes time to the Summit Historical Society and to wandering scholars and their projects.

INTRODUCTION

Downhill west on Interstate 70, just beyond Eisenhower Tunnel, the new Dillon, Colorado, embraces the Lake Dillon shoreline, the pride of Denver Water. Continuing with the transportation linkage are Silverthorne, Kremmling, Frisco, Vail, Aspen, and Leadville. Silverthorne, the youngest Colorado town at only 42 years, has become a shopper's paradise with its new Target department store and clusters of factory outlet boutiques.

Tucked beyond the view of tourists, but well known to locals, is one of the highest, longest, biggest, and most secretive transmontane tunnel. This Denver Water project, using the natural law of gravity, rushes fresh mountain water 23.3 miles down from Lake Dillon to Denver through a steel and concrete water pipe boasting an inside diameter of 10 feet, 2 inches.

Old Dillon, once only a trading post, stage stop, and the mountain route of the Denver and Rio Grande Railroad, assumed the name from the romantic tale of a lost Golden City (today's Golden) miner, Tom Dillon, who in the 1840s wandered over what is now called Loveland Pass and down into the Blue River Valley. Early winter forced Tom into accepting help from Native Americans. The Ute tribe took care of Tom that winter and, when it was time, sent him back to where he originated. Tom Dillon reemerged in Idaho Springs the next spring, blurry-eyed and crammed full of exciting survival tales.

The Ute Tribe hunted the Blue River Valley and occasionally, for trading purposes, shared a strategic location at the confluence of three streams—the Blue River, Snake River, and Ten Mile Creek—with fur trappers. One trapper, La Bonte, has been memorialized with his name on a street sign in the new town of Dillon.

An idea of diverting water from the western high mountain slopes was present in the minds of Denver's early fathers. On October 29, 1907, George Bancroft and W. H. Meyers filed plans with the state engineer to bring Snake River water through a tunnel near Montezuma. The plan, as re-filed on January 13, 1909, would have a western portal elevated at 10,322 feet. Ditches no doubt would have brought water from the Blue River, Ten Mile Creek, and Snake River to the Swan River. Fortunately nothing was approved, but Denver Water did begin buying water rights west of the Continental Divide. A version of the Bancroft plan using the Blue River was filed by the state engineer on May 13, 1923. This idea was short-lived because of its cost. However, an alternate plan was filed by Denver Water with the state engineer on October 19, 1927. This ingenious plan featured a 23.3-mile tunnel with the western portal at an elevation of 8,845 feet and a dam across the Blue River, using the Ten Mile Creek and the Snake River as support feeders. The plan was adventurous, creating a water storage area encompassing all of old Dillon, including its school, church, saloons, city market, blacksmith shop, gas station, post office, motels, and numerous ranches. Denver Water recognized it was now or never to start purchasing old Dillon property rights, especially during the economic depression. It was the timely thing to do.

Early construction began September 17, 1942, on the tunnel and resumed after World War II. When Denver Water engineers recommended on February 16, 1946, that the project proceed again, but this time because of the need to regulate stream flow, along with water storage, the diversion could also provide power to facilitate a hydroelectric plant producing a minimum of 1.7 megawatts, which would feed power into the Public Service Company's electric grid.

In 1952, Denver Water retained attorney Harold D. Roberts to assist in securing water supplies from the Blue River. After several years in court, Denver won this struggle against Western Slope interests and also the federal government, who tentatively claimed prior rights to the supply question.

In 1955, Denver issued construction bonds for $75 million and, with the political savvy of Mayor Bill Nicholson, was able to secure finances for the "Blue River Plum." The transmontane project was later officially named Harold D. Roberts Tunnel after the Denver Water attorney who was most responsible for buying water rights on the Blue River and securing congressional approval for the project.

Bids for construction went out, and a contract was awarded to Potashnick Construction of Cape Girardeau, Missouri, on October 27, 1959. A higher dam was finally settled upon with an elevation of 9,031 feet and a width of 32 feet. The same dam with a height of 9,031 feet and width of 70 feet could accommodate the proposed Interstate Highway 70. But this was turned down.

The dam construction was engineered by R. Y. Tipton and Olin Kalmbach. The dam consists of three sections built upon a trapezoidal-shaped central section (series of triangles) extending from floor to crest. It became a 231-foot-tall earth-fill dam to impound 252,678 acre-feet of water. Clearing the land began April 22, 1960. Borrow areas were chosen to provide 12 million tons of earth fill. Also large boulders called riprap were placed on the upstream face of the dam wall from crest to bottom to prevent erosion from the elements.

Clearing the willow bushes proved to be the most difficult because, when pushed by heavy equipment, their limber branches just bent over, causing the construction worker to attach the necessary equipment to pull the willows out by the roots. They were then set ablaze or, in some unavoidable situations, buried.

The Blue River needed to be diverted alongside the construction area to allow land development and construction of a safety overflow port, the "glory hole." The river's outlet tunnel was to be cut into stable rock on the west side. When completed, the Blue River diversion measured 1,700 feet and 15 feet in diameter, leading to a 233-foot shaft that angles 90 degrees at the bottom to allow horizontal flow downstream. The only part visible is the glory hole, designed and constructed by Colorado State University. This engineering marvel allows water to overflow in such a way as not to spin or form whirlpools and cause damage to the shaft.

Robert's Tunnel, a construction and engineering wonder, was a continuing process since 1946. To ensure gravity flow, an acceptable gradient of 7 feet per mile required precise surveying. The elevation of the west portal at 8,844 feet above sea level placed the entrance to the tunnel below that of the Blue River's channel. The tunnel's inside diameter's dimensions of 10 feet, 3 inches would allow 1,000 cubic feet of water per second or 680 million gallons per day to flow to Denver.

The labor-intensive effort of building the tunnel consisted of pneumatic jack hammers drilling dynamite holes, loading charges, exploding the dynamite, removing the shattered rock (muck), inserting steel supports, drilling feeler holes, and pumping cement while engaging fans to blow out the dust and reversing the fans to bring in fresh air. To expedite the removal of muck and hasten transportation of supplies, railroad tracks were installed along the bottom of the tunnel.

New Dillon, a village-like atmosphere emerging out of the old town of Dillon at the expense of Denver Water, was relocated on the ridge north of old Dillon and south of Straight Creek. A circular plan with a shopping area in the center, designed by Trafton Bean, with one access road to and from relocated Highway 6, as mandated by the highway department, prevented future string or strip developments.

Old Dillon was erased by lug, tug, push, pull, and fire. The most difficult and expensive was the Dillon Cemetery. Three-hundred and twenty-seven cemetery residents and their grave sites had to be moved to a new 39-acre site east of new Dillon, facing the route of the new location for U.S. Highway 6. The Dillon Community Church was transported to new Dillon; Antlers Café and Bar was hauled to neighboring Frisco; the Arapahoe Café moved to new Dillon; Kremmling Store was moved and renamed Frisco Drug and Department Store; Graff's Hall was renamed Three Rivers Rebekah Lodge and relocated in new Dillon; Hamilton-Dillon Hotel moved to Breckenridge; Lucky Horse Saloon was demolished; and Dillon's schoolhouse was razed. The Mint Bar, Old Dillon Inn, Wildwood Bar, a general store, and the post office were moved downstream from the dam.

Two-hundred and fifty feet below the dam embankment where the Blue River emerges from its Dillon Dam Channel, the town of Silverthorne surfaced. The area was inhabited by mostly ranchers and men who lived in trailer houses and worked at the Climax mine near Leadville or on the construction of the Dillon Dam. City fathers, like Clayton Hill, envisioned the town as a four-season sports destination and voted to incorporate the town September 1967. But Silverthorne also had a placer mining legacy. The heart of the town grew up on Judge Marshel Silverthorn's 1881-patented placer mining claim on the west side of the Blue River. Judge Silverthorn was many things in addition to being a miner and a rancher; he was also a judge on the 1860s miner's court for the Blue River diggings. (An "e" was later added to the town's name to be fashionable. Also Marshel was never Marshall.)

Water diversion from the western slope to the eastern side of the Continental Divide is what has allowed Denver to become the major city it is today. The first major transmontane diversion was through David Moffet's rail track tunnel bore. After purchasing the rights, Denver Water retrofitted the eight-foot bore with steel rebar and concrete, channeled surface land sufficient to gather western slope water, constructed reservoirs in which to store the water, and welded together a long pipe to carry the water into the city. The first water rushed through in 1936.

Poet-essayist Tomas H. Ferril expressed many Coloradoans' feelings regarding water. "I was born in Denver," Tom says. "I love every square inch of Colorado's 66,718,080 acres, but when some body writes to me, asking how to spend a pleasant vacation in our beautiful Rocky Mountains, my innards tie up into knots. I loathe tourists. I hate myself when I get crowded into being one. From my window, as I write, I see two huge new skyscrapers and more are on the way. They too must have water, but every drop of water is already appropriated. . . . Colorado's water war seems insoluble."

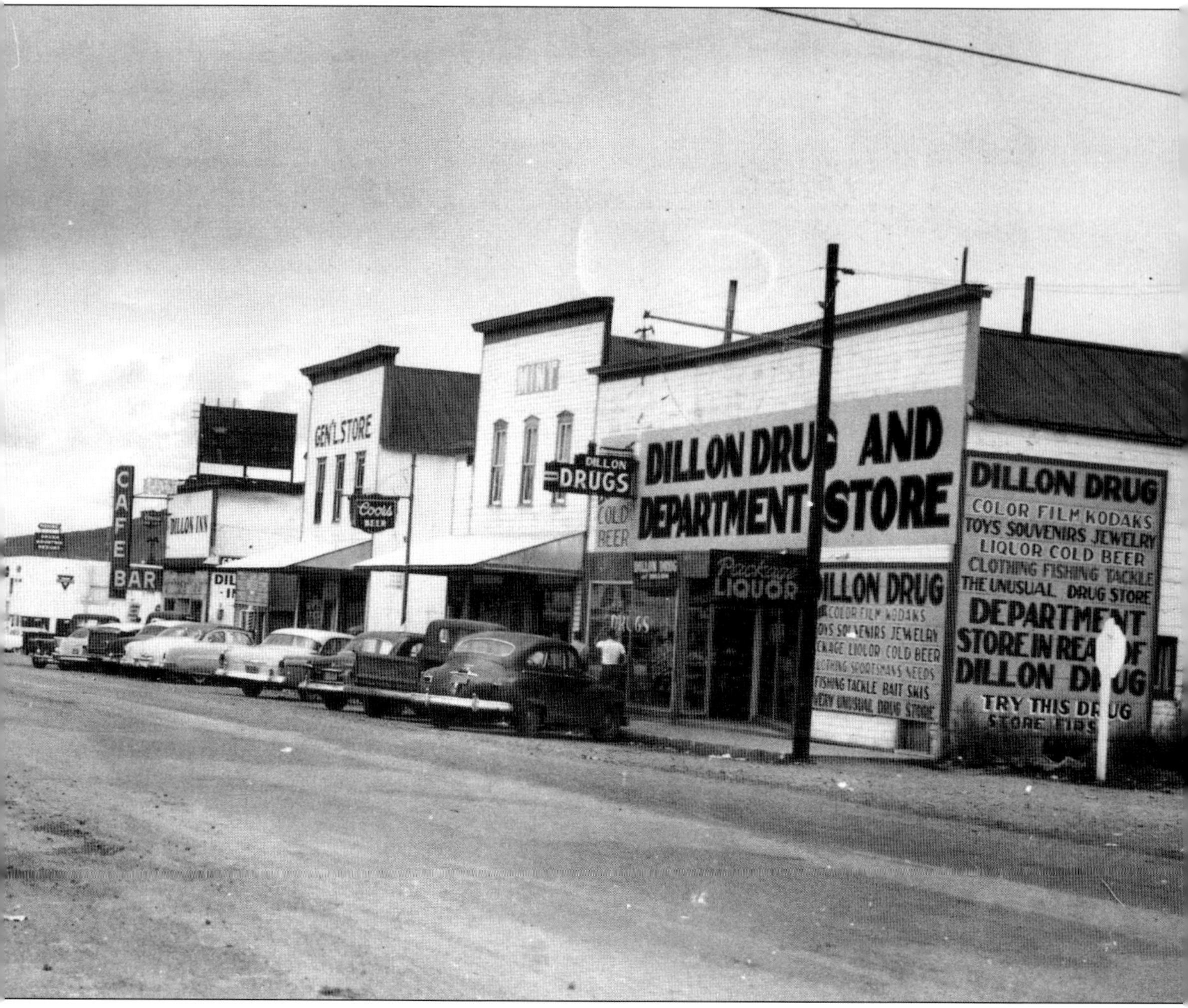

Main Street, Dillon. This photograph was taken sometime during 1957. The view is north, offering one last look at old Dillon.

One

Old Town Before the Dam

There was an old town of Dillon before the coming of the railroads, and there was another one after they left. It was merely older and poorer because the mines up and down the once beautiful Blue River had played out.

Mid-20th-century Dillon—a mere shell of its former self—consisted of two main streets going north and south for five blocks, with five streets going east and west. Businesses that were breaking even were located on Main Street, which was also U.S. Highway 9 leading to Breckenridge. At one time, this street boasted four saloons, one pool hall, two general stores, a butcher shop, a drugstore, two blacksmith shops, two cafés, a telephone office, a doctor's office, two livery barns, two hotels, the post office, and the *Dillon Enterprise.*

"Back Street" Dillon consisted of Hamilton Hotel, the IOOF Hall, the *Blue Valley Times*, town hall, the church, and the school.

Dillon was always a town getting ready to be "something," but it never could get over the tipping point. Sam Mishler, William Teller, Hal Sayre, and Harper Orahood initially built a stage stop/trading post at the old La Bonte Hole, where the Blue, Snake, and Ten Mile Rivers meet. In early 1873, cabins sprang up, and by 1879, a road was developed from Dillon over Loveland Pass and down through Georgetown. Bustling mining traffic earned Dillon a post office, the Denver and Rio Grande Railroad, and permanent development interests on the Dillon site.

According to Mary Ellen Gilliland, author of *Summit: A Gold Rush History of Summit County Colorado*, "July 6, 1881, The Dillon Mining Company was awarded a patent for a 320-acre town site on the northeast side of the Snake River. The Denver & Rio Grande (D. & R. G.) railroad arrived at Dillon in 1882 and its rival, Denver, South Park & Pacific (D.S.P.) chugged into town in 1883. The new town rated a place on 1880's maps. Incorporation came January 26, 1883, with John Jones as first mayor. The town was named Dillon, and like the legend young Tom Dillon would endure many hardships."

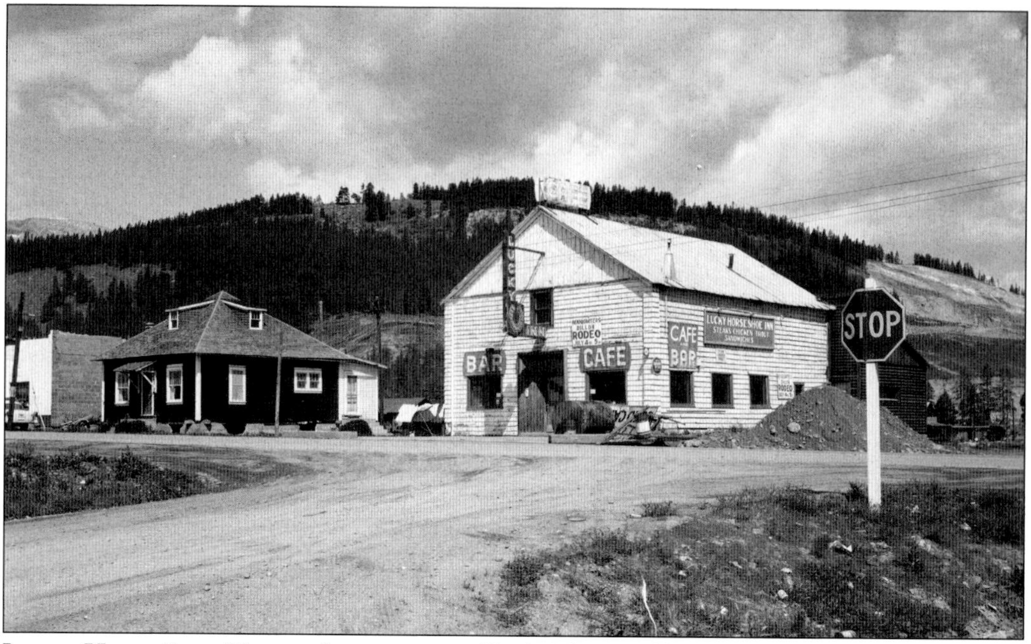

Lucky Horse Inn. The inn has run out of luck. The establishment was one of the favorite watering holes of Summit County tourists and ranchers for years. It served steaks, chicken, trout, and sandwiches. This photograph was taken on July 1, 1961, just before the inn's demise. The view is to the northwest. Notice the tar paper finishing on the home with a gabled roof next door.

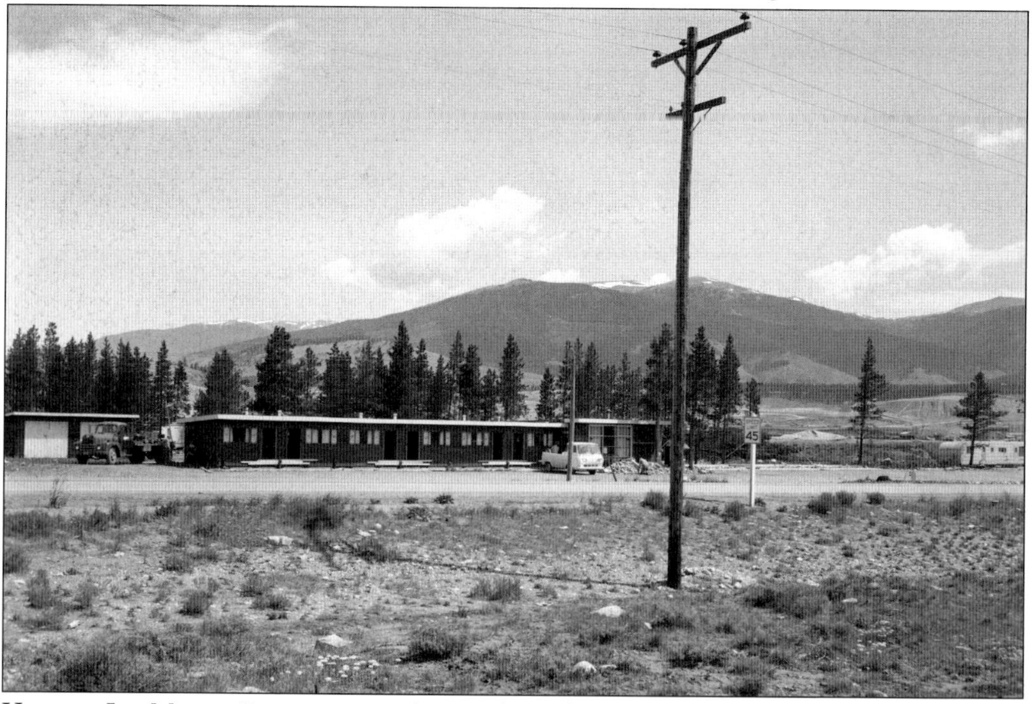

Holidays Inn Motel. Construction trailers, trucks, and equipment can be seen, which were the sign of the times for the ending of old Dillon. At this late date—July 1, 1961, looking northeast—there remains public service and telephones. In the foreground is a telephone pole.

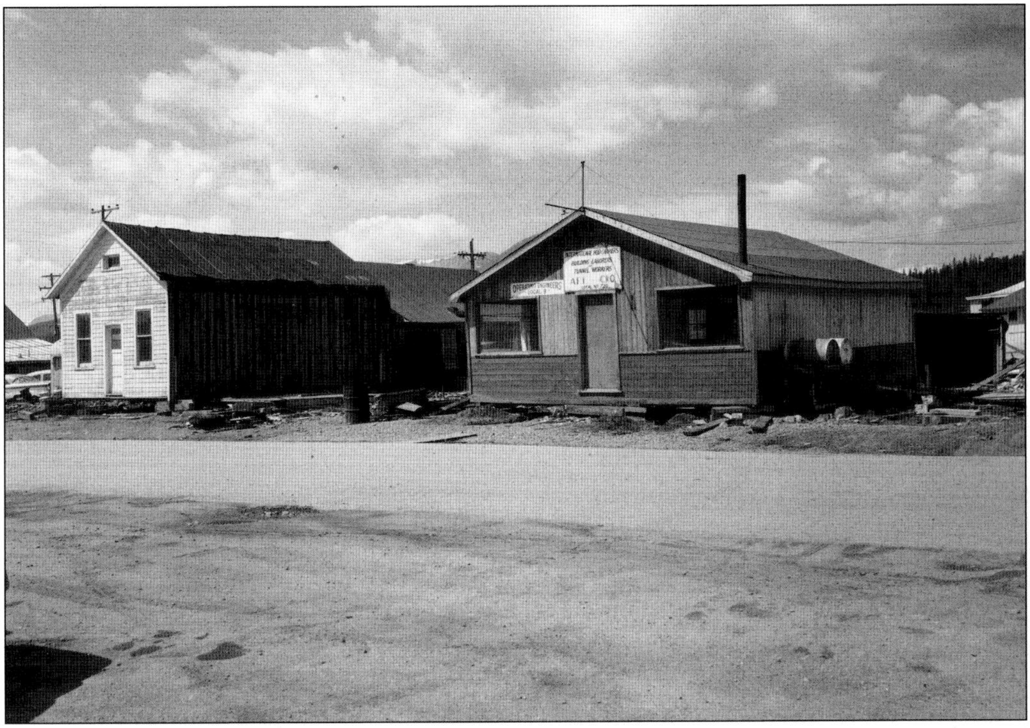

UNION HALL. Still standing tall near the northwest corner of the junction of U.S. Highway 6 and State Highway 9 is Union Hall. The view is looking southwest on July 1, 1961.

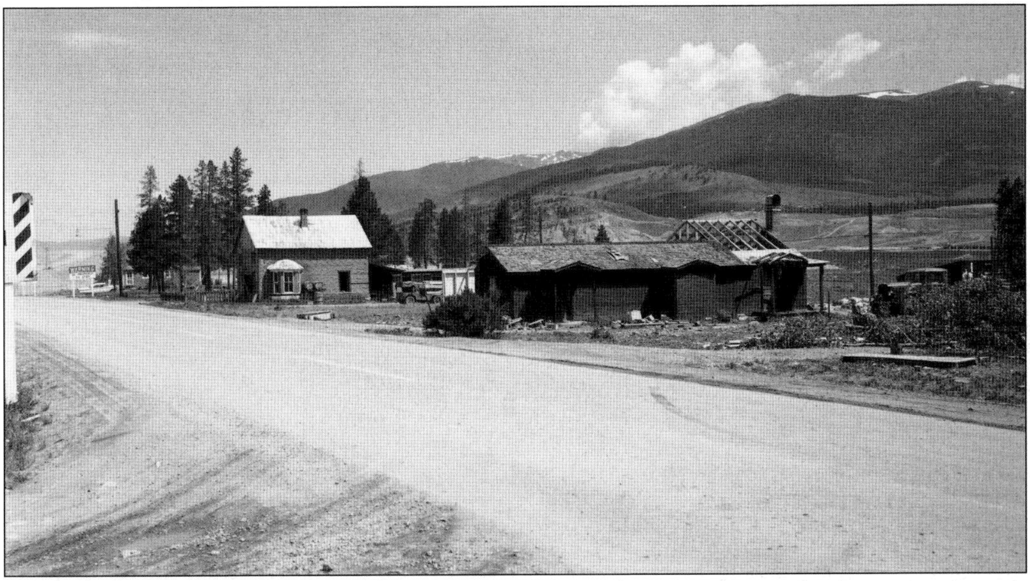

ABANDONED HOUSE. Looking northeast along State Highway 9, just north of its junction with U.S. Highway 6, this abandoned house marks the end of the highway's 50 years of usage. An uncompleted roof on a shed can be seen just under the view of the dam site excavation. Just beyond the road warning sign, one can see a small residence with an automobile parked out front. Within months, the site was underwater. Obviously, on July 1, 1961, the long-term residences of Dillon were still clinging on.

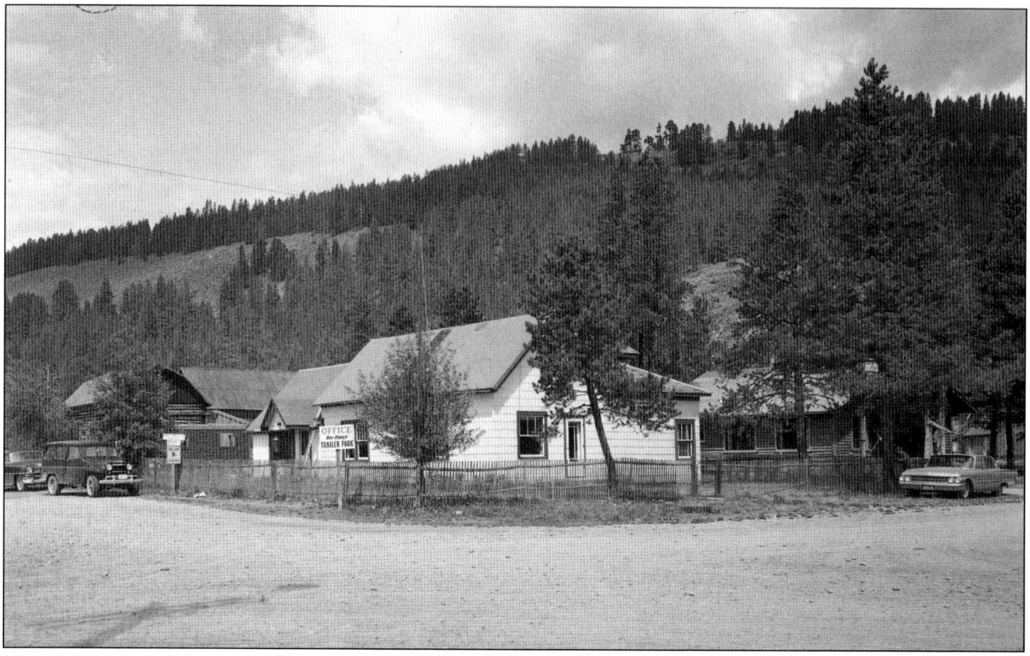

Fence Repair. The mountain retreat and trailer court is depicted. Only Main Street in Dillon was paved. The view is to the northwest. Look closely to see an unidentified person on the far right-hand side, near the automobile, repairing a fence. He obviously thought it needed it. The photograph is dated July 1, 1961.

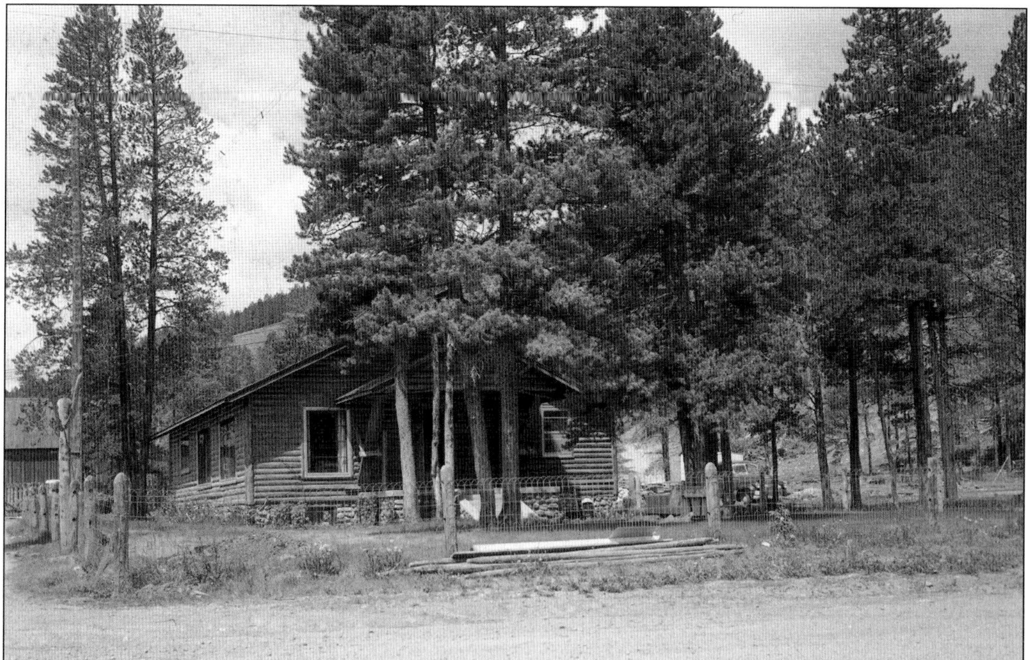

Residence of Ray Hill. The home was made from local lodge pole pines and has wire fencing and additional lodge pole pines in the front yard. The corner of the barn can be seen the background. The July 1, 1961, point of view is due west.

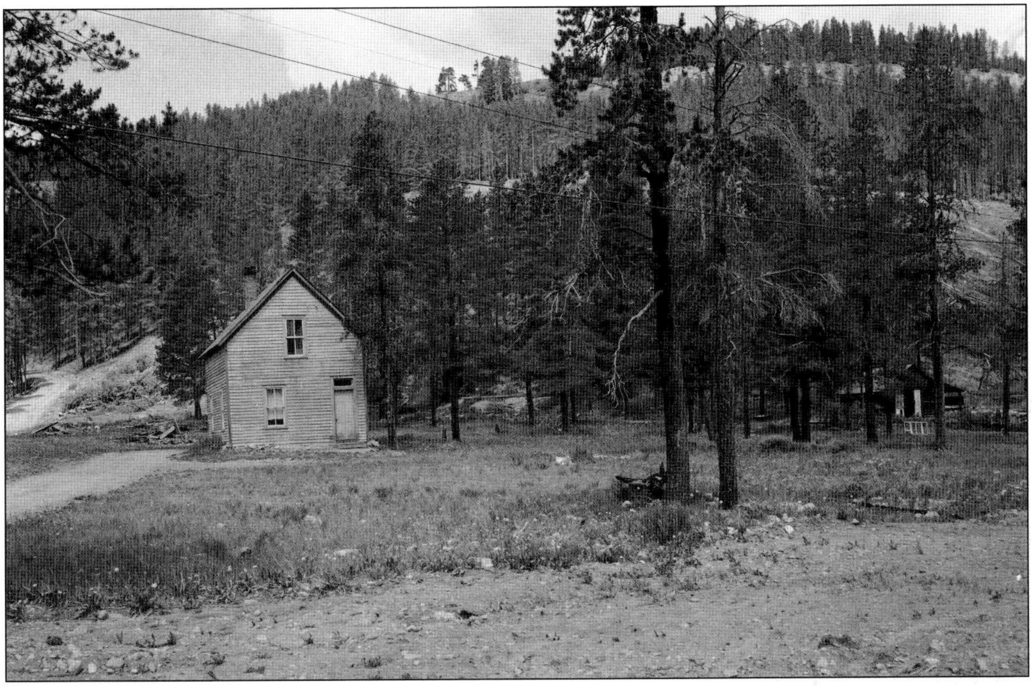

THE RICE HOUSE. This is the Rice House, situated north of Ray Hill's place. The view of the steep gable-roofed house looks west. The chimney shows an abundance of usage. A small woodshed can be seen in the rear. This photograph was taken on July 1, 1961.

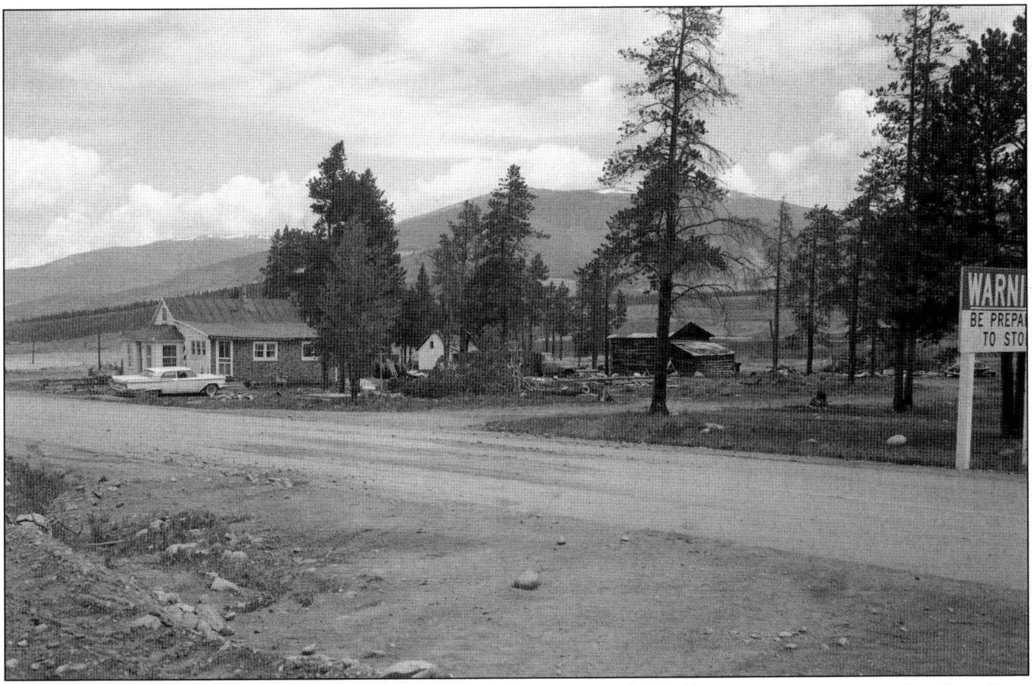

REFUSED TO MOVE. One of the few remaining homes in old Dillon is seen prior to the flooding of the site. The automobile parked along the front demonstrates how intense the Dillon resident was in clinging on until the last moment. The photograph was not dated.

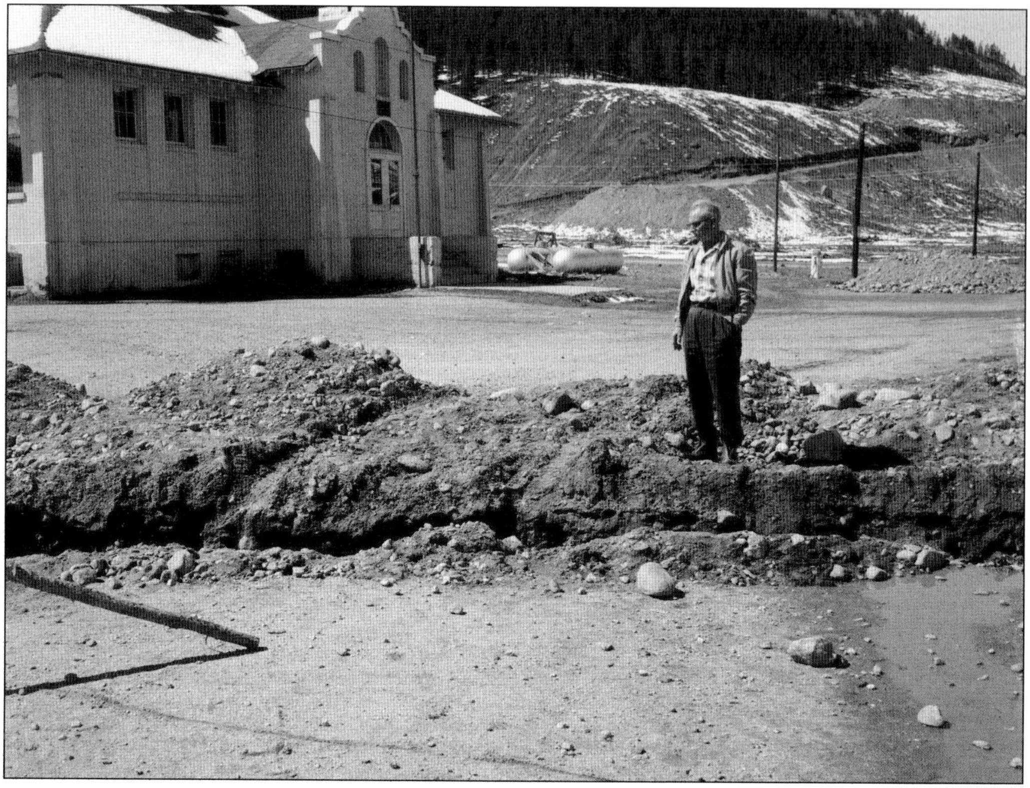

DILLON WATER MAIN. An unidentified man is inspecting the Dillon water main's interconnection removal ditch near the Dillon schoolhouse. Interesting unidentified vehicle tracks somehow crossed the ditch. The photograph was taken on September 5, 1961.

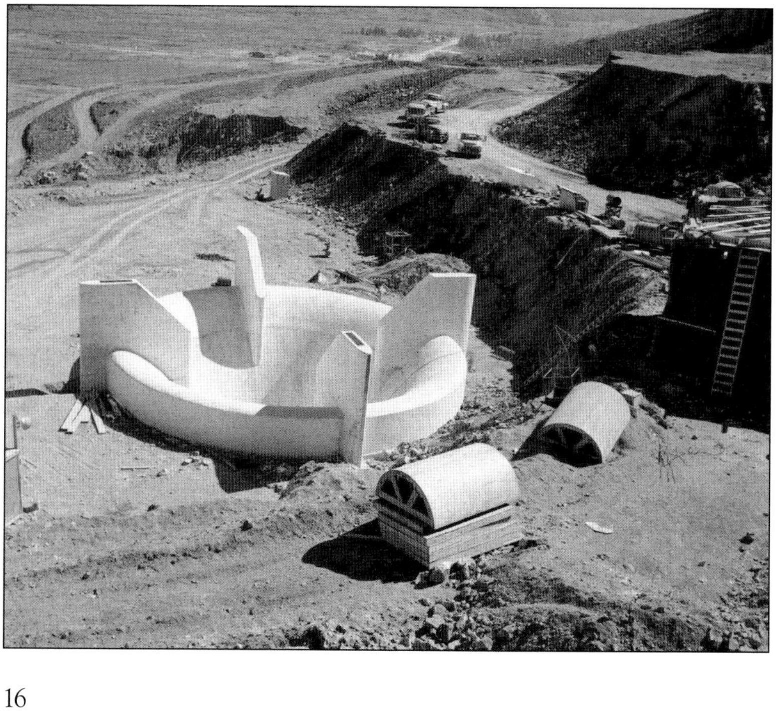

DILLON DAM SPILLWAY. The distribution crest has been put into its permanent place. The point of view is southwest from the highway cut on October 5, 1961. On the far right-hand side, in the distance, the remains of old Dillon can still be seen.

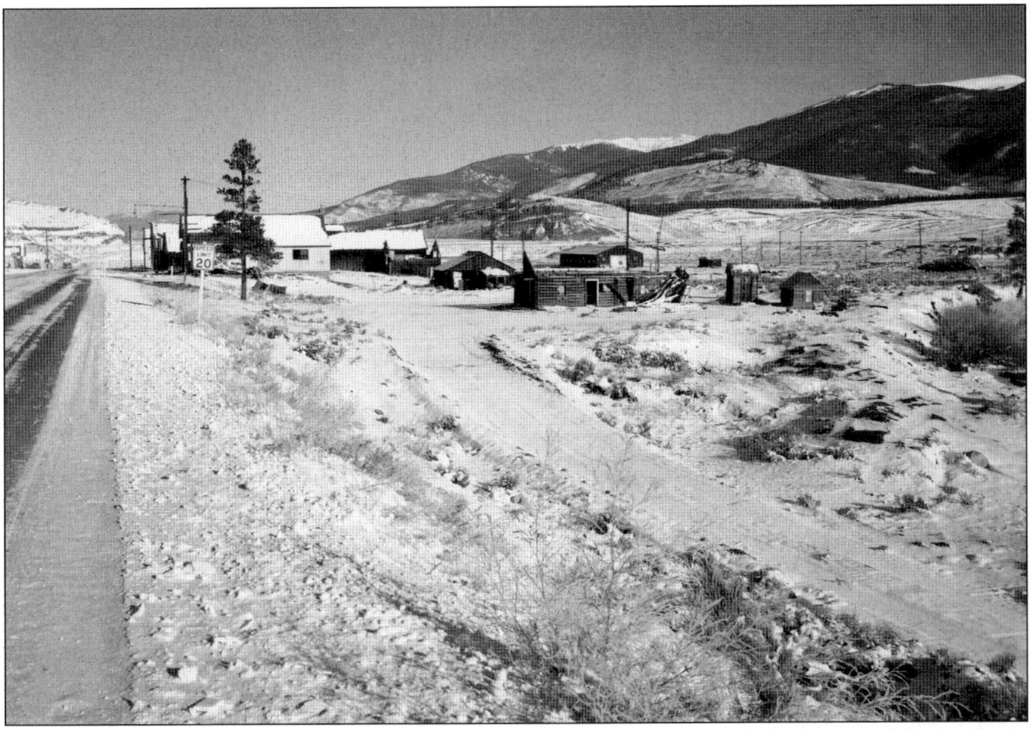

OLD HIGHWAY 9. The highway also served as Dillon's Main Street. The buildings on the east side of Main Street appear to have been abandoned just prior to Thanksgiving. The view is north. The photograph is dated November 14, 1961.

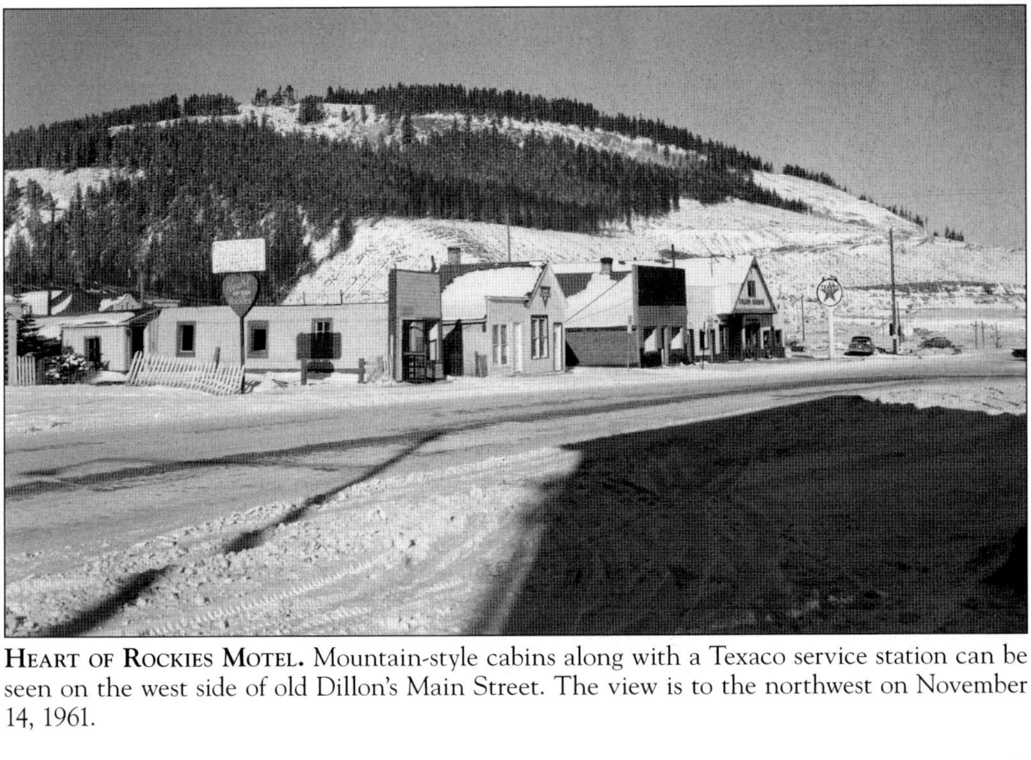

HEART OF ROCKIES MOTEL. Mountain-style cabins along with a Texaco service station can be seen on the west side of old Dillon's Main Street. The view is to the northwest on November 14, 1961.

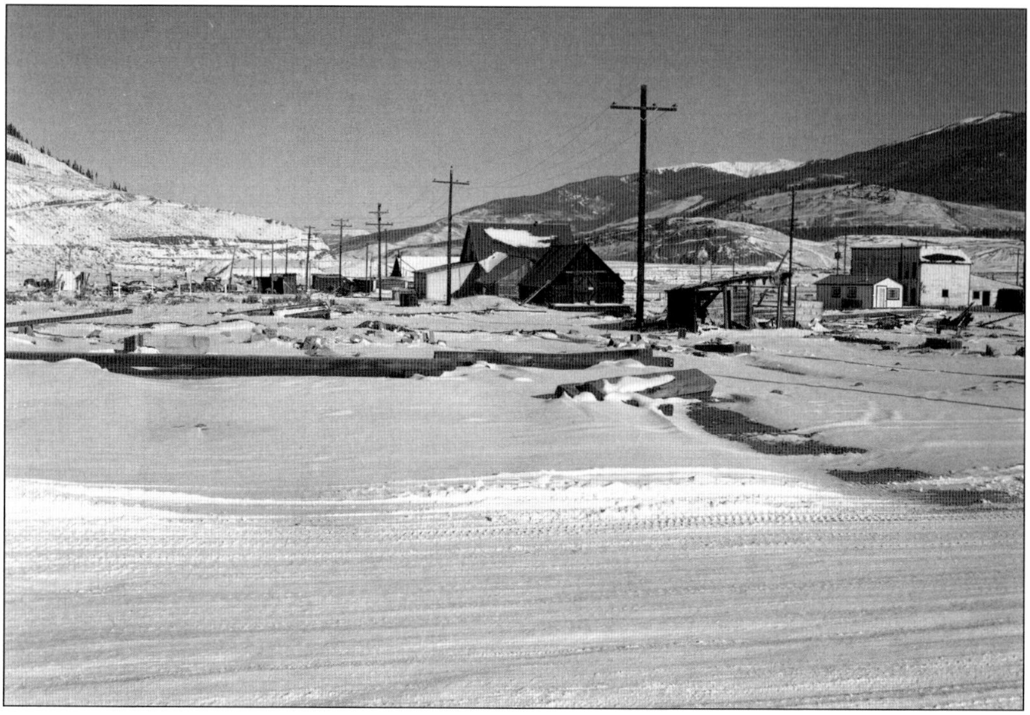

Back Street. Locally known as Back Street, this was officially known as Hamilton Street, where the Hamilton Hotel held the dominant position. This view looks northwest. The date of the photograph is November 14, 1961.

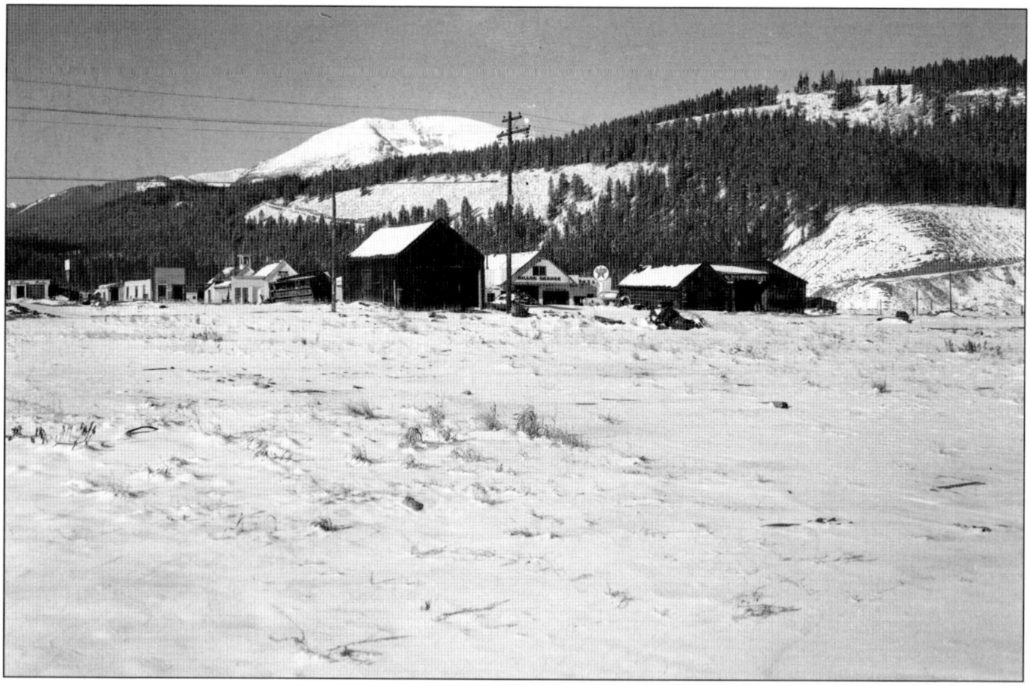

Winter in Old Dillon. This general overview depicts the town during one of its last winters. The view is east alongside Main Street, taken on November 14, 1961.

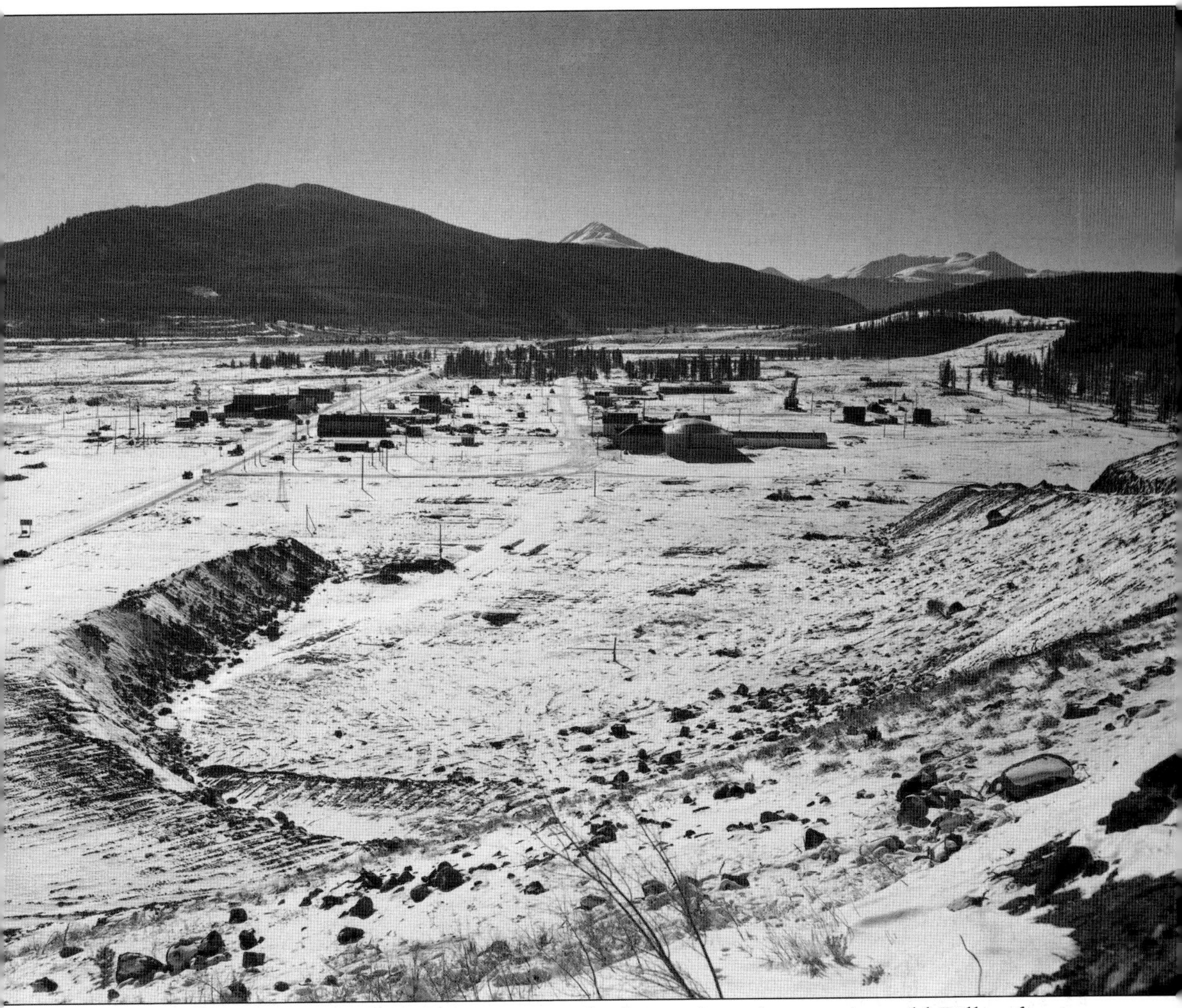

Strategic Point of View. This vantage point looks south at the one-time old Dillon from a crow's nest. The photograph was taken November 14, 1961.

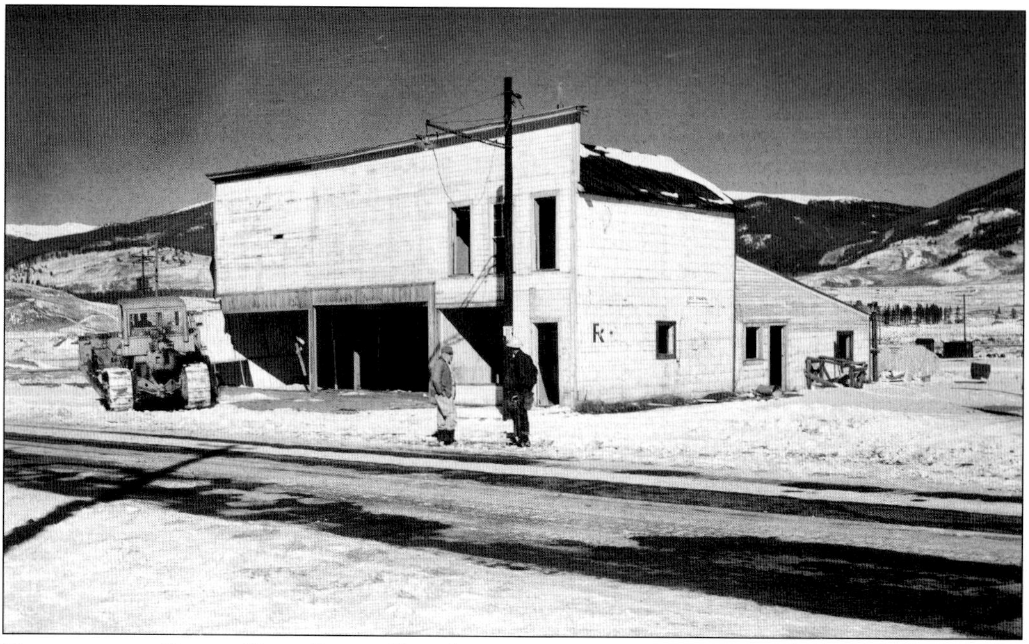

Demolition of Dillon Drug Store. Demolition experts are seen on November 14, 1961, discussing how not to hit the electric light pole while they plan to demolish the Dillon Drug Store. John Strong dispensed remedies here for years.

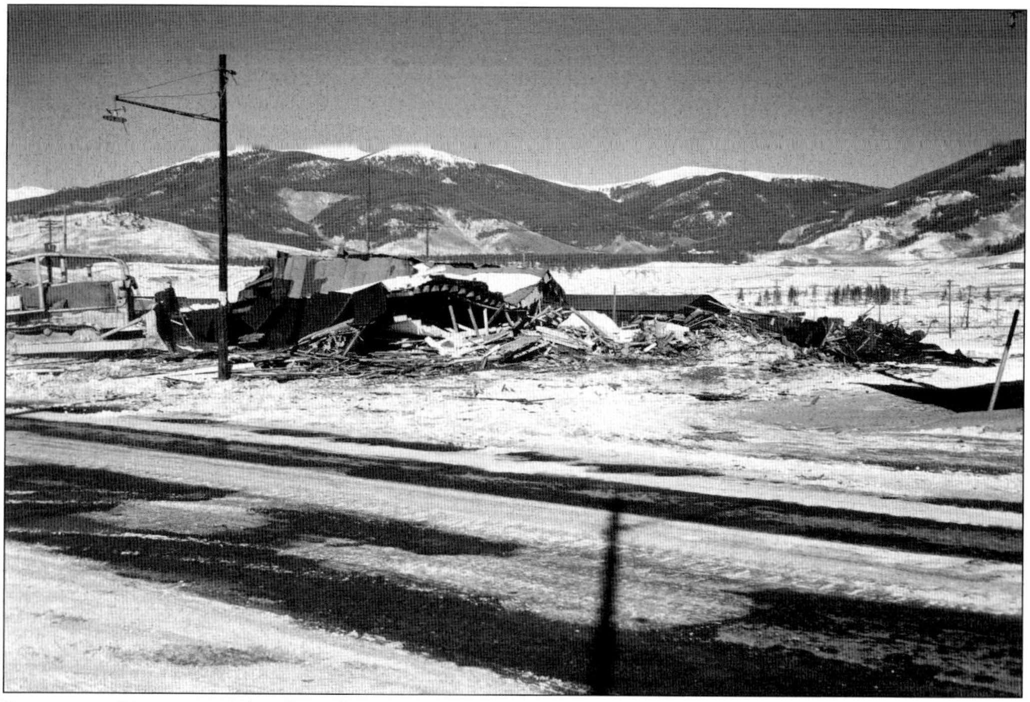

Burn the Remains. The demolishing process was to first push the buildings off their moorings and then crush the remains by running the tractor cleats over the rubble several times. Then the demolishers burnt the remains so only ashes would be at the bottom of Lake Dillon. The photograph was taken on November 14, 1961.

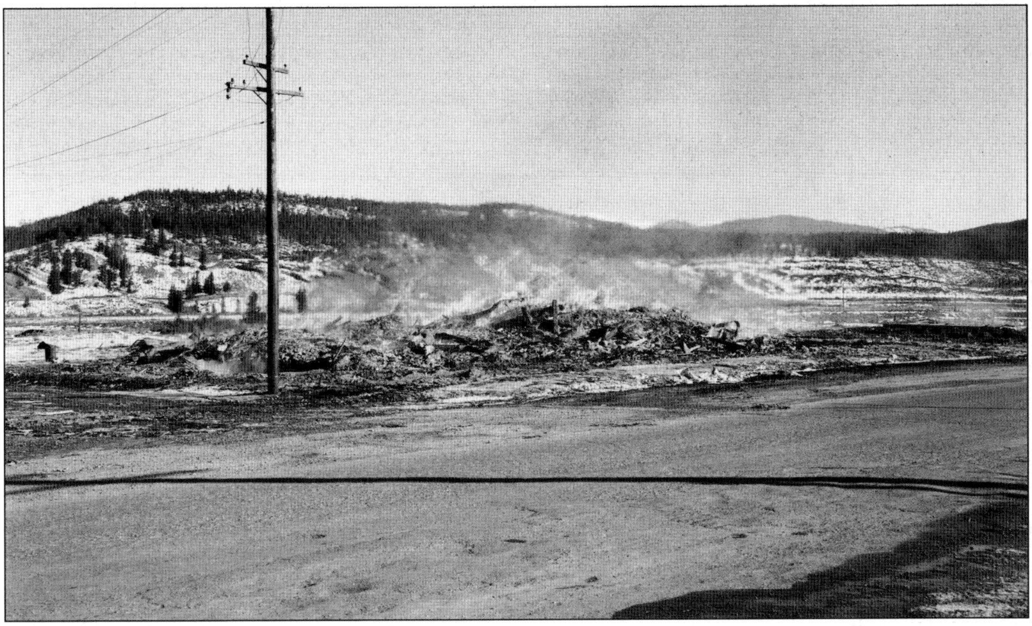

Central Grocery Store. Dillon went through many types and owners of grocery stores. A. B. Tubs and his son operated a meat and grocery store. The Albers' store gave way to the new General Supply House, which locals called "City Market," and Saul Baron, an orthodox Jew who kept a strict kosher product line, also ran a store. This photograph was taken on November 28, 1961, and depicts the burning of the remains of General Grocery Store. The view looks southeast.

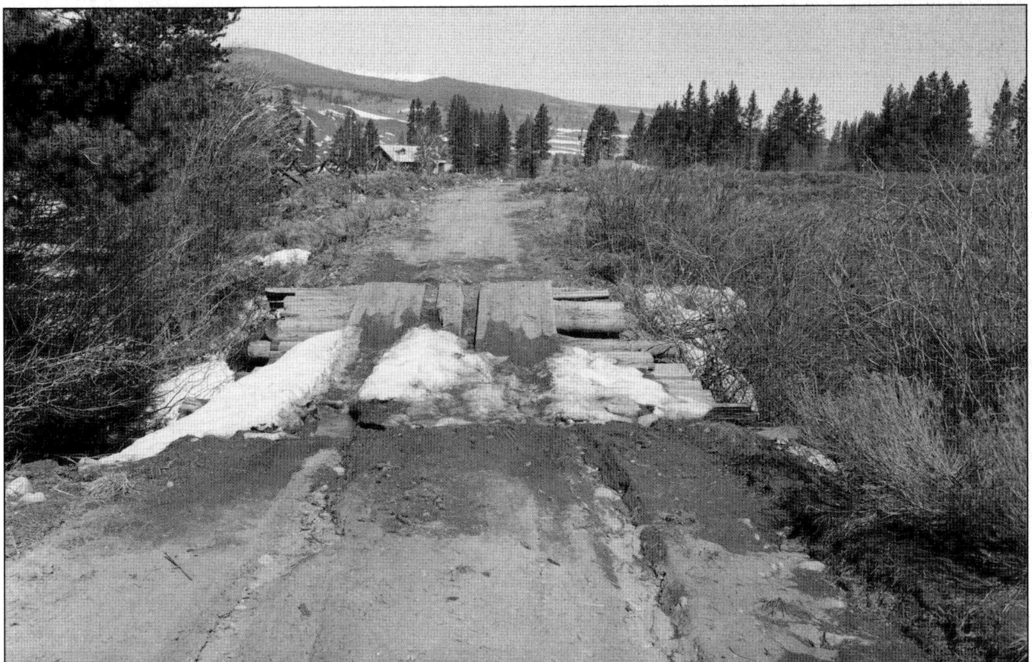

Abandoned Bridge. The bridge on an abandoned Summit County road north of the gauging station appears broken and in need of repairing. However, when news came of the new dam that was to be built, there was no need to fix the bridge. This view looks north on April 23, 1962.

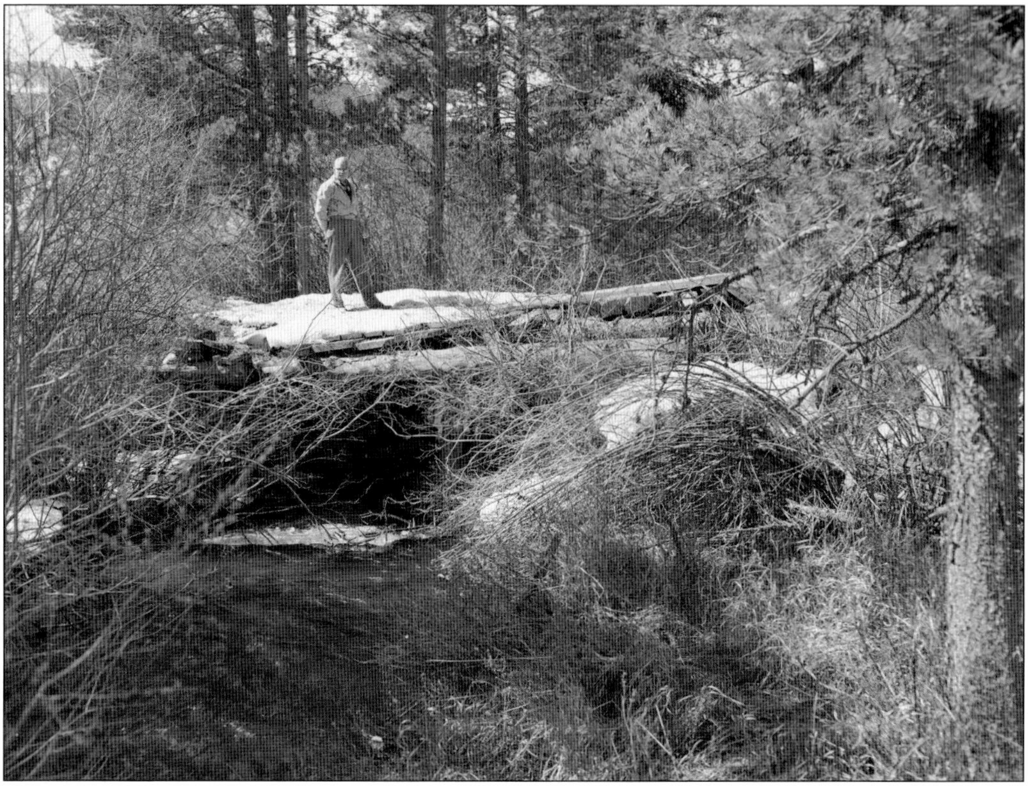

STRAIGHT CREEK BRIDGE. Knotted and weathered sagebrush has begun to overrun the bridge in this view. The unidentified man wearing street clothes stares into the camera lens. The point of view is east on April 23, 1962.

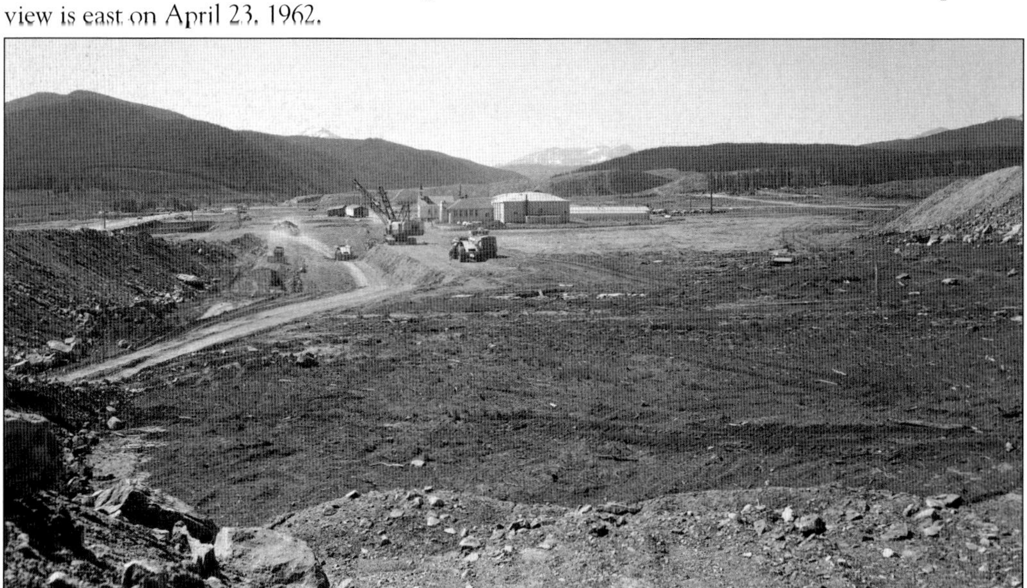

CROW'S NEST VIEW. The image looks across Borrow Area No. 7, which was a designated fill-soil source. The Dillon Dam took many years to build and went through many seasons. This photograph was taken on June 15, 1962.

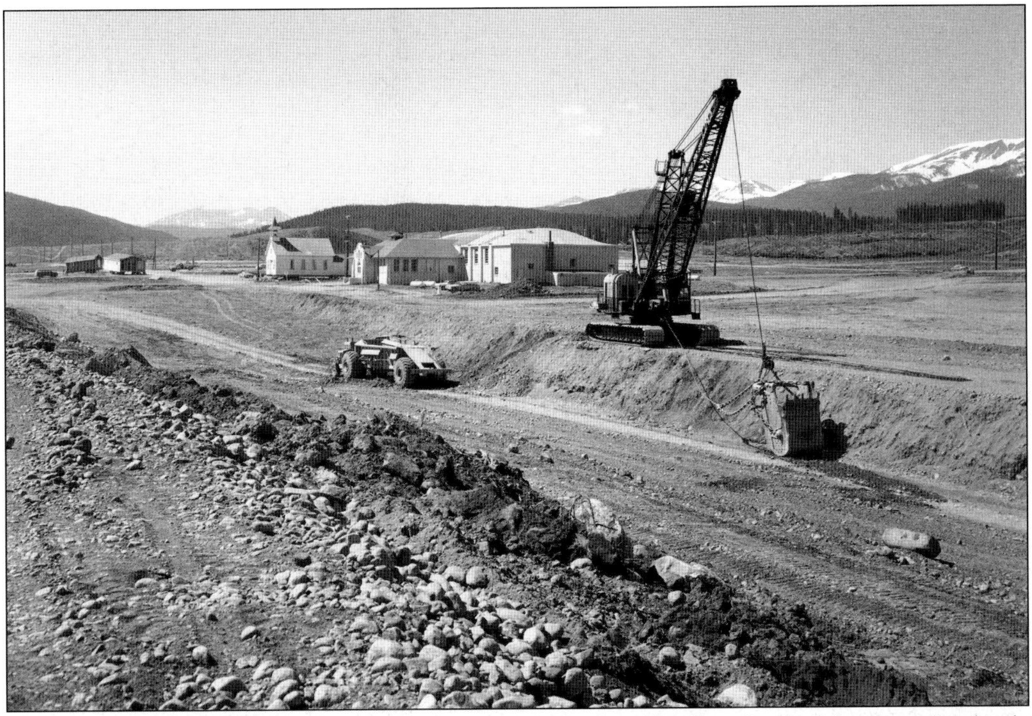

Excavating Old Town. The Dillon Community Church and Dillon Grade School can be clearly seen to the right of the excavation site in this June 15, 1962, photograph.

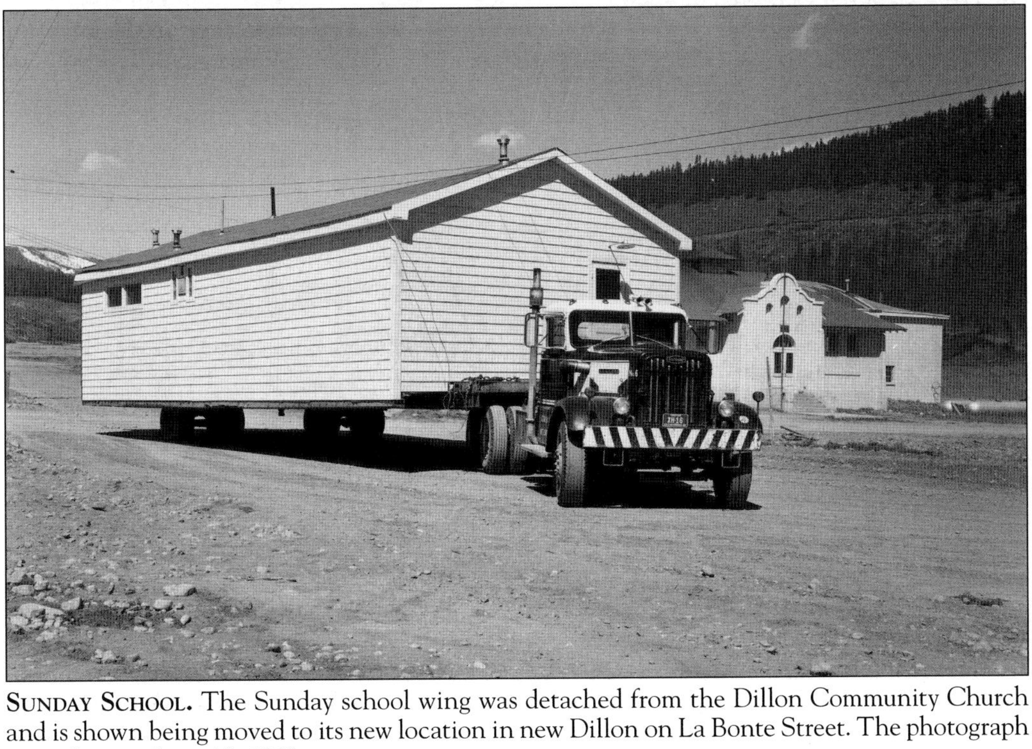

Sunday School. The Sunday school wing was detached from the Dillon Community Church and is shown being moved to its new location in new Dillon on La Bonte Street. The photograph was taken on June 15, 1962.

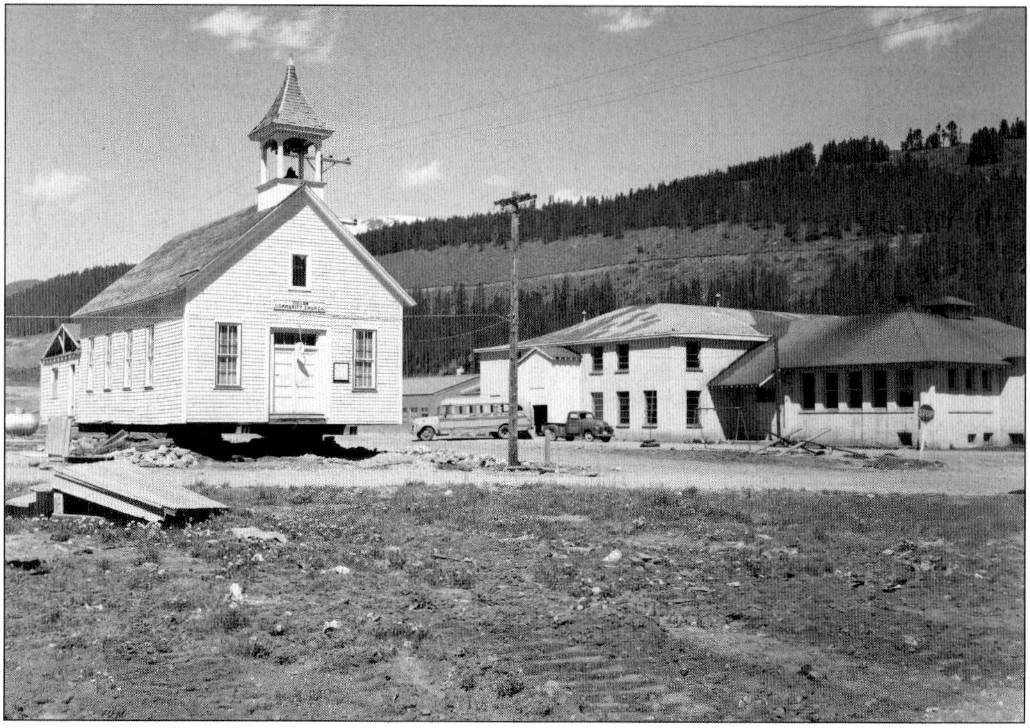

DILLON COMMUNITY CHURCH. The church had been prepared for its relocation to the new town of Dillon on La Bonte Street. At one time, the well-traveled itinerant Methodist preacher John Lewis Dyer stayed in Dillon and preached in Dillon. This photograph was taken on June 15, 1962.

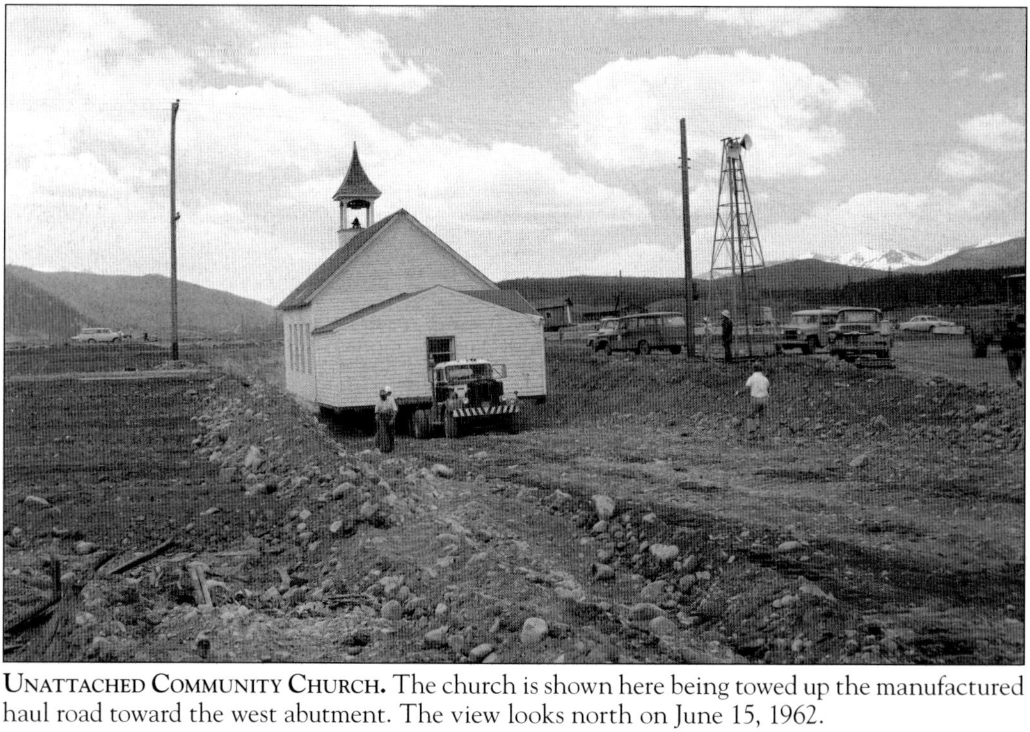

UNATTACHED COMMUNITY CHURCH. The church is shown here being towed up the manufactured haul road toward the west abutment. The view looks north on June 15, 1962.

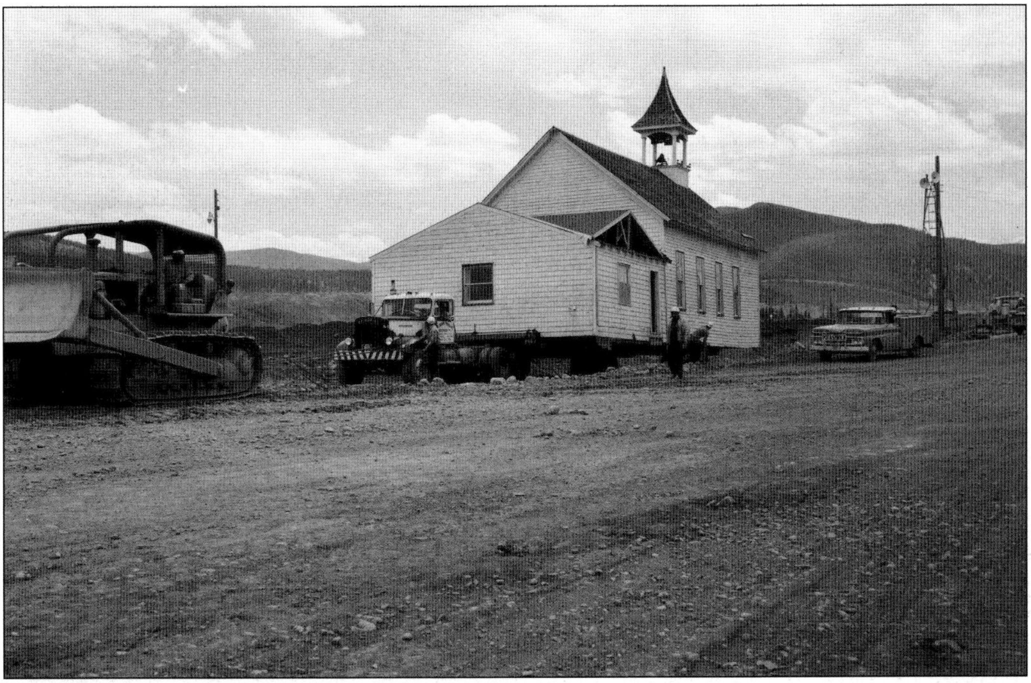

Spiritual Moment. Rumor has it that an unidentified preacher refused to leave the Dillon Community Church, fearing for its life as it was towed over gullies and rocks across the downstream Zone 2 embankment on June 15, 1962.

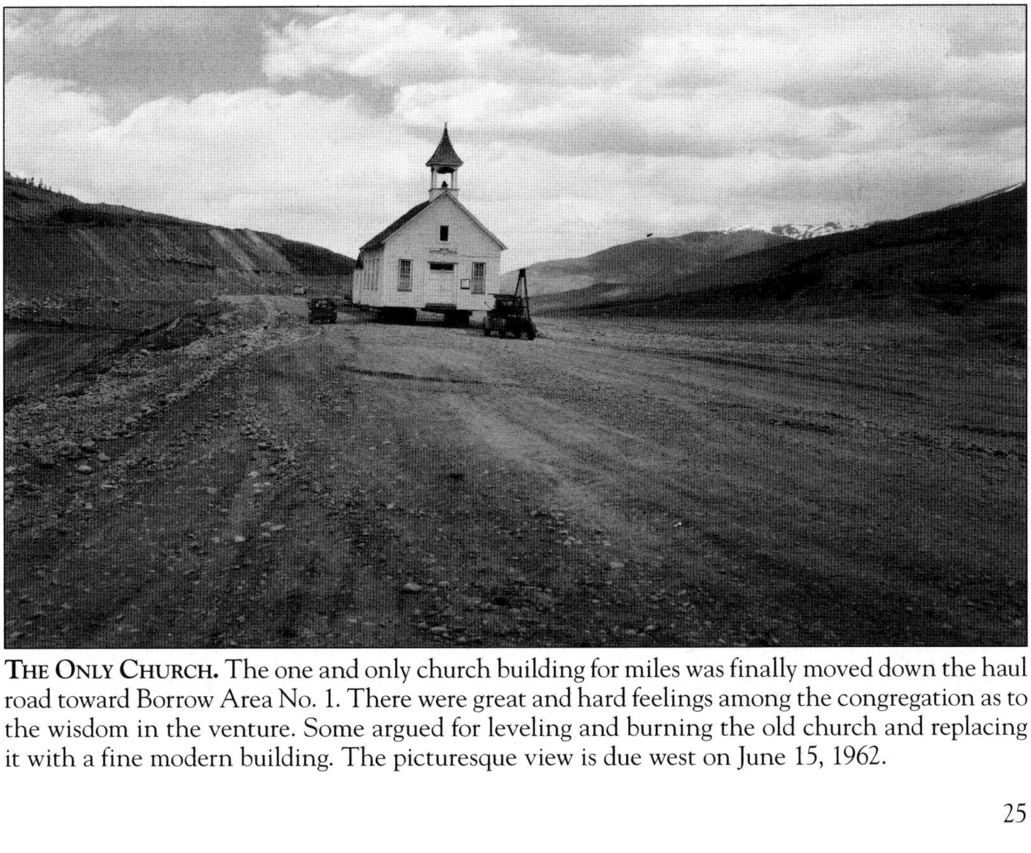

The Only Church. The one and only church building for miles was finally moved down the haul road toward Borrow Area No. 1. There were great and hard feelings among the congregation as to the wisdom in the venture. Some argued for leveling and burning the old church and replacing it with a fine modern building. The picturesque view is due west on June 15, 1962.

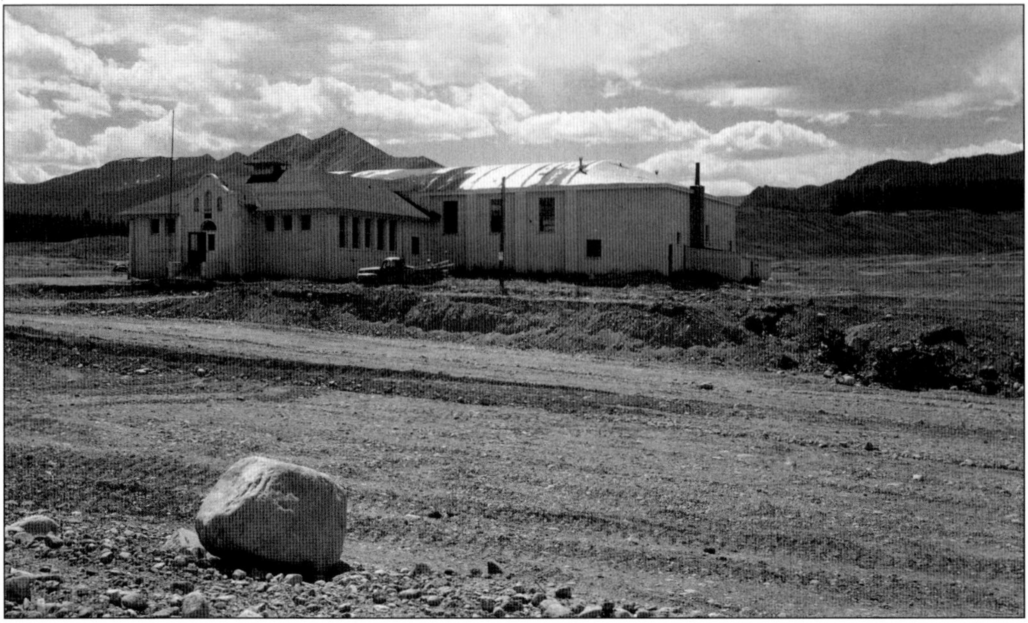

DILLON GRADE SCHOOL. Summit School District No. 8 was established, and a new white-framed wooden building opened its doors in 1884. R. N. DeBuque was the first teacher. Seven boys and six girls were the first students. This newer 1910 building is the one being demolished. The large boulder in the foreground is now on the bottom of Lake Dillon. The photograph was taken looking southwest from Borrow Area No. 7 on September 4, 1962.

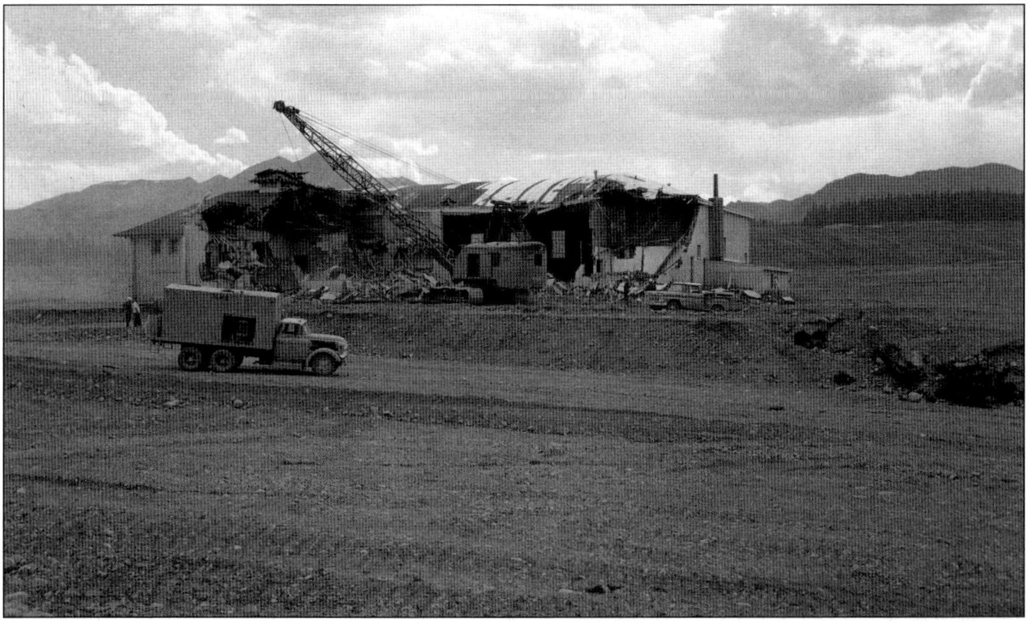

DILLON GRADE SCHOOL DEMOLISHED. Only the demolition crew showed up to see the old school being torn down on September 4, 1962, because all the children had moved away. At one time, children from all over the area walked to Dillon's school, especially those students who had discipline problems. Frisco schools couldn't control some students, and they were sent to Dillon to be rehabilitated.

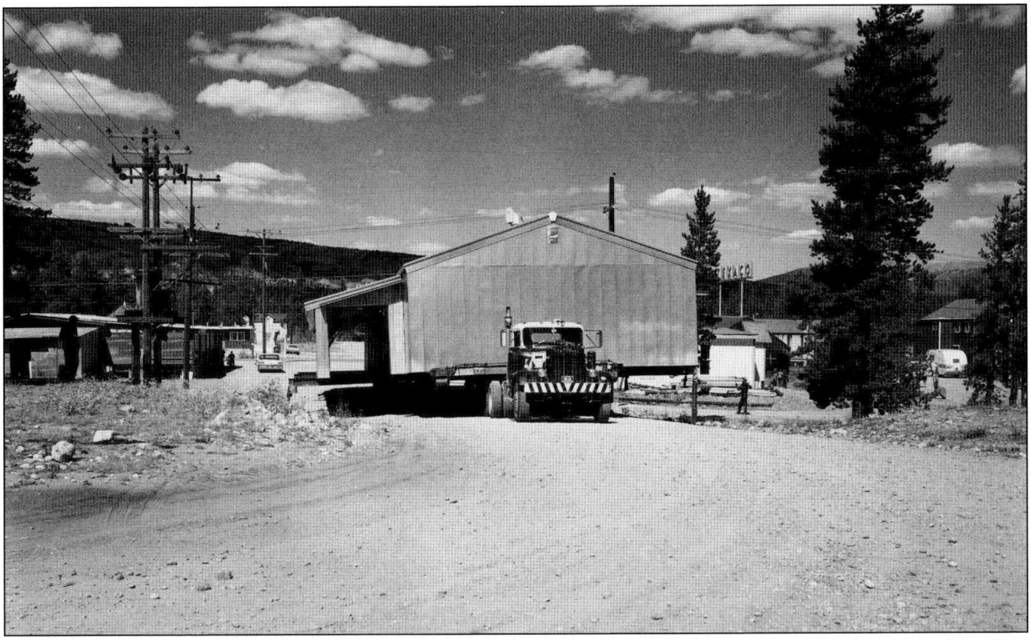

Blue River School Addition. The wooden-framed building, which was part of the old Dillon School, is shown being moved southwest on U.S. Highway 6, near the site of the former Alexander Motel, on September 18, 1962.

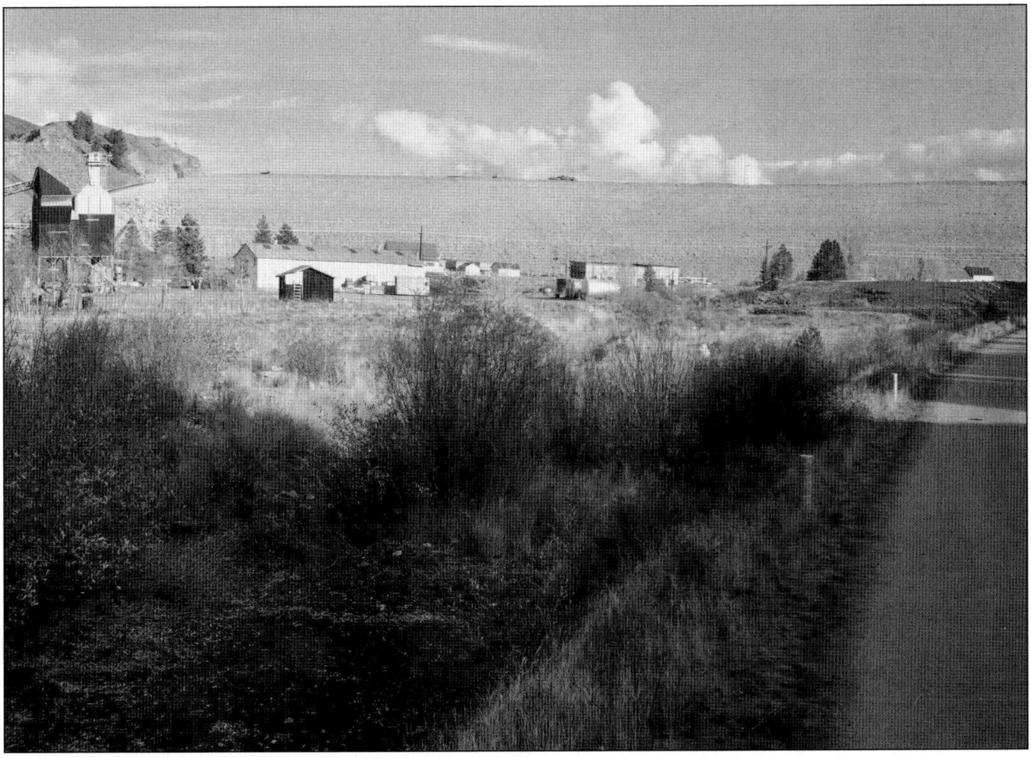

New Dillon Dam Embankment. This October 17, 1962, view looking north at the upstream face of the dam was taken from old Highway 6 at Ten Mile Creek.

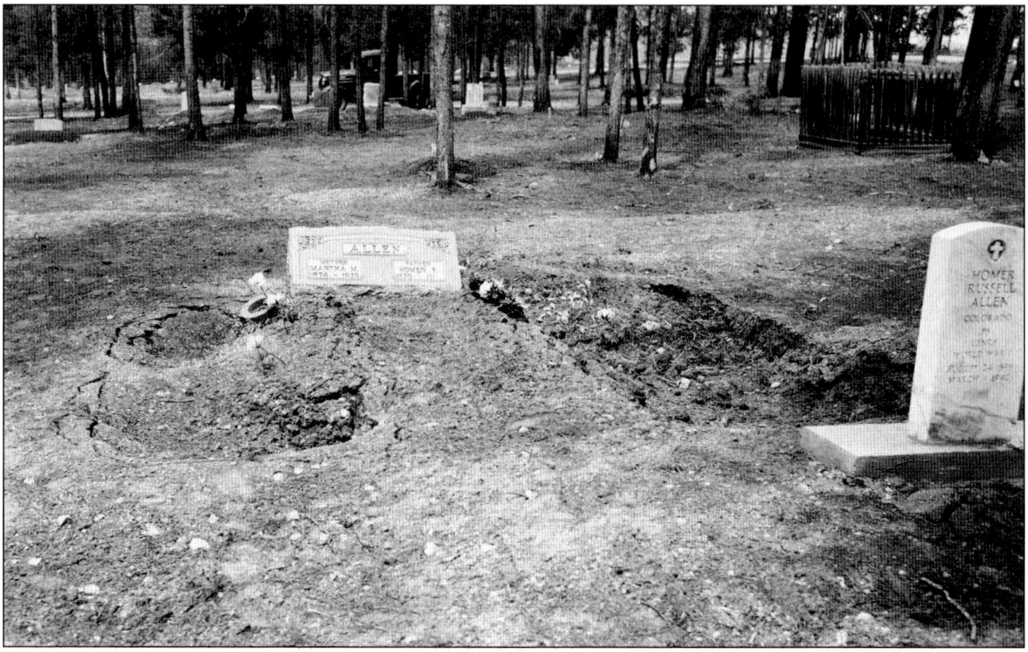

Old Town Cemetery. Very obviously untended and sunken grave sites and headstones were found all over the old cemetery site. This documented photograph was taken on May 14, 1963.

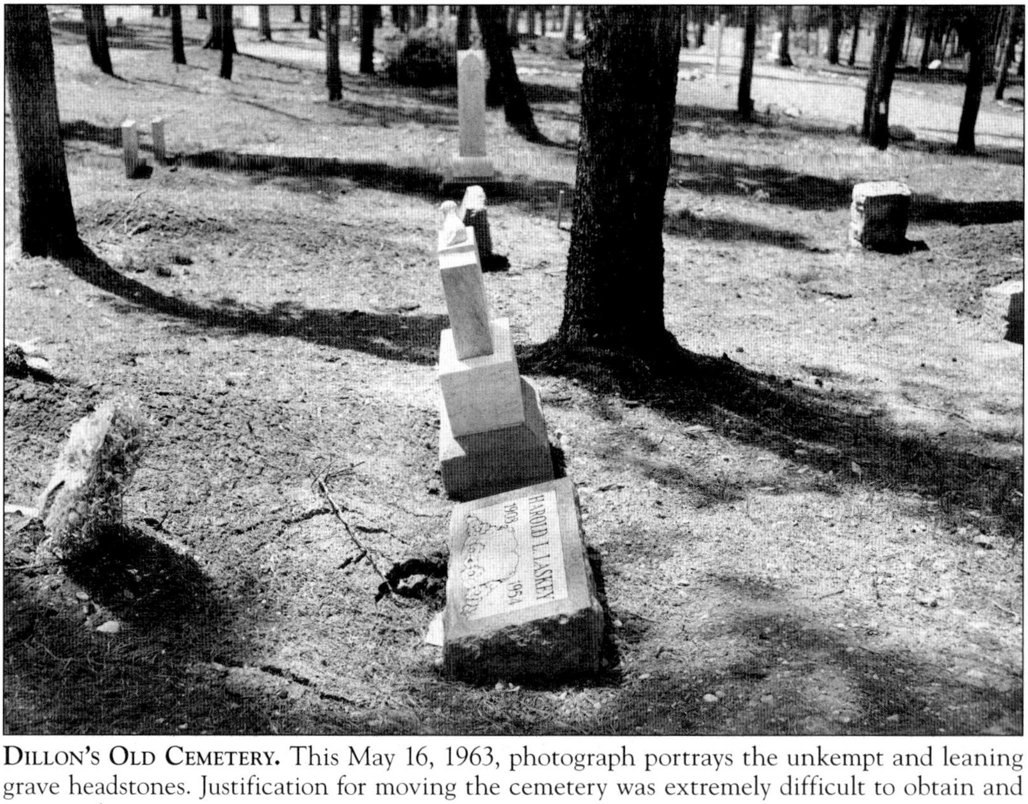

Dillon's Old Cemetery. This May 16, 1963, photograph portrays the unkempt and leaning grave headstones. Justification for moving the cemetery was extremely difficult to obtain and very costly.

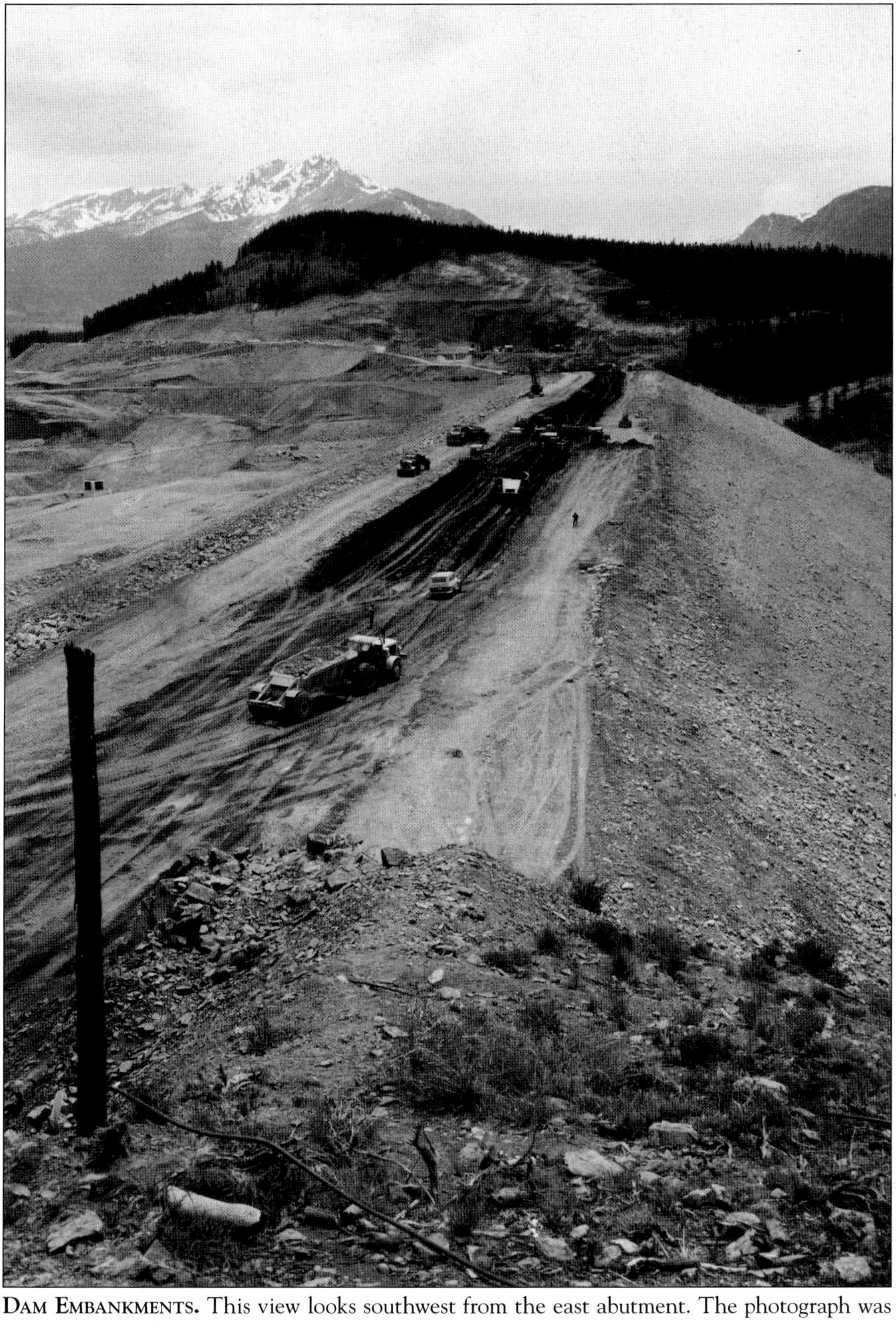

DAM EMBANKMENTS. This view looks southwest from the east abutment. The photograph was taken on May 28, 1963.

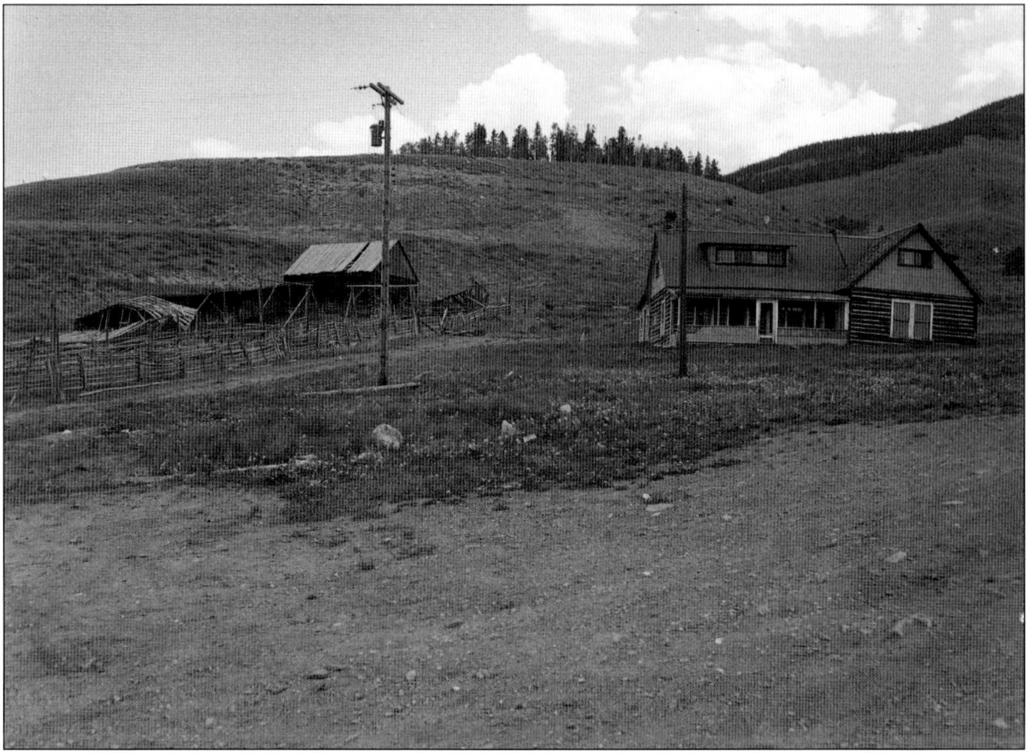

Byers Ranch. The view here is due north, and the photograph was taken on July 1, 1963. This site became the headquarters for the Denver Water Board and its maintenance staff.

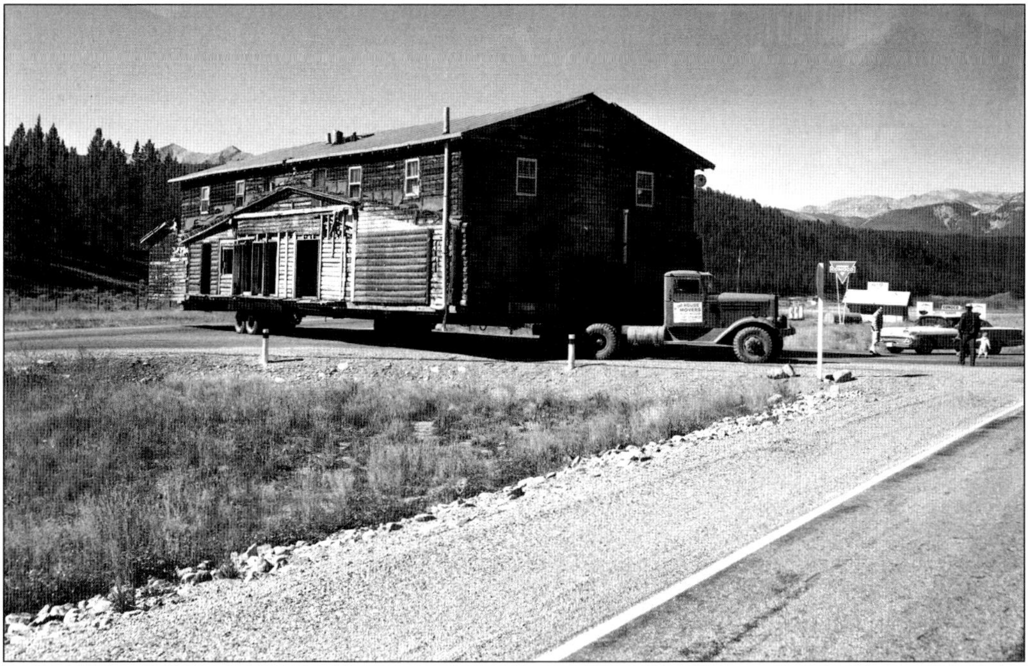

Wildwood Lodge. This building was located at the junction of former State Highways 6 and 9. It is depicted en route to Silverthorne. The view is looking north on September 30, 1963.

Two

DILLON DAM SITE

A dam is a designed barrier across a stream for the purpose of confining and controlling the flow of water. The Dillon Dam is an embankment type of dam. It includes spillways, outlet works, and control facilities. It also includes hydropower and other project purposes.

The inflow of water into the reservoir is monitored continuously, and the outflow is controlled to obtain maximum benefits. Normally, the reservoir is controlled by the outlet works, consisting of a large tunnel and a spillway, called a "glory hole."

The dam was designed and constructed to meet specific requirements. First, it was built from locally available materials. Second, it was stable under all conditions during construction and operation, both at normal reservoir operating level and under flood and drought conditions. Third, the dam and foundation are sufficiently watertight to control seepage and maintain the reservoir level. A trench, dug on the water side of the embankment, is 30 feet wide at the base and 90 feet deep. Finally, it has a sufficient spillway and outlet works capacity as well as a free board to prevent floodwater from overtopping it.

Full credit should be given to Denver Water and the citizens of Denver and its suburbs for their joint efforts in funding and building the dam, hiring Tipton and Kalmbach, Inc., to design it. The designers considered the stream flow around or through the dam site during construction. Stream flow records determine the largest flood to divert during construction. Diverting water initially involved constructing the temporary, and then permanent, outlet works—at first a conduit and later a tunnel in the abutment along portions of the dam adjacent to the abutments. In the first construction period, the Blue River was diverted into the outlet works by a cofferdam, which was high enough to prevent overtopping during construction. The downstream cofferdam was also required to keep the dam site dry.

Sandra F. Mather, in *Dillon-Denver and the Dam*, said, "In determining the location of the dam, the Water Board considered geologic structures at and below the surface. But geomorphology overruled geology. The confluence of the three rivers and the ability to maintain gravity flow," dictated the dam site. Constructing a large dike across the Blue River was necessary in preparation for construction.

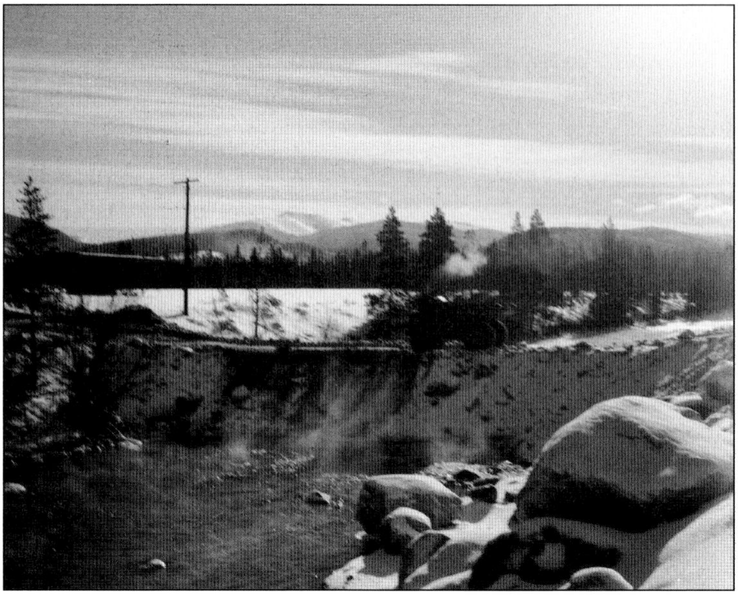

Dillon Dam Dike. Throughout history, there have been instances of dam failure and the discharge of stored water. Dillon is a rock-filled dam consisting of an embankment of loose rock, a 90-foot-deep concrete trench line, and core dam material impervious to water. This photograph taken on February 12, 1960, looking south, shows preparations were underway for the construction of the water outlet.

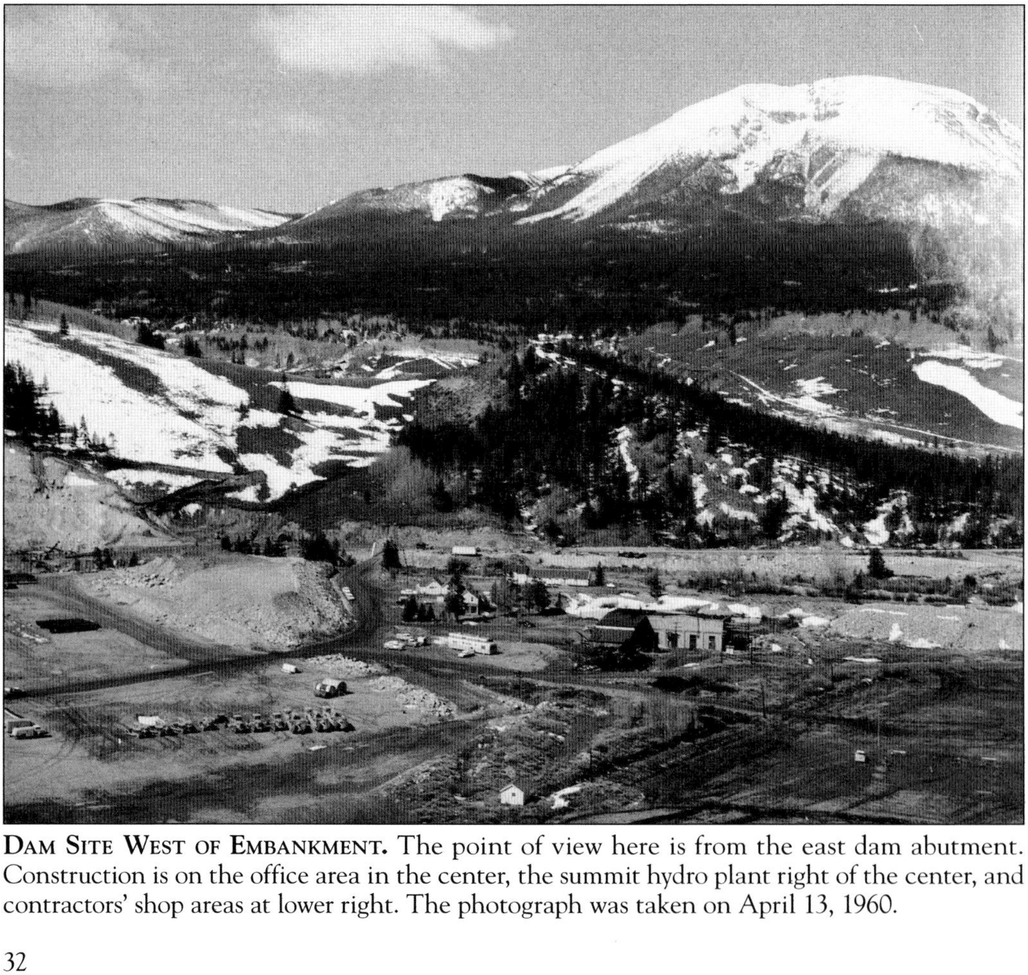

Dam Site West of Embankment. The point of view here is from the east dam abutment. Construction is on the office area in the center, the summit hydro plant right of the center, and contractors' shop areas at lower right. The photograph was taken on April 13, 1960.

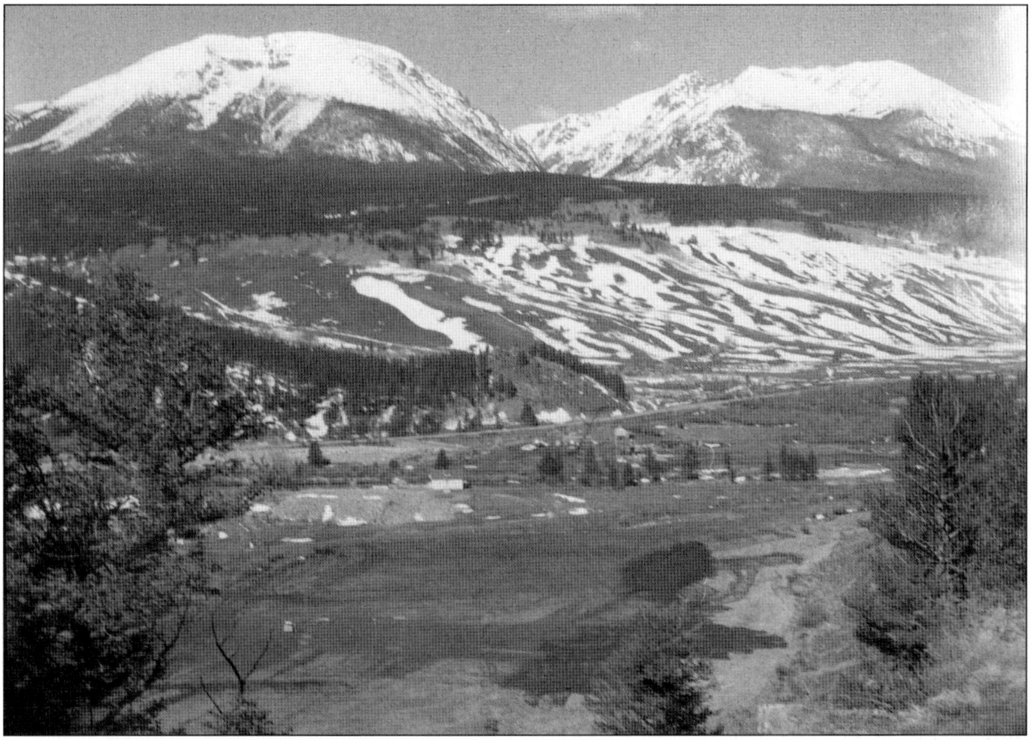

SITE OVERVIEW. The Dillon Dam site overview is seen looking northwest from the east dam abutment, at the confluence of Straight Creek and the Blue River, on April 13, 1960.

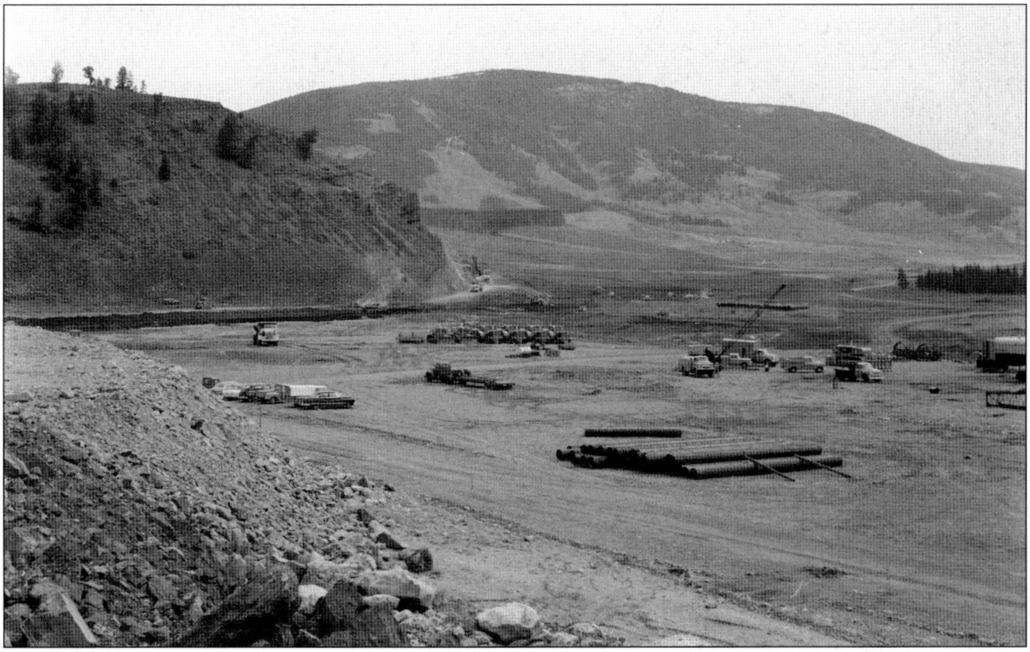

SUMMIT COUNTY HYDROELECTRIC PLANT. The view here looks east at the west face of the east dam abutment at the Dillon Dam site. The Summit County Hydro Plant piped water from the former penstock, stored in the foreground. The photograph was taken on May 17, 1960.

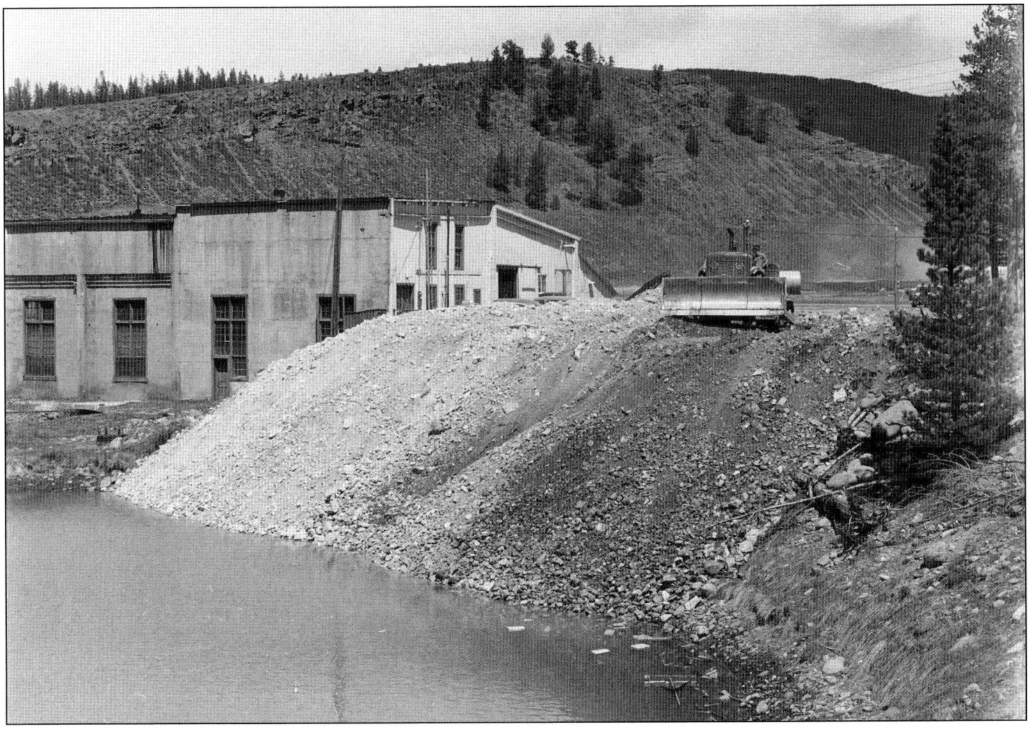

Muck from Outlet Works Tunnel. This point of view looks northeast across the pond west of Summit County Hydro Plant, showing the placement of muck from the outlet works tunnel. The photograph is dated May 25, 1960.

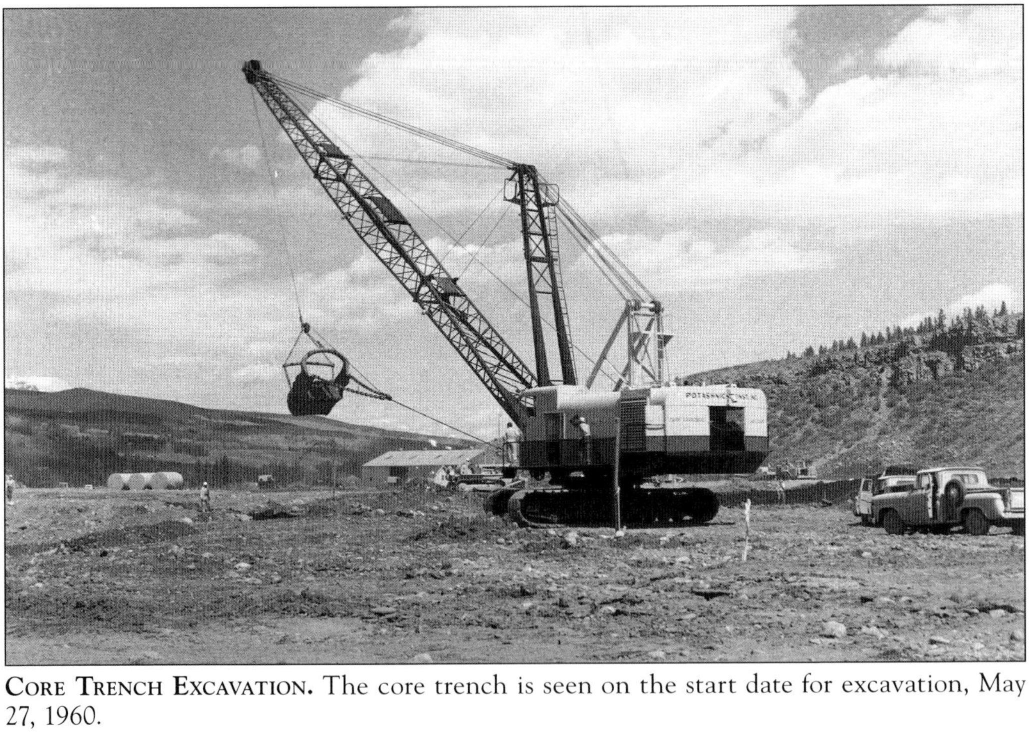

Core Trench Excavation. The core trench is seen on the start date for excavation, May 27, 1960.

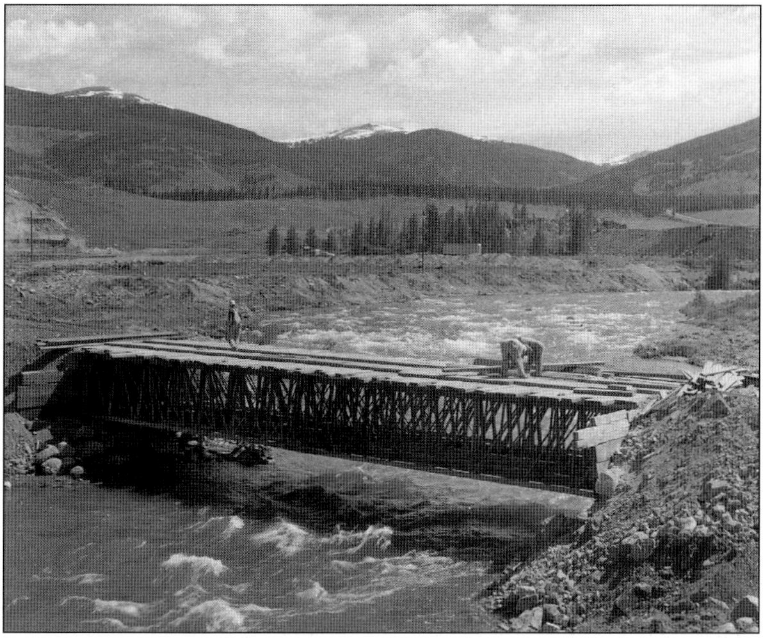

Temporary County Road Bridge. Construction workers install decking on a temporary County Road Bridge at the Dillon Dam site on May 27, 1960.

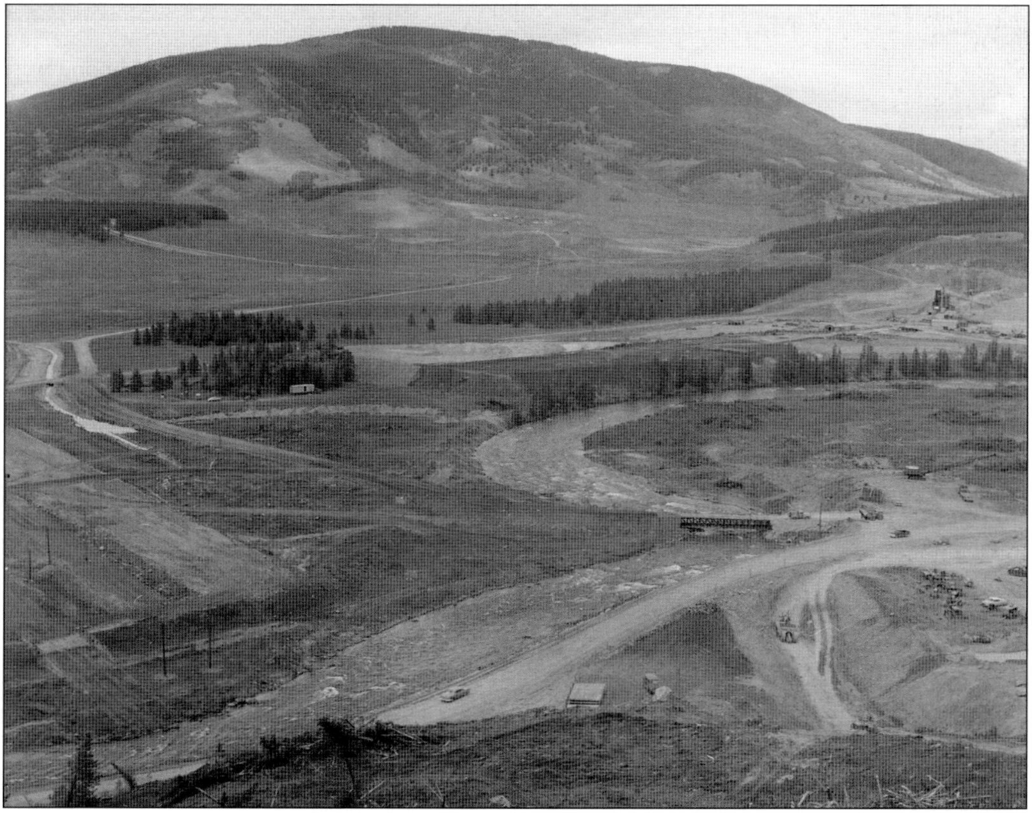

Overview of Spillway Area. Seen are the County Road and bridge, located east from the spillway area, at the Dillon Dam site on June 14, 1960.

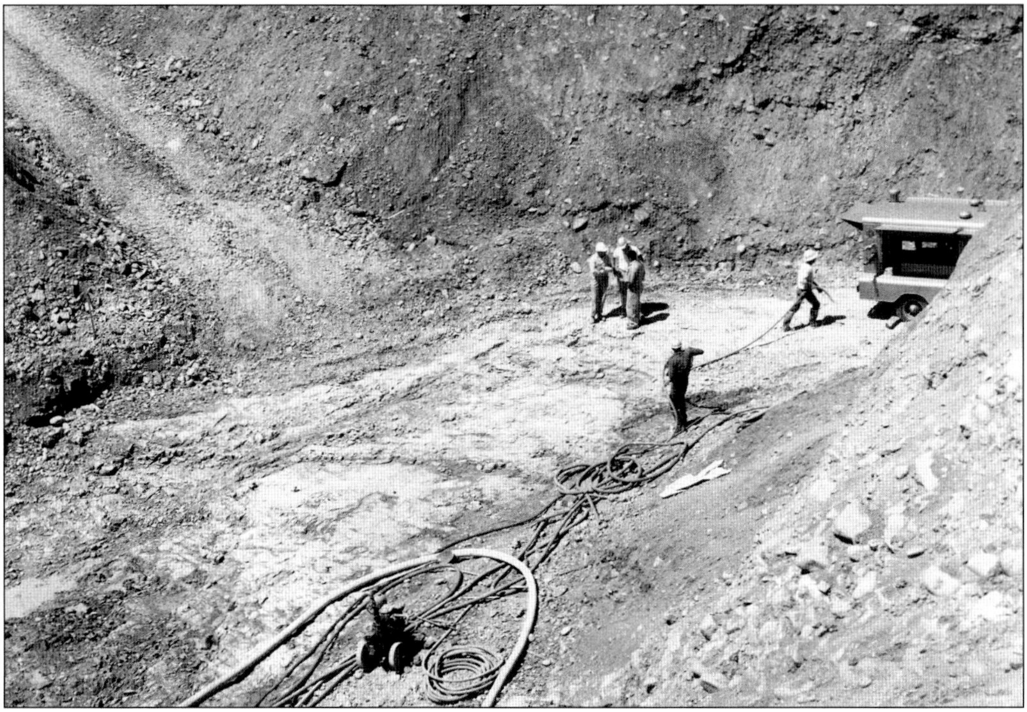

Setting Sub-base Forms. Cleaning rock and setting sub-base forms takes place, readying the Dillon Dam site for intake. The view is southeast on June 23, 1960.

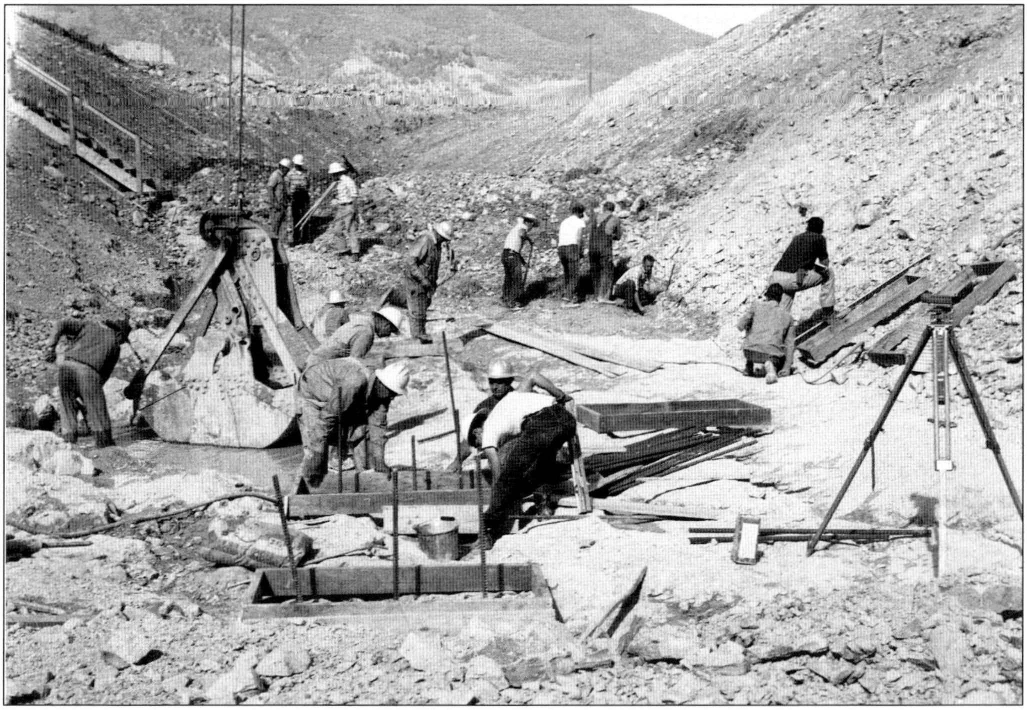

Beginning Core Trench. This July 1, 1960, view is looking east from the east bank of the Blue River toward the core trench at the Dillon Dam site.

Construction Accident. An accident at the Dillon Dam site is seen here as one of the Euclids tumbled into the Blue River. The driver got out in time to avoid being hurt. The photograph was shot on July 5, 1960.

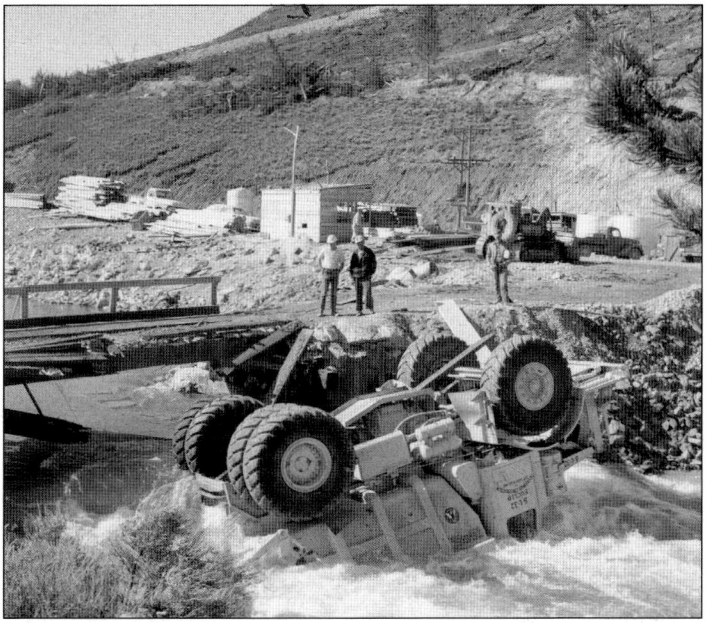

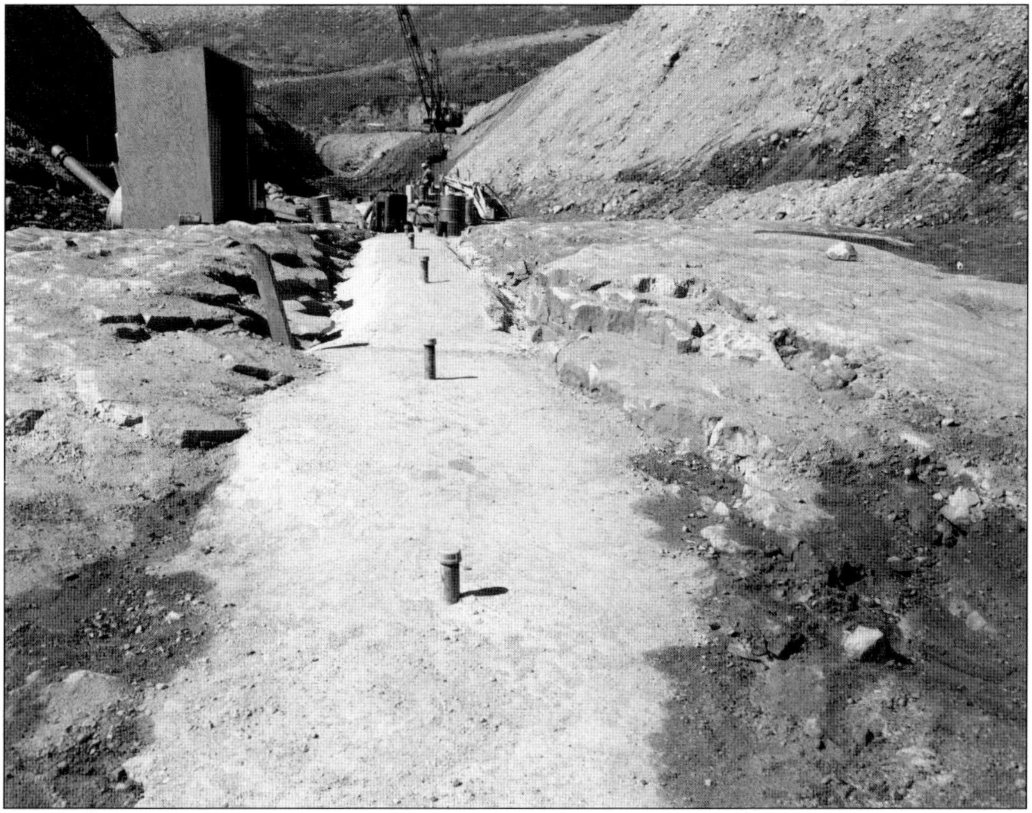

Core Trench with Stabilization Rods. Looking west along the cut-off trench from Station No. 16, the viewer can see the grout cap in fractured Entrada sandstone. The photograph was taken on August 26, 1960.

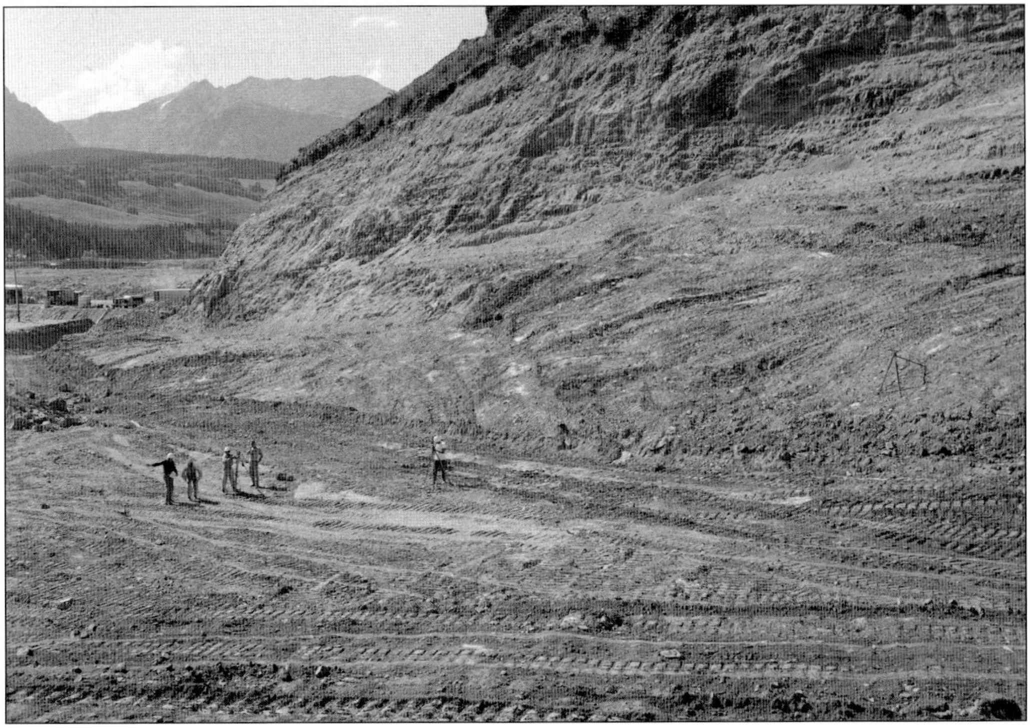

South Face, Final Stripping. The final stripping of the south face of the east abutment takes place in this August 26, 1960, view looking northwest, on the left side.

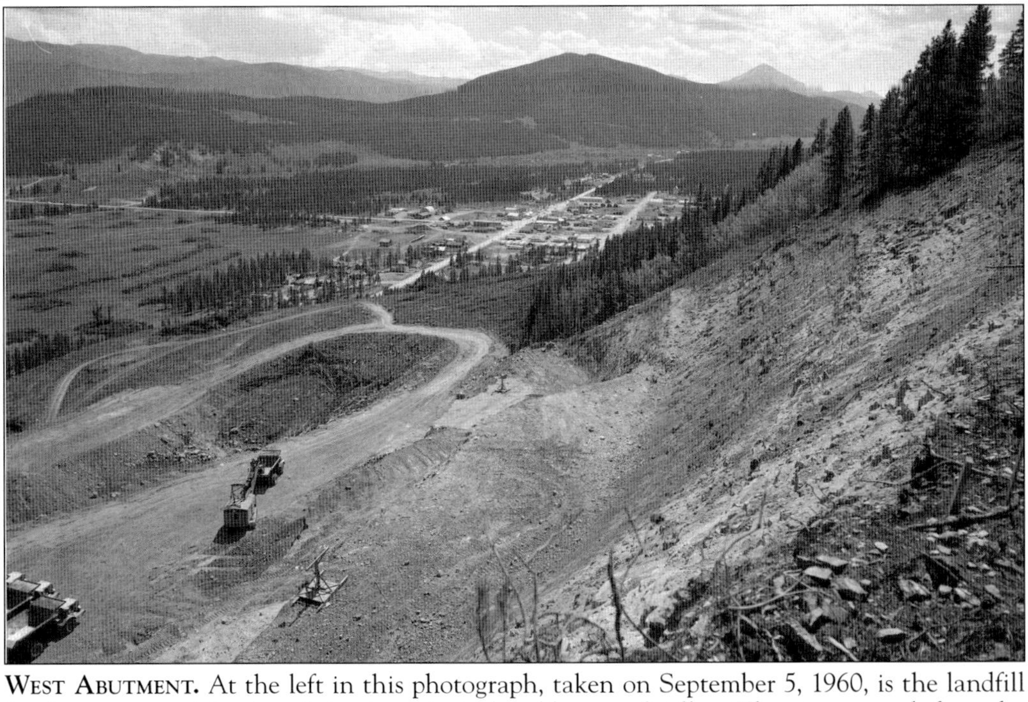

West Abutment. At the left in this photograph, taken on September 5, 1960, is the landfill for the contractor's haul road. At the right is the old town of Dillon. The view is south from the west abutment.

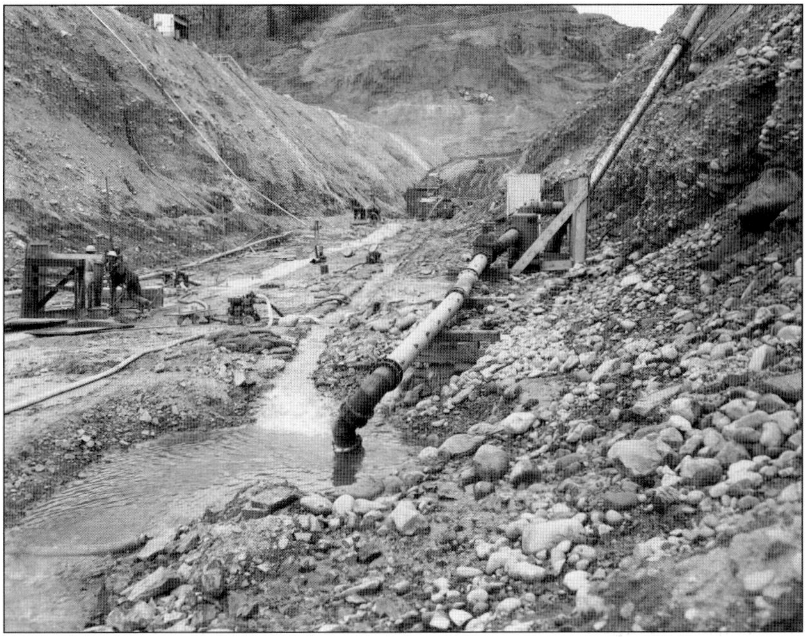

Sump Pump Action. The in-core trench is seen at location Station No. 13. The view is facing east on September 28, 1960.

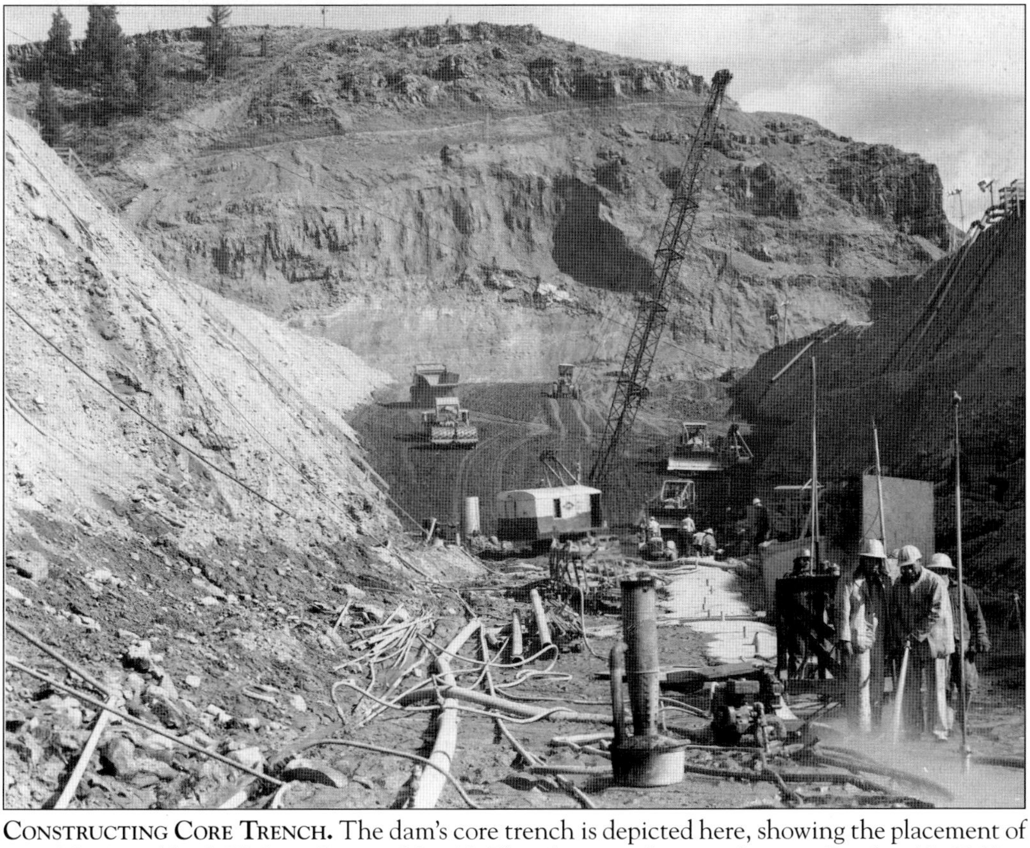

Constructing Core Trench. The dam's core trench is depicted here, showing the placement of zone No. 1 and backfill from Station No. 16. The photograph was taken on October 13, 1960.

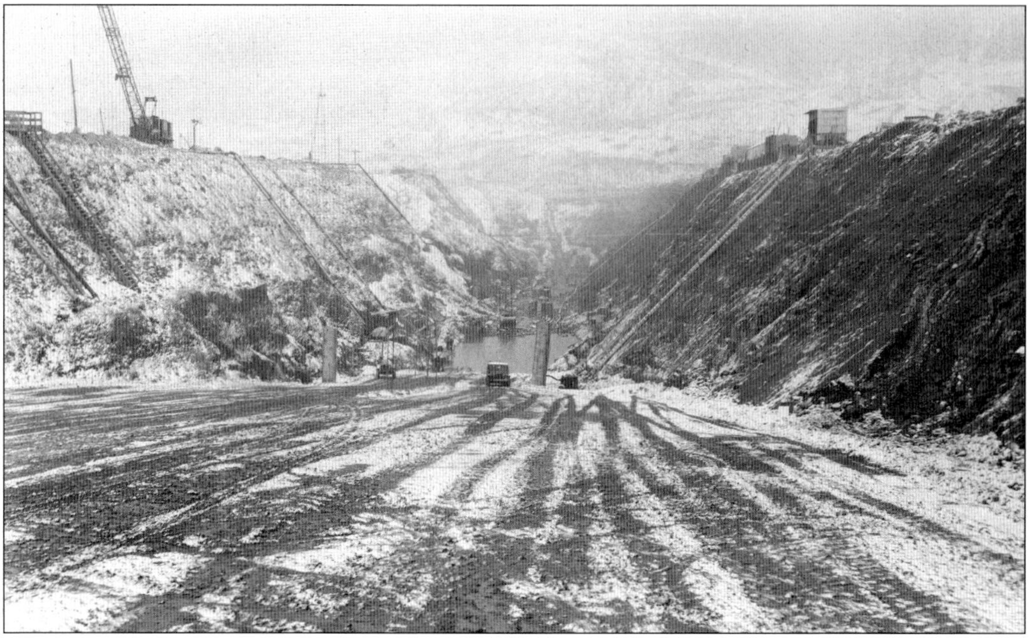

General View of Core Trench. The general view is southwest from Station No. 20 during the first snow of the season on October 14, 1960.

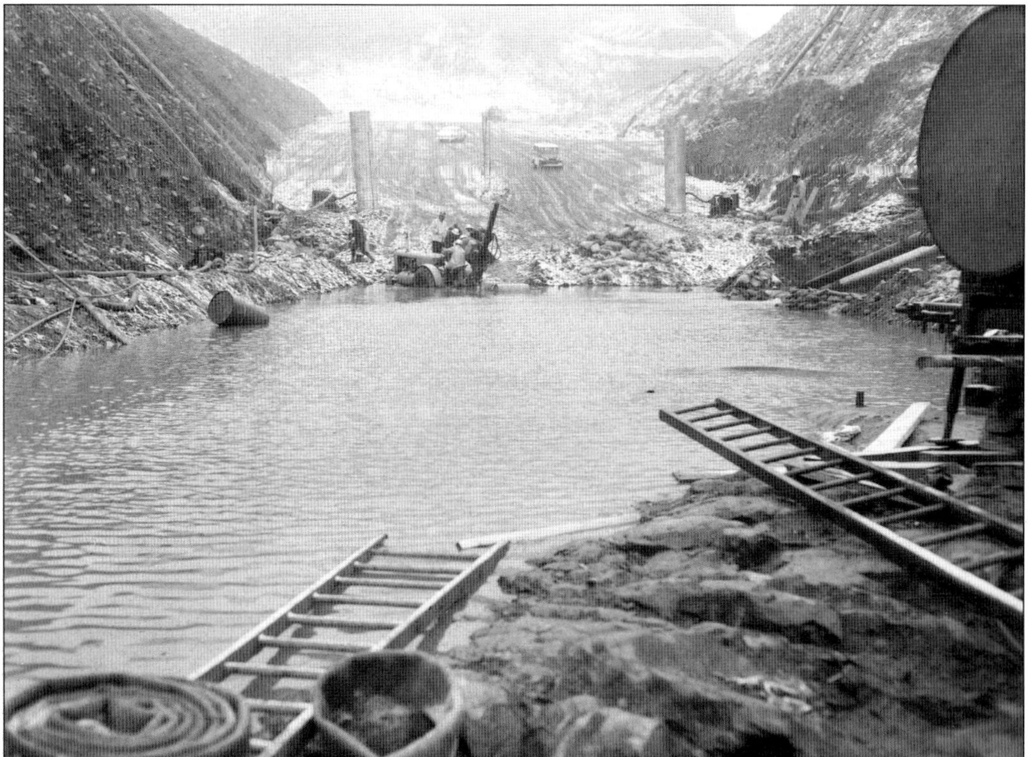

Flooding Problems. Serious flooding occurred after an electrical supply failure to the sump pumps in the core trench of Dillon Dam on October 14, 1960.

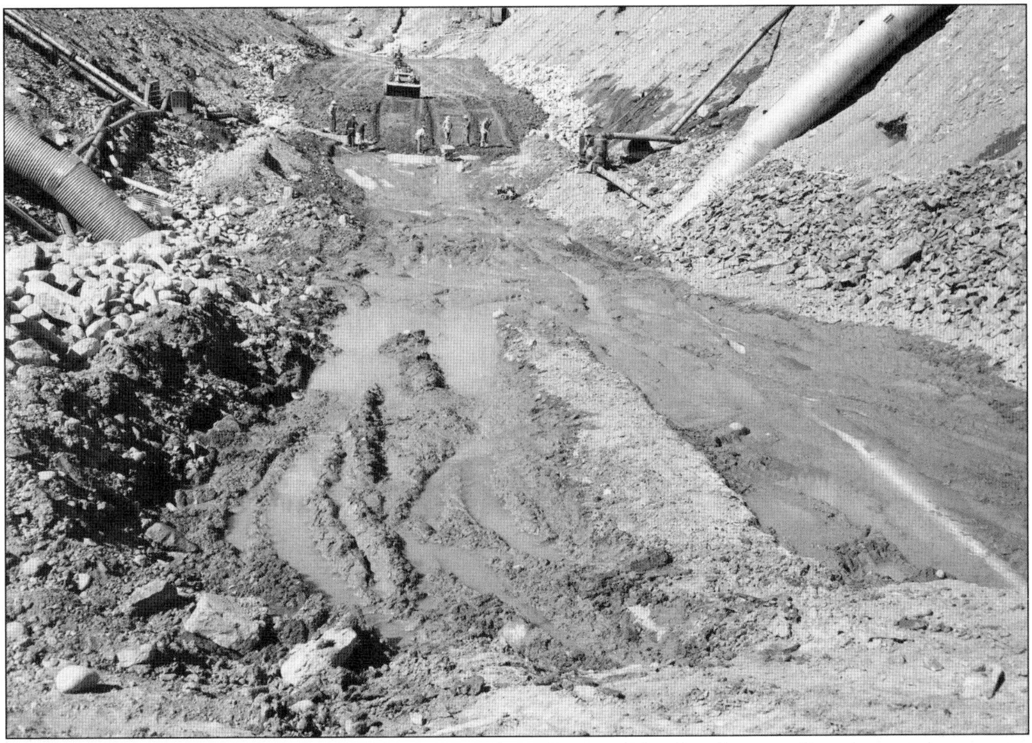

Fill Placing. The vantage point here is south at Station No. 9, where a 40-cubic-yard-capacity Euclid places fill in zone No. 1. The photograph is dated June 26, 1961.

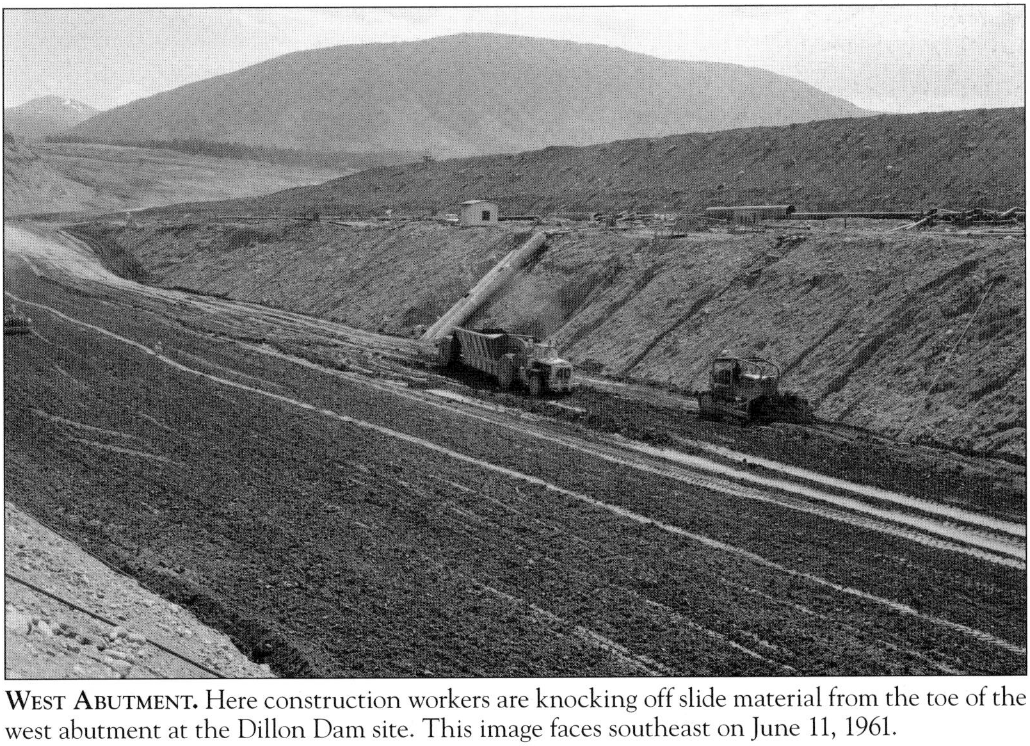

West Abutment. Here construction workers are knocking off slide material from the toe of the west abutment at the Dillon Dam site. This image faces southeast on June 11, 1961.

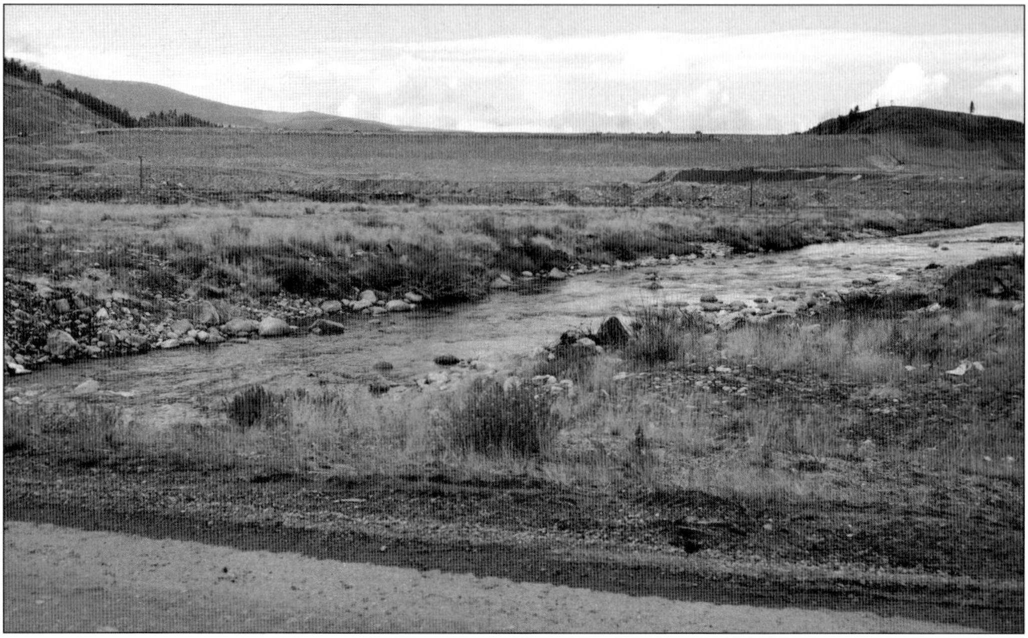

Ten Mile Creek. The point of view seen here is north, looking at the upstream face of the dam from old Highway 6 at Ten Mile Creek. The photograph is dated October 17, 1962.

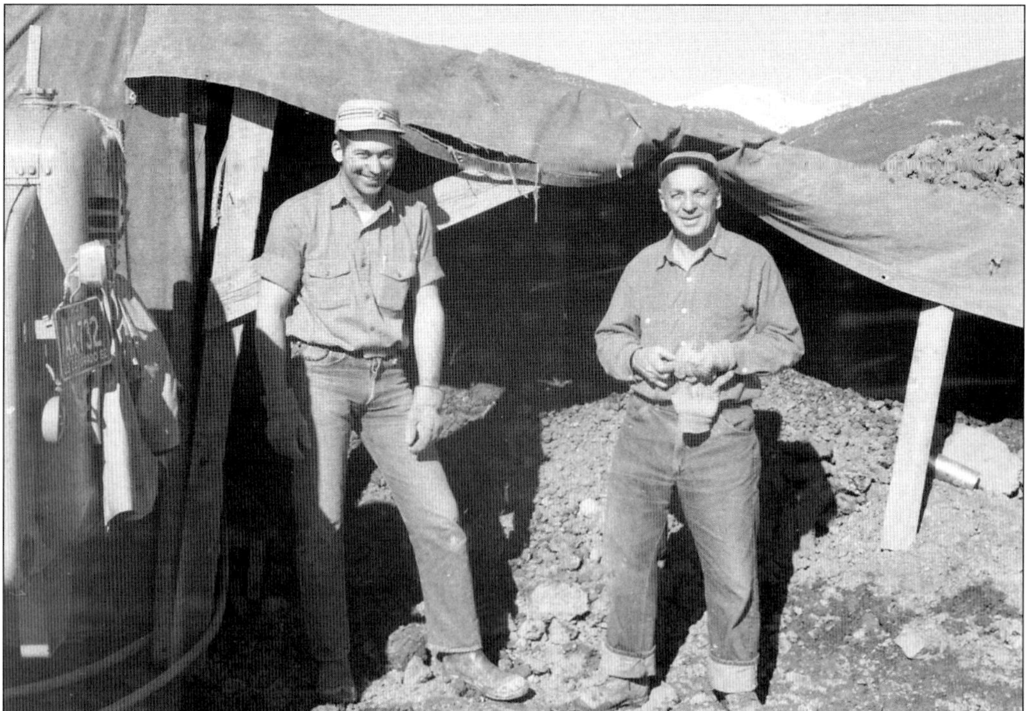

Future Mayor of Silverthorne. Future mayor Warren Alloway is seen here on the left side, and resident of old Dillon Ray Hill is on the right side. They are in the test pit of the Zone No. 1 embankment area at the Dillon Dam site on April 2, 1963.

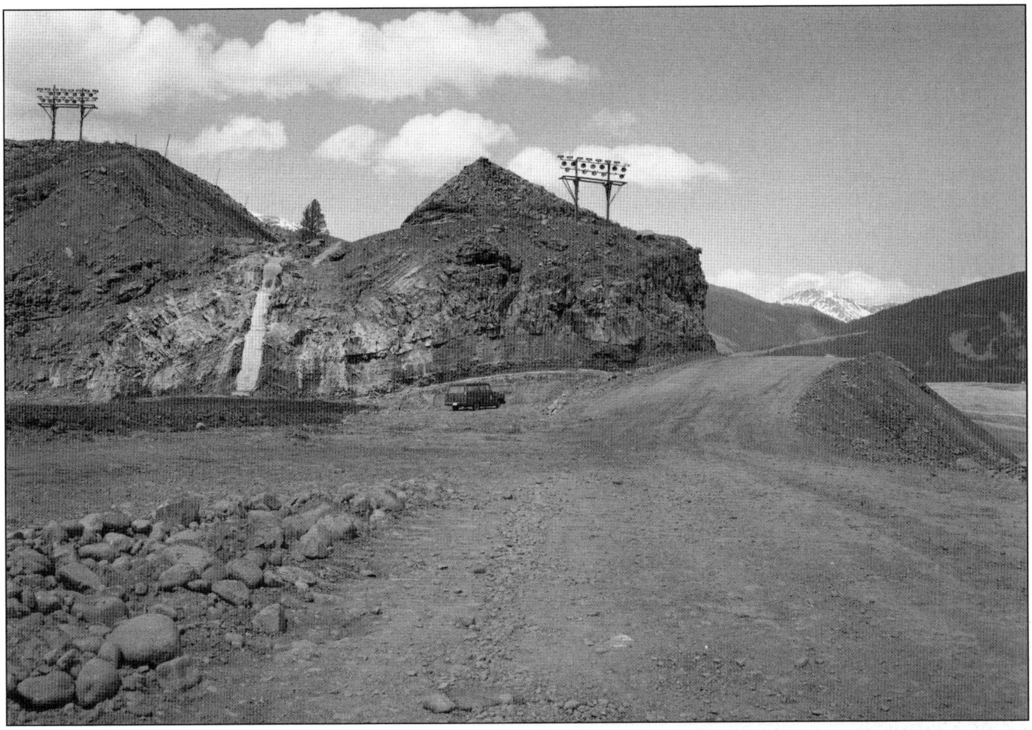

East Abutment. The east abutment of the Dillon Dam site is seen here as well as the cut for the highway and the haul-road fill at the right side of the photograph, which is dated May 9, 1963.

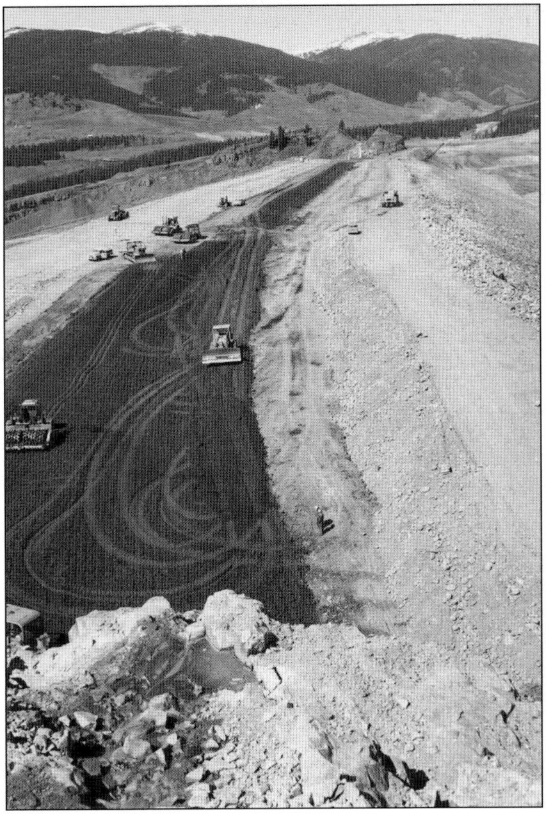

Riprap. The application of riprap to the dam slope is pictured on the right side of the Dillon Dam embankment. This May 9, 1963, view looks northeast from the west abutment of Zone No. 1.

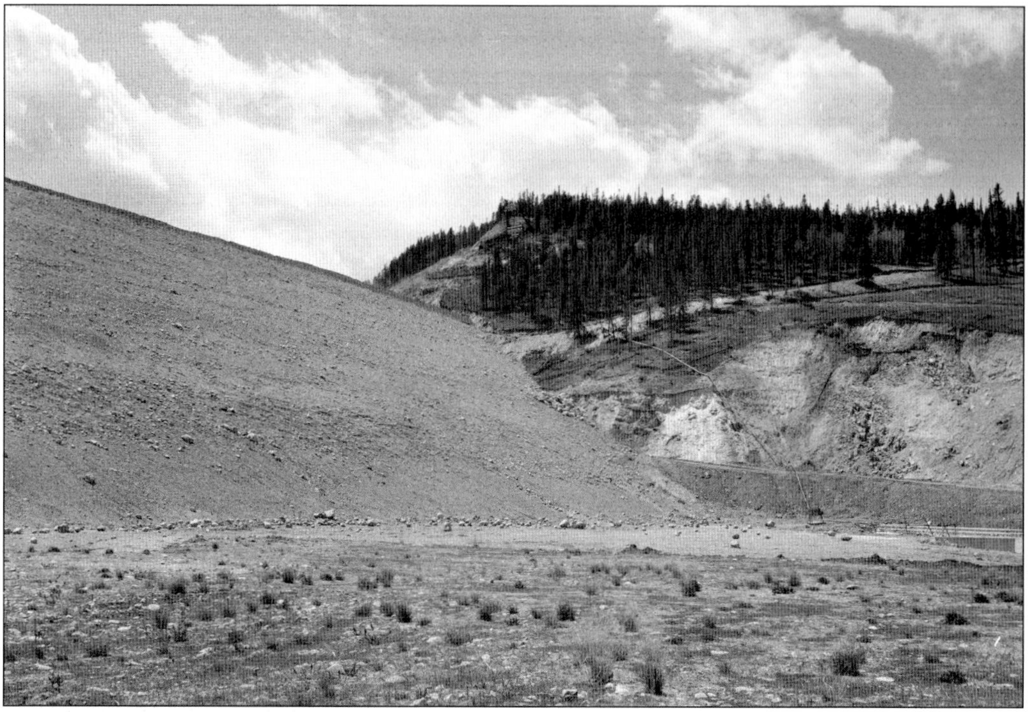

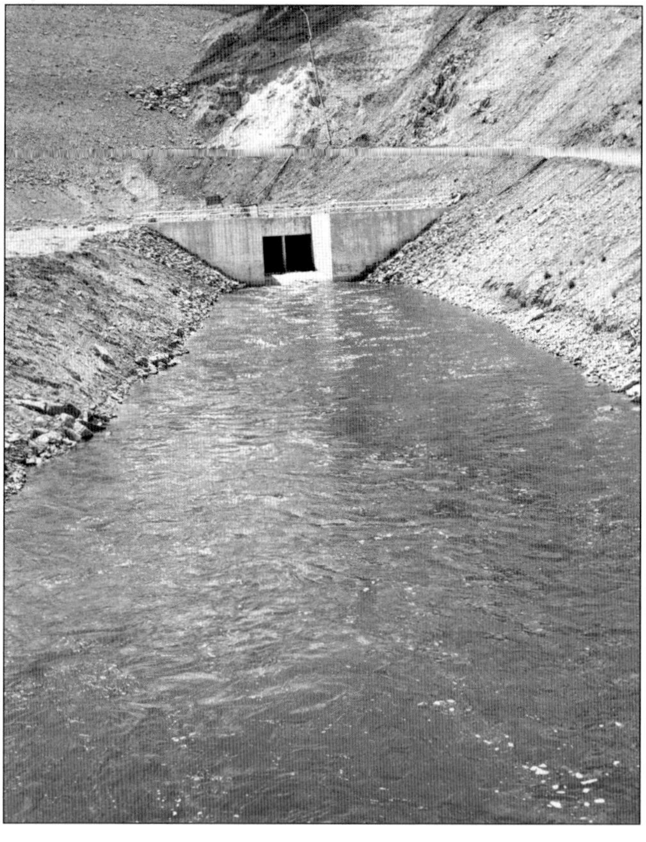

West Side of Dam. The Dillon Dam embankment is seen on the Silverthorne side, downstream from the face of the dam. The photograph, facing southwest at the west abutment, is dated May 16, 1963.

Downstream Side. The downstream faces of the dam embankment are seen from the Silverthorne side of the Dillon Dam site on the same day as above.

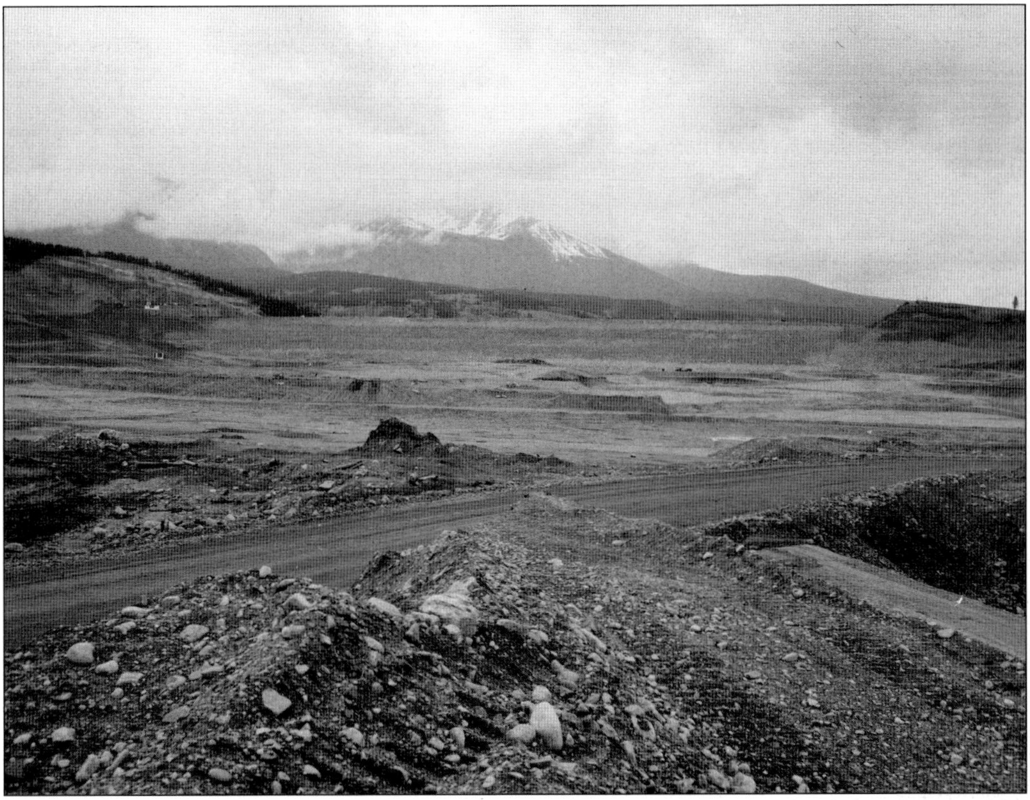

General View of Dam Site. This vantage point looks northwest at the downstream face of the dam across Borrow Area No. 2 on May 22, 1963. In the far distance, Buffalo Mountain can be seen topped with clouds.

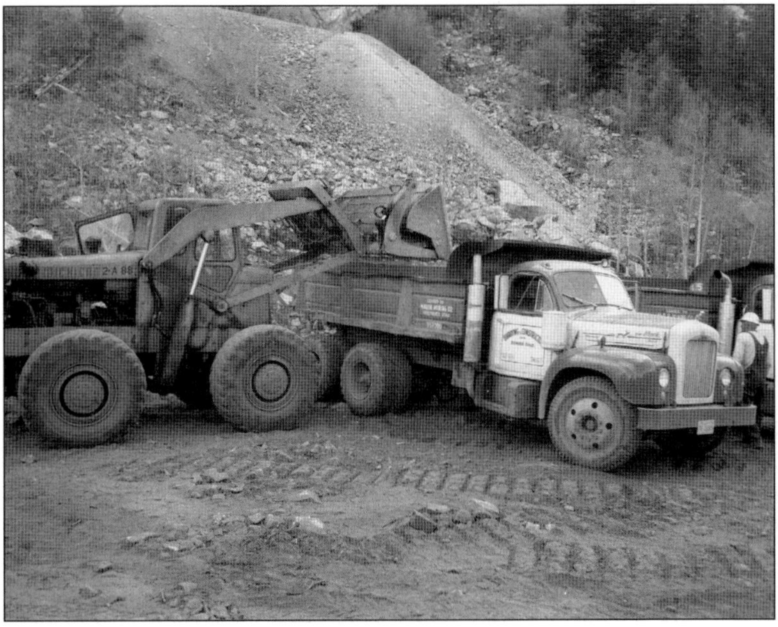

Loading Riprap. The men seen here are loading riprap at the nearby Frisco quarry on May 27, 1963. It was applied to the Dillon Dam embankment.

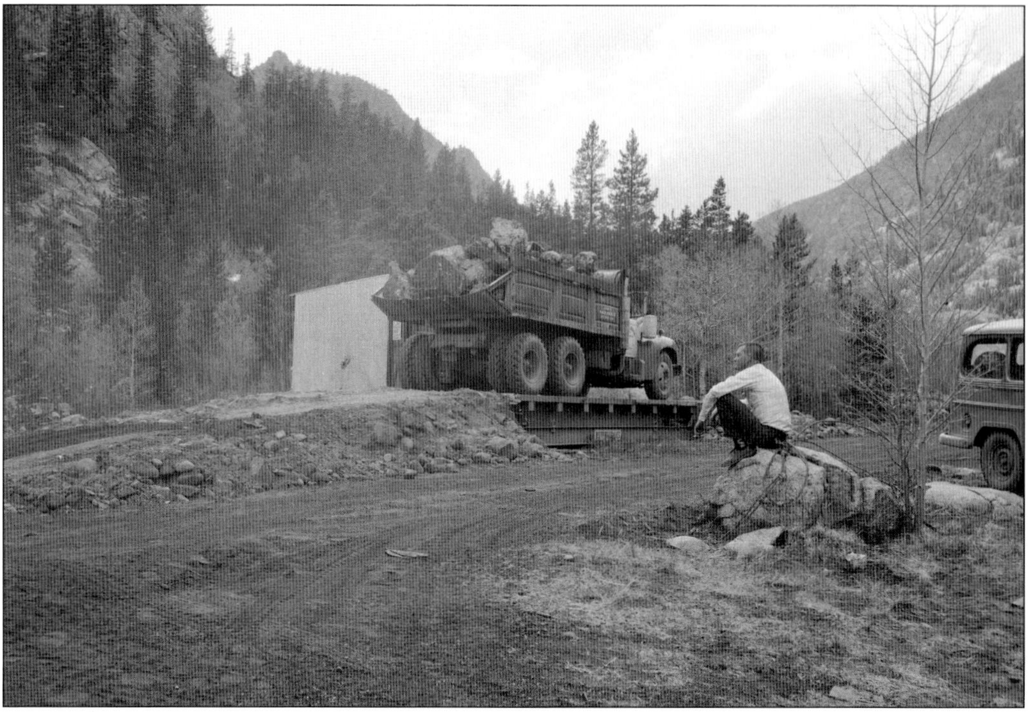

Weighing Riprap. Weighing riprap occurred at Frisco quarry for its subsequent application to the Dillon Dam embankment. The view is due west, and the date is May 27, 1963.

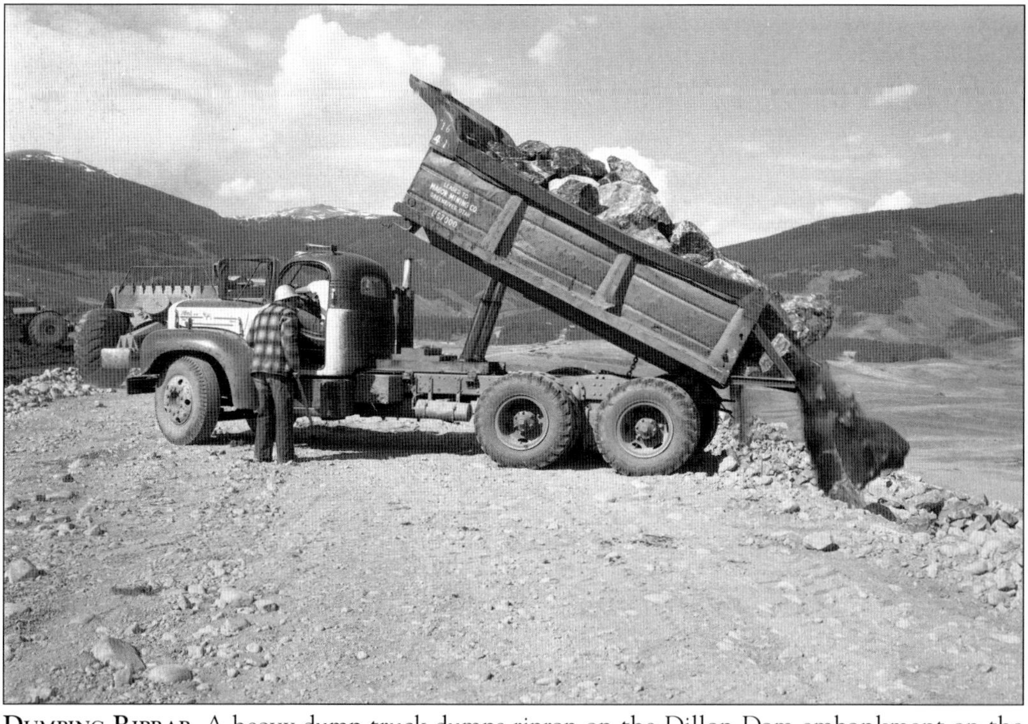

Dumping Riprap. A heavy dump truck dumps riprap on the Dillon Dam embankment on the upstream face of the dam at its west end. The photograph is dated May 27, 1963.

Survey Place Marker. Here is the placing of the location marker on Zone No. 1 in the Dillon Dam embankment area. The view is southwest from the east abutment and was taken on May 28, 1963.

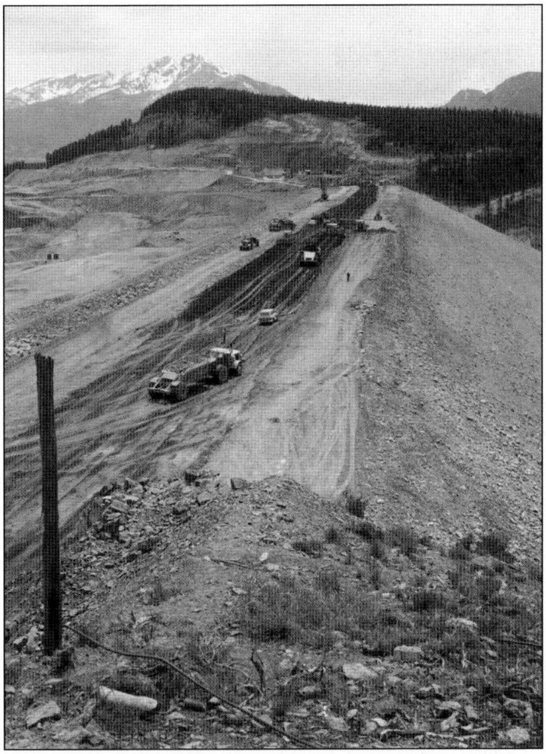

Density Samples. Workers are performing density testing sequence No. 3 on the Dillon Dam embankment. The engineer is using an auger to pull an earth sample on June 5, 1963.

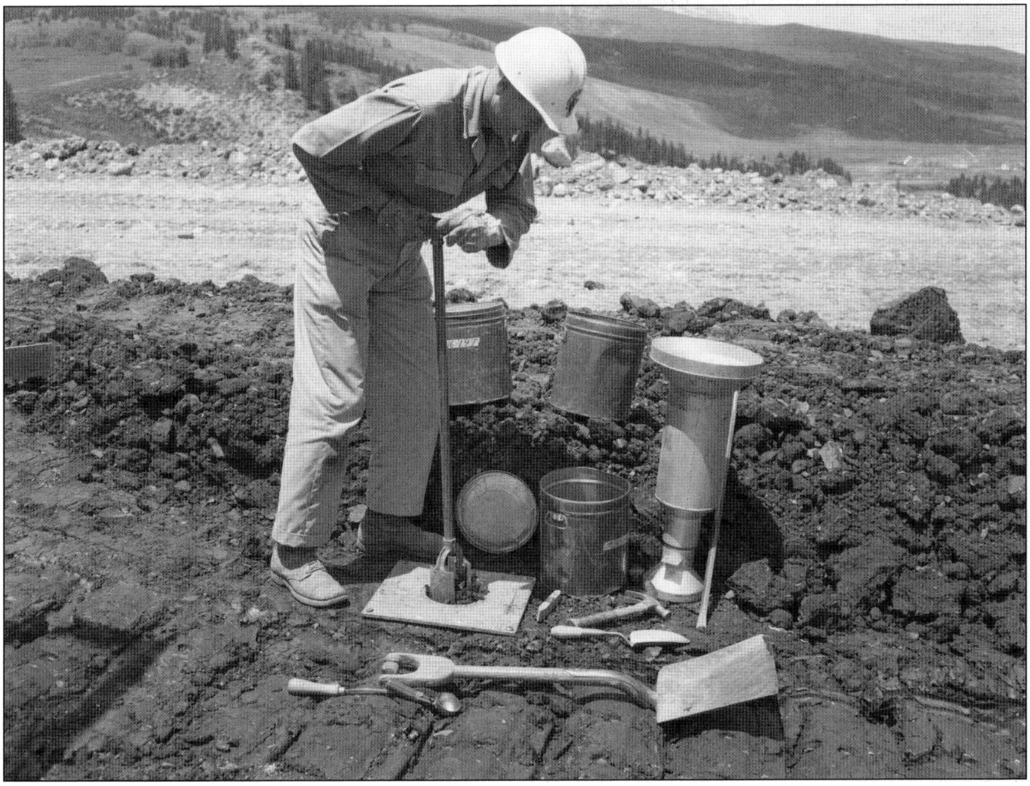

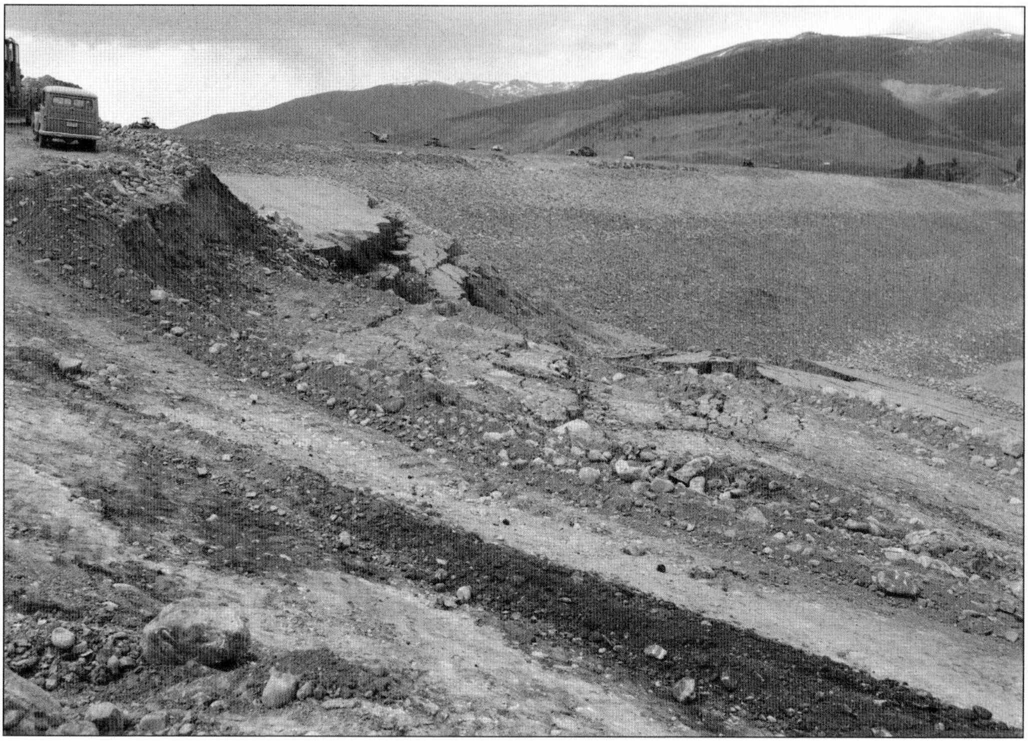

Haul Road. The old haul road is seen here across the central portion of the slope above the intake. The June 6, 1963, view looks northeast at the slippage area of the Dillon Dam site.

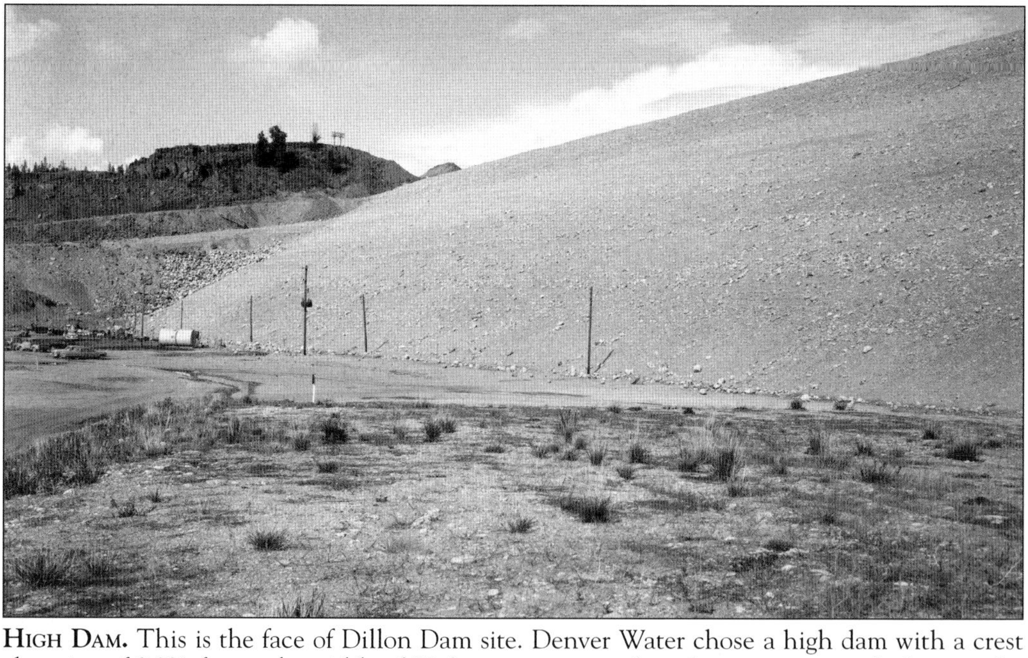

High Dam. This is the face of Dillon Dam site. Denver Water chose a high dam with a crest elevation of 9,031 feet and a width of 70 feet to accommodate the prerequisites for having the proposed Interstate 70 down the mountainside. The riprap was a 3-foot-thick layer of large boulders to protect from erosion. This photograph was taken on June 17, 1963.

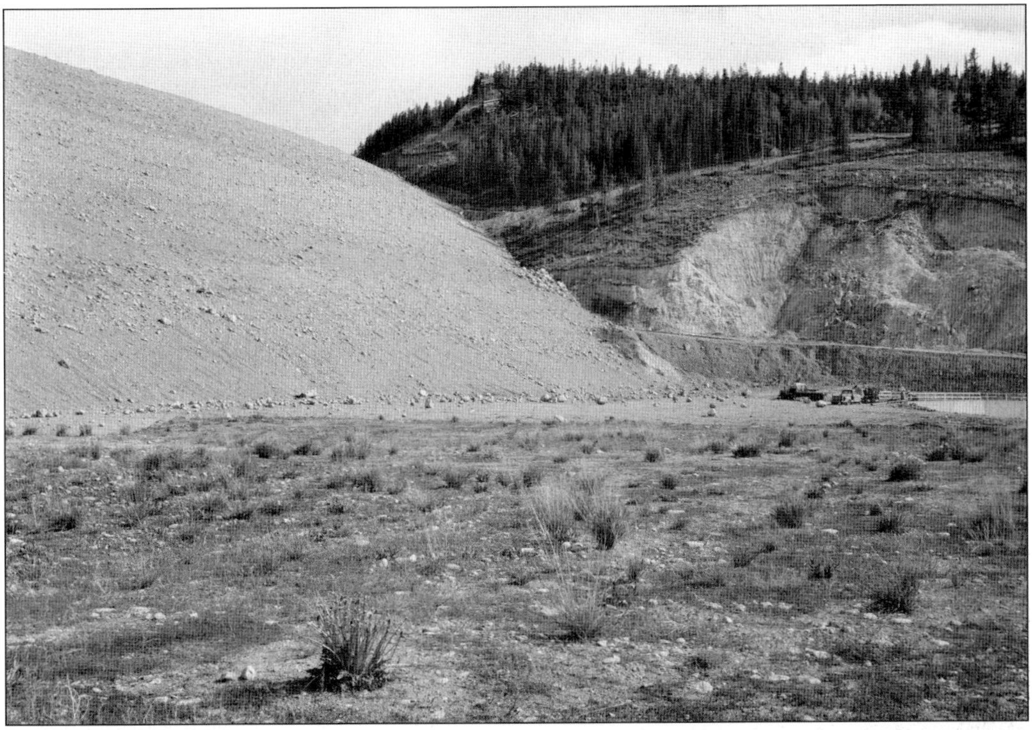

The 231-Foot-Tall Dam. The earth-filled dam would contain 12 million tons of earth-fill and 252,678 acre-feet of water. This is the Silverthorne side of the embankment pictured on June 17, 1963.

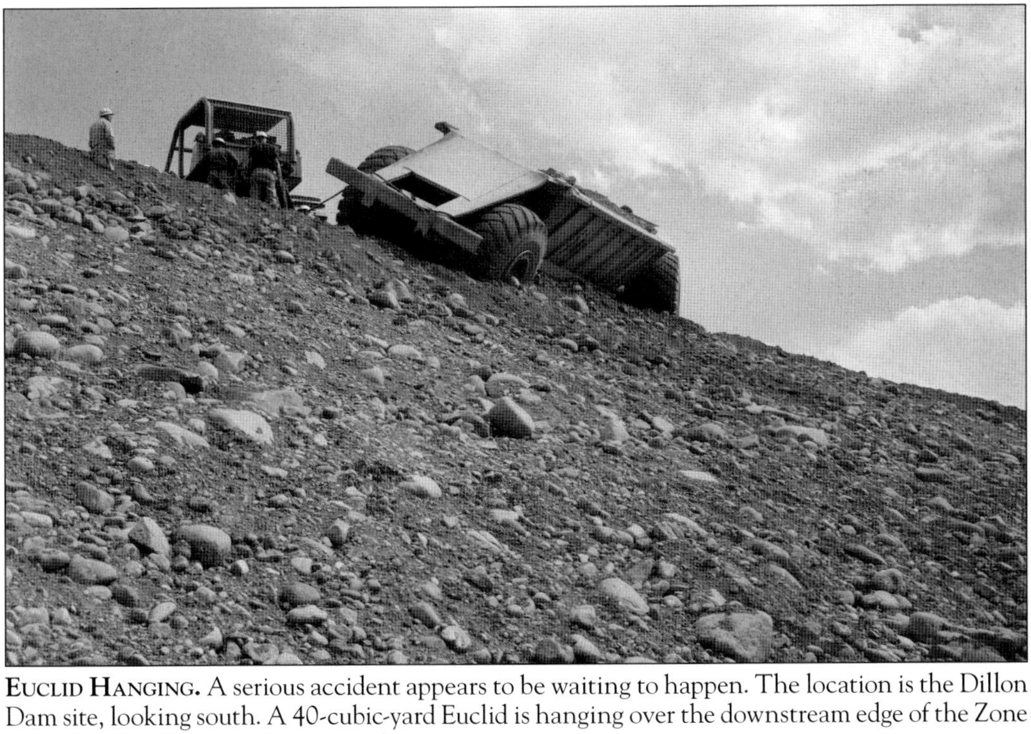

Euclid Hanging. A serious accident appears to be waiting to happen. The location is the Dillon Dam site, looking south. A 40-cubic-yard Euclid is hanging over the downstream edge of the Zone No. 2 embankment on June 27, 1963.

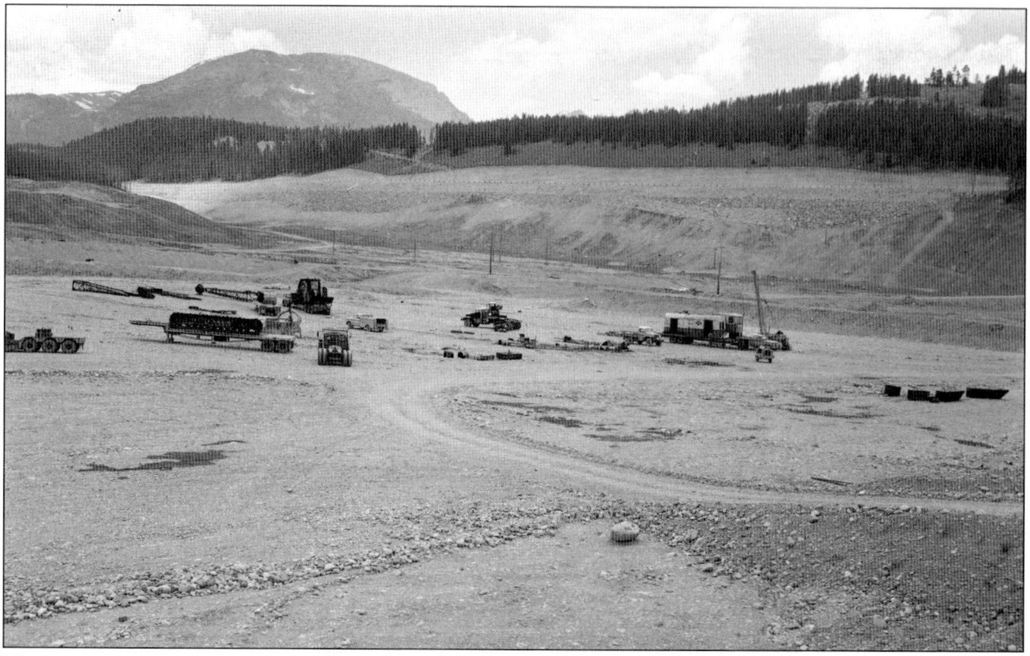

NORTHEAST OVERVIEW. This vantage point looks northeast along the upstream face of the dam from the west abutment on July 8, 1963.

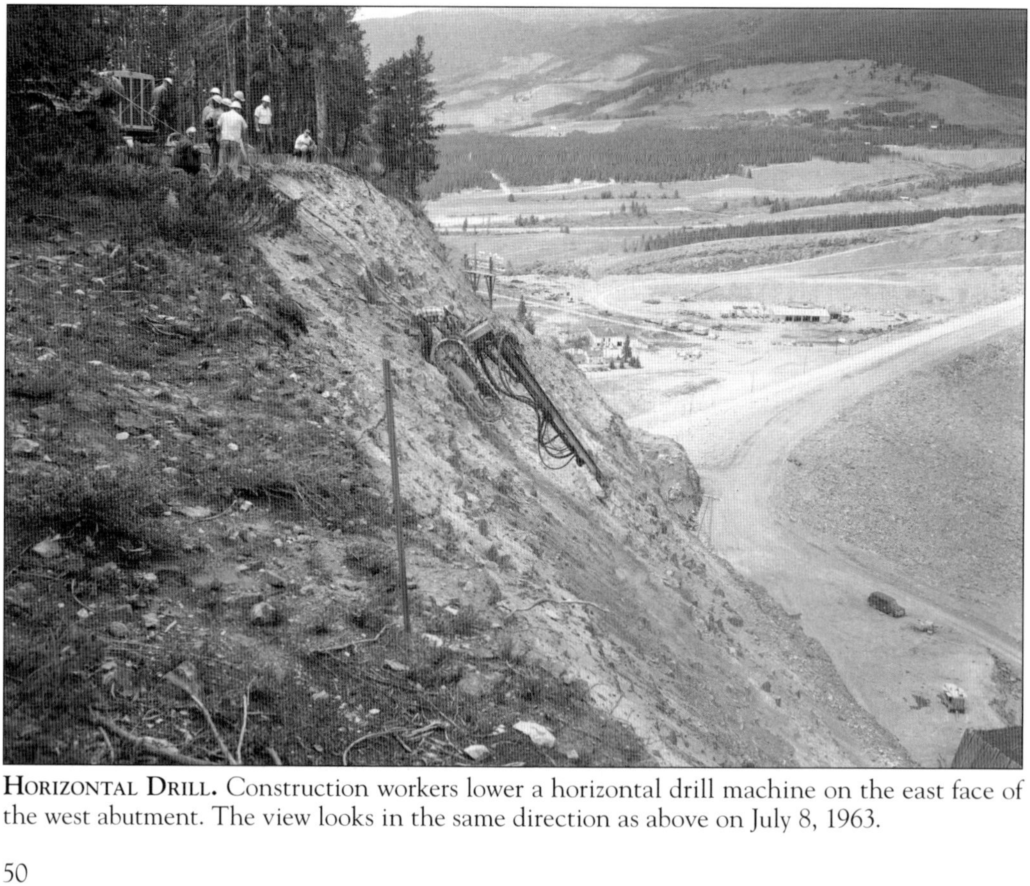

HORIZONTAL DRILL. Construction workers lower a horizontal drill machine on the east face of the west abutment. The view looks in the same direction as above on July 8, 1963.

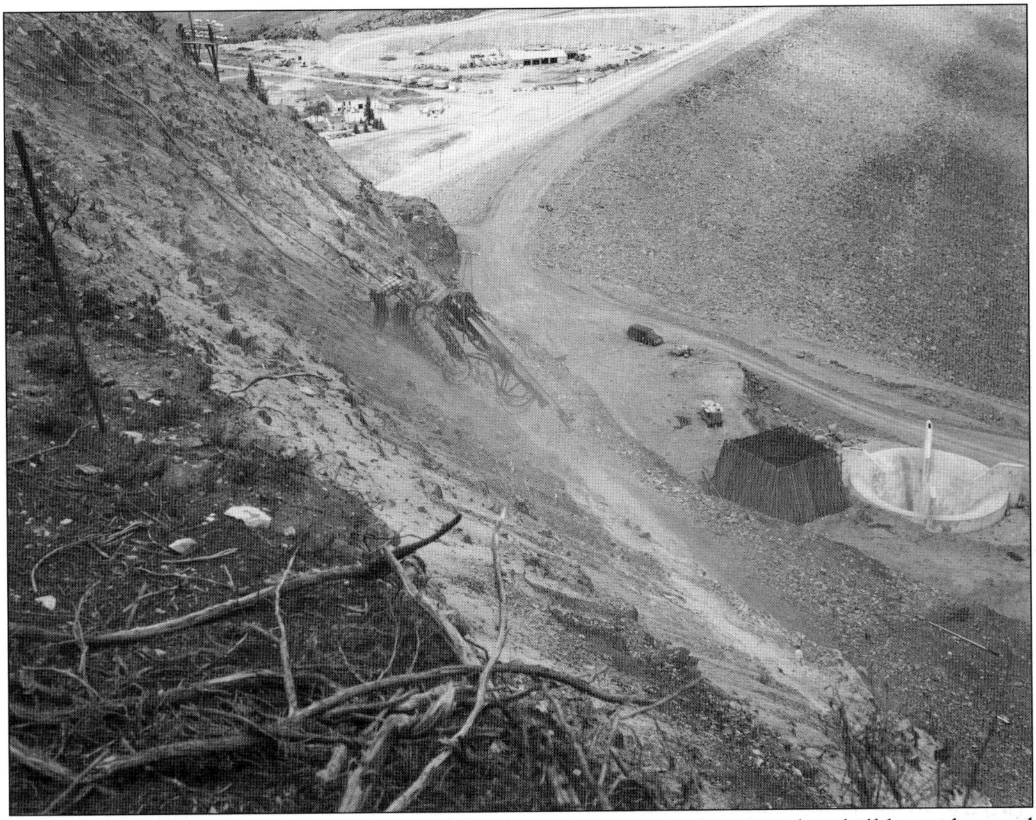

COMPOUNDED DRILLING. The east face of the west abutment is shown with a drill being lowered to a scale abutment on the Dillon Dam. The photograph is dated July 8, 1963. The view is to the north.

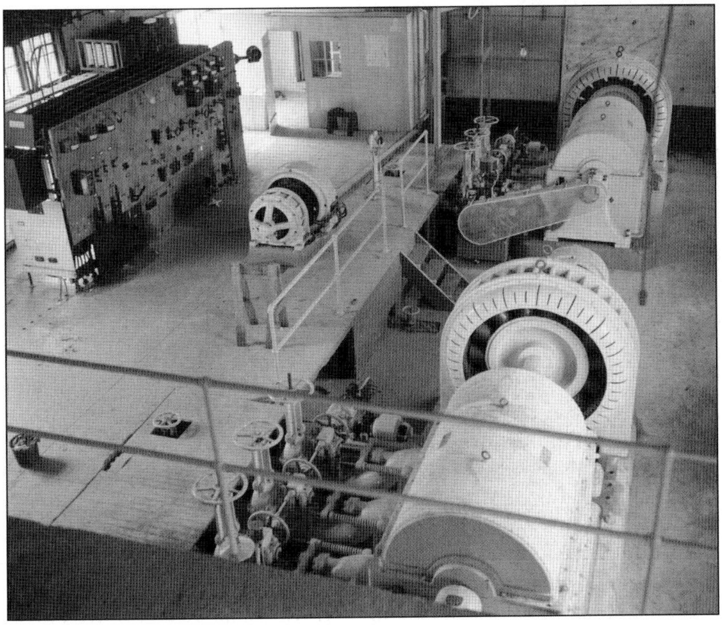

HYDROELECTRIC PLANT. The Summit County Hydro Plant is located on the Dillon Dam site. The view here is south from the transformer gallery area on July 11, 1963.

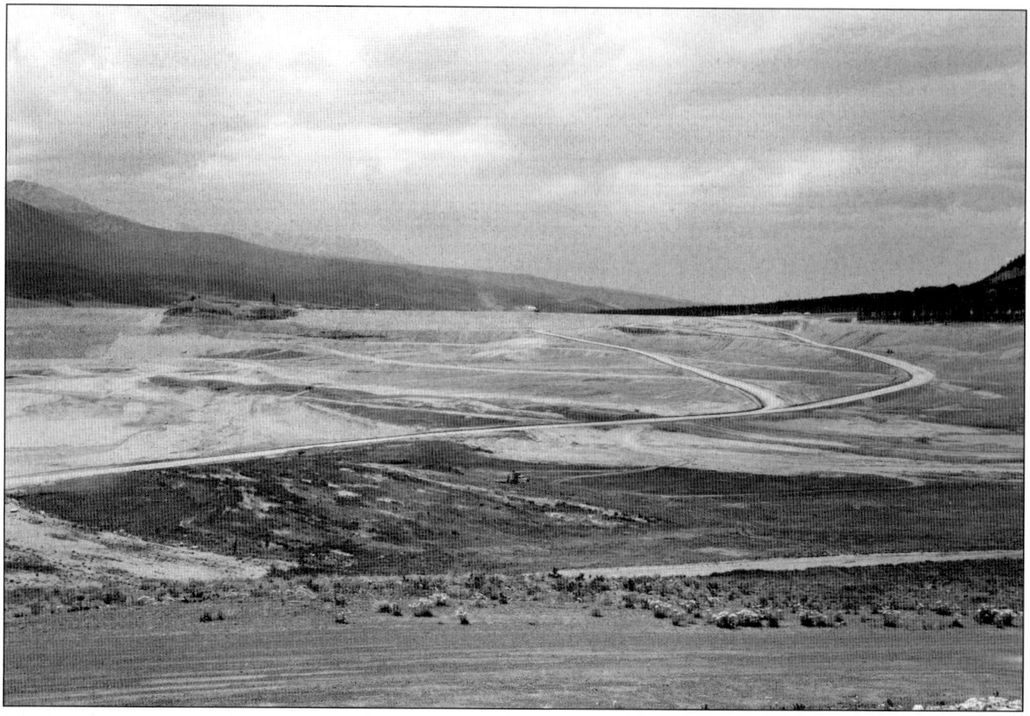

GENERAL VIEW. Looking north at the upstream face of the dam, this view shows the area between Dillon and the east abutment from the Roberts Tunnel Gate House on July 12, 1963.

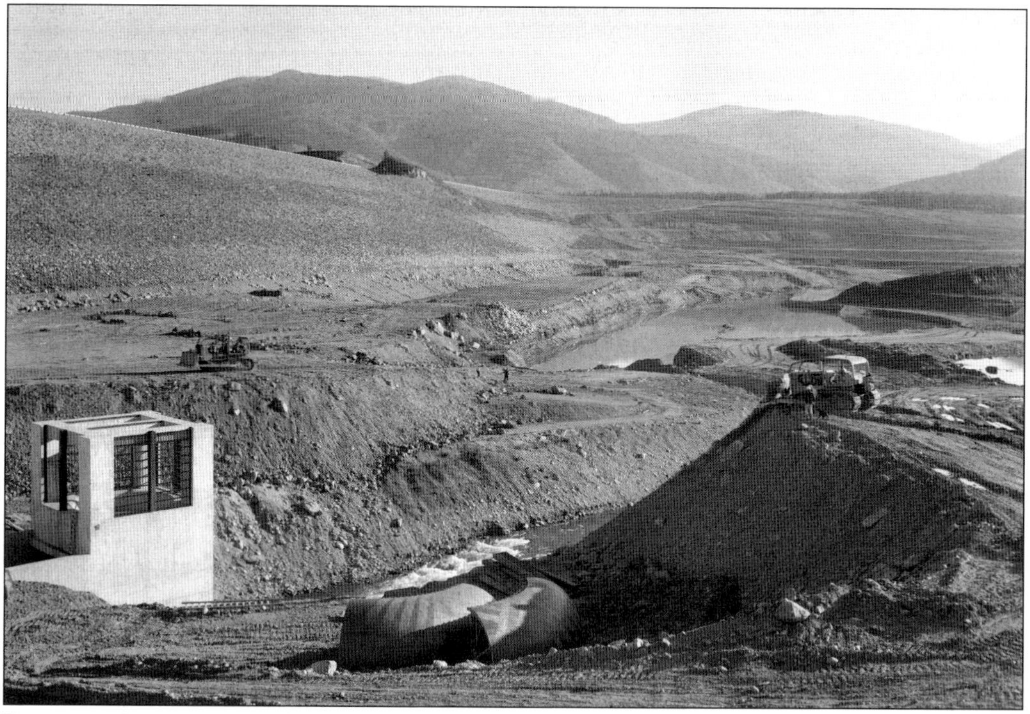

PLUGGING BLUE RIVER. The new cofferdam is being installed at the works outlet site here on August 5, 1963.

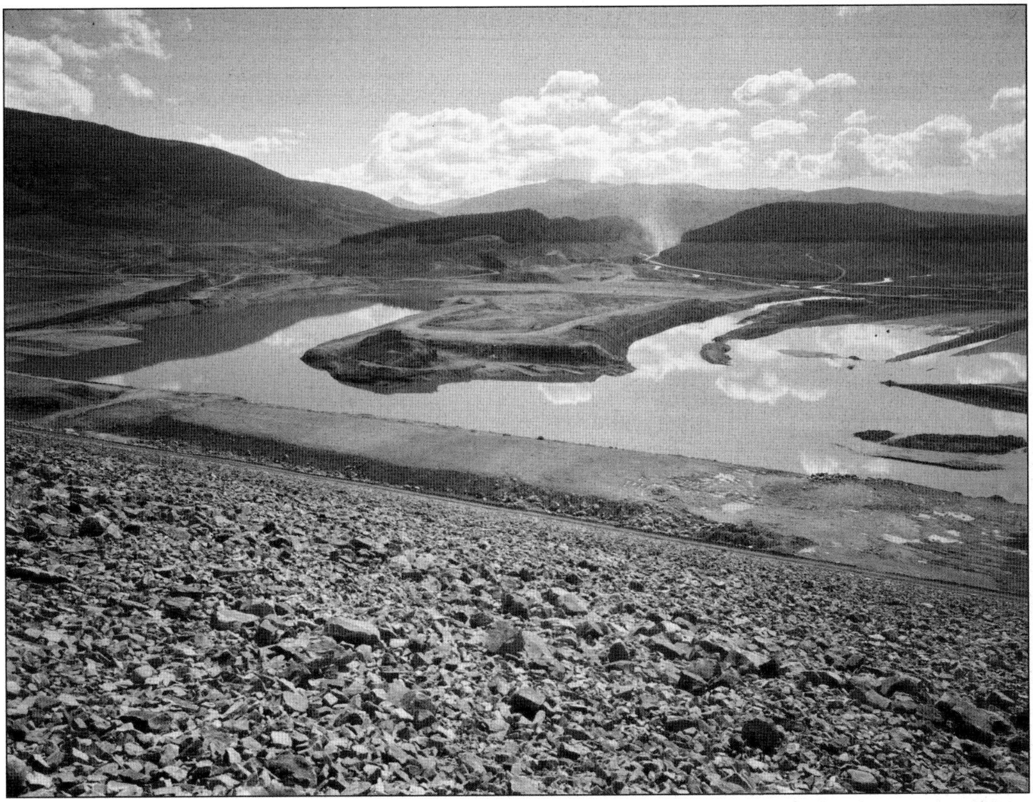

Crow's Nest View. The Dillon Dam site is seen in this southeast view from the dam at the filling of the reservoir in September 1963. The riprap shows up well in this view.

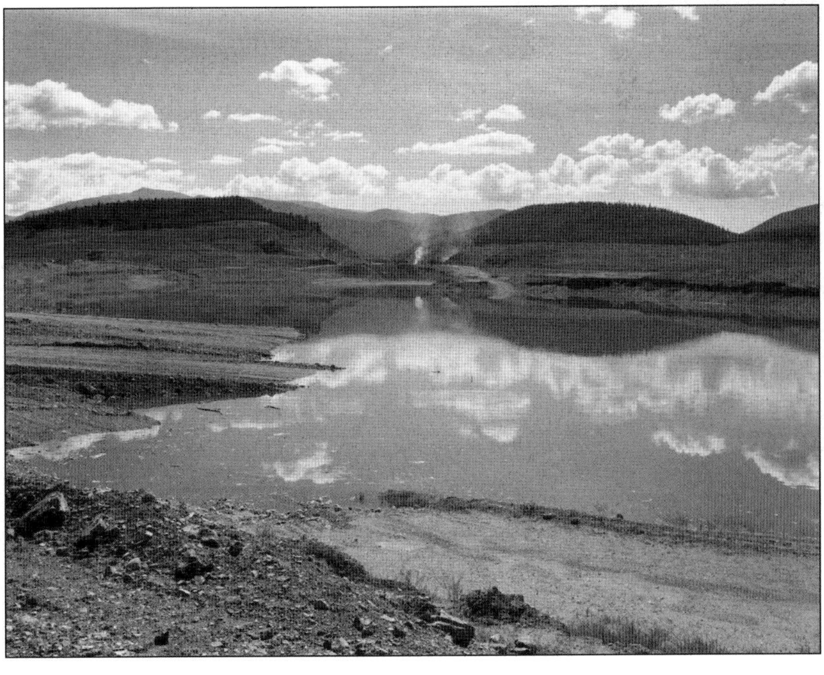

Dillon Dam Overview. The point of view of this photograph, taken on September 4, 1963, is toward Snake Canyon, which can be seen far out in the distance from the toe of the dam as the reservoir continues to fill.

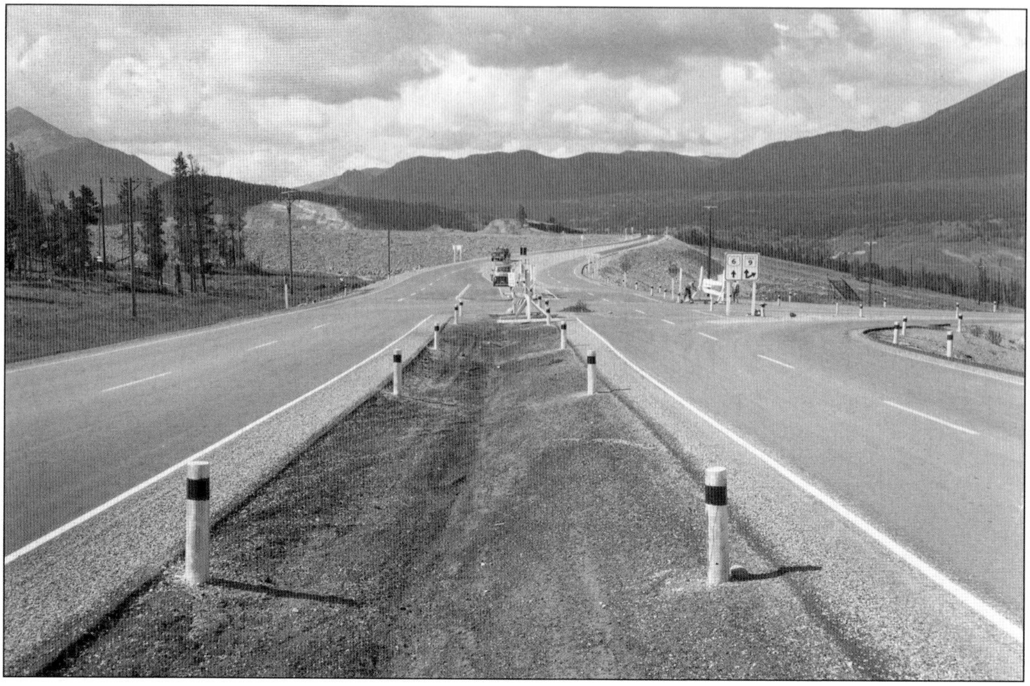

Snake River Canyon. This is the Dillon Dam site looking toward Snake River Canyon from the toe of the dam. The new U.S. Highway 6 is clearly visible. This photograph is dated September 4, 1963.

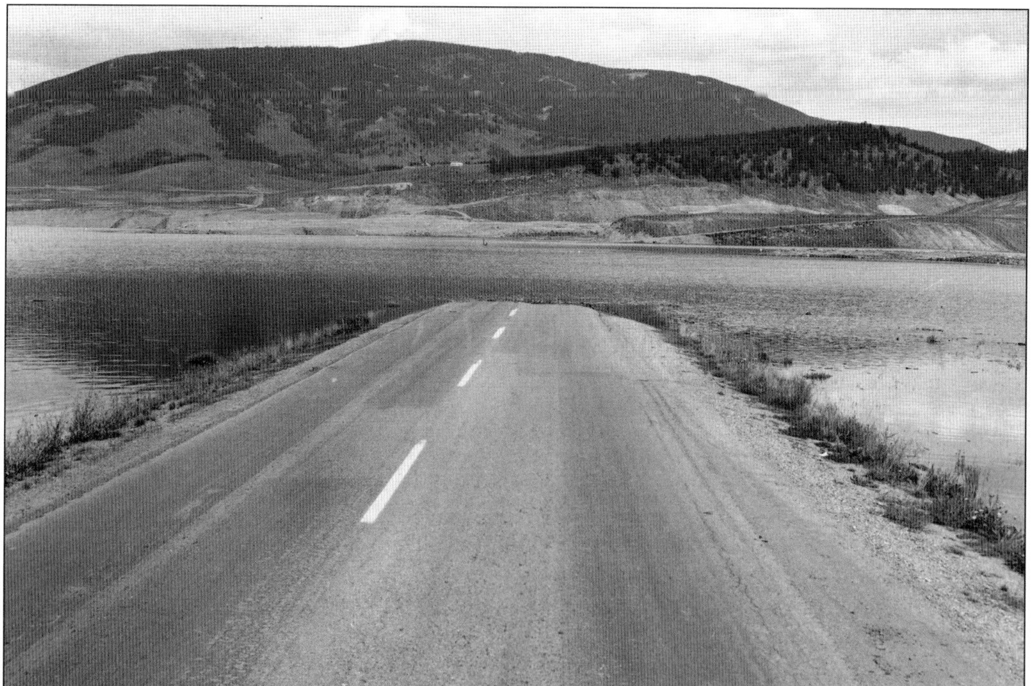

Old U.S. Highway 6. This view looks southeast toward Snake River Canyon, showing the reservoir slowly filling. The photograph is dated September 11, 1963.

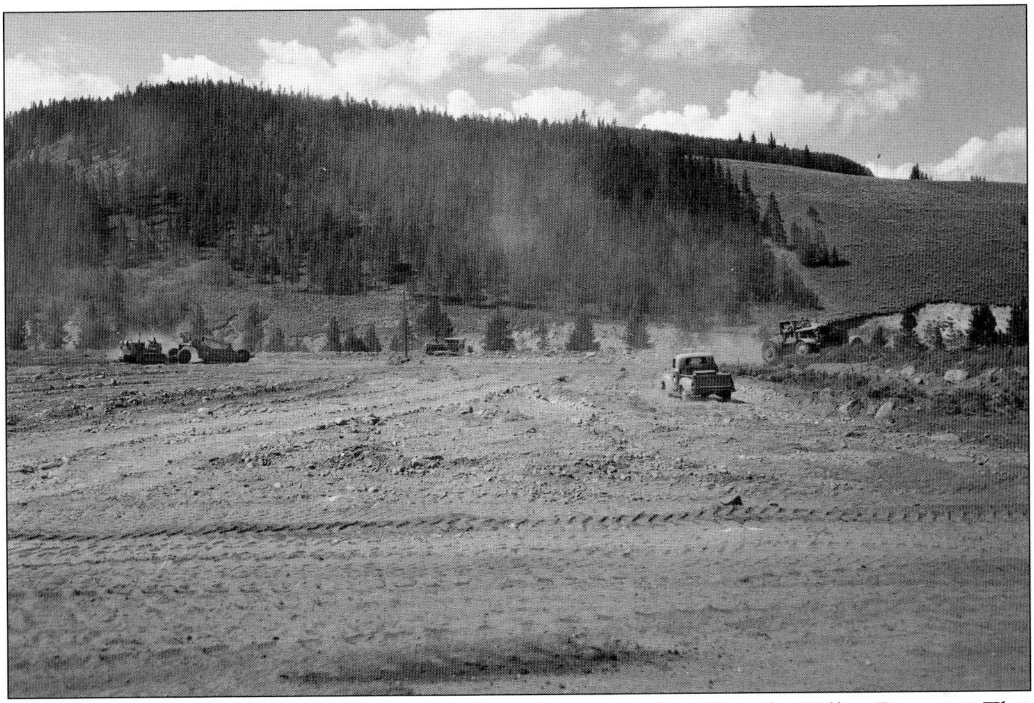

Euclids. Caterpillar earth-movers are seen here clearing and leveling the Dillon Dam site. This photograph is dated September 11, 1963.

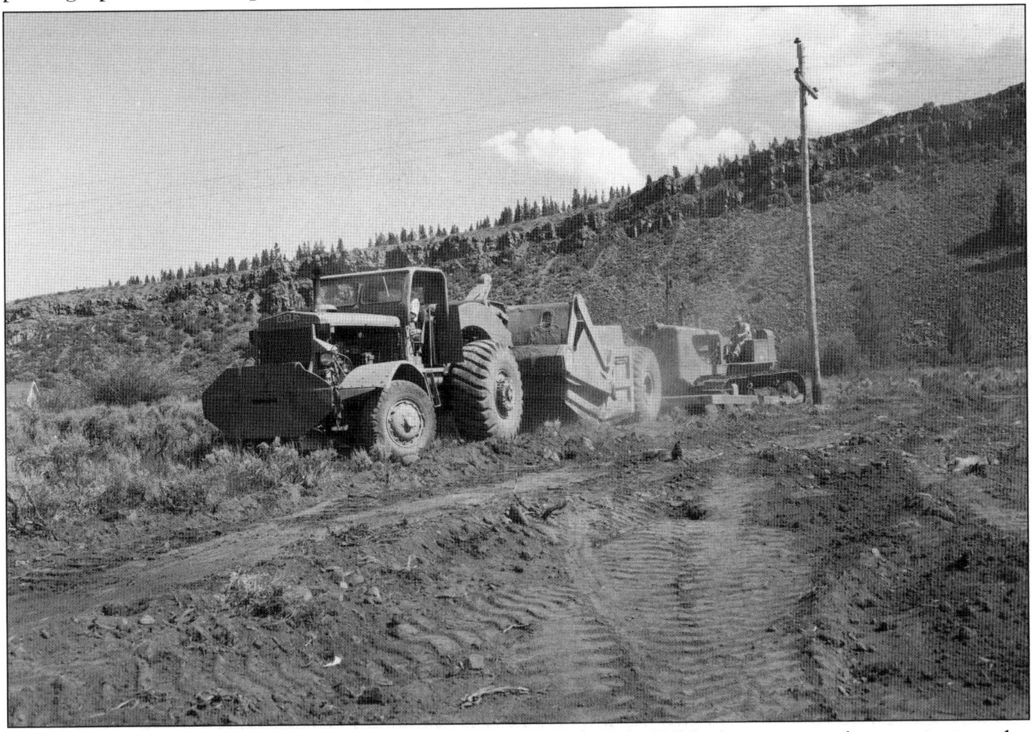

Stripping Foundation. This photograph dates to July 26, 1956, showing workers stripping the foundation area of sagebrush and willows at the Dillon Dam site.

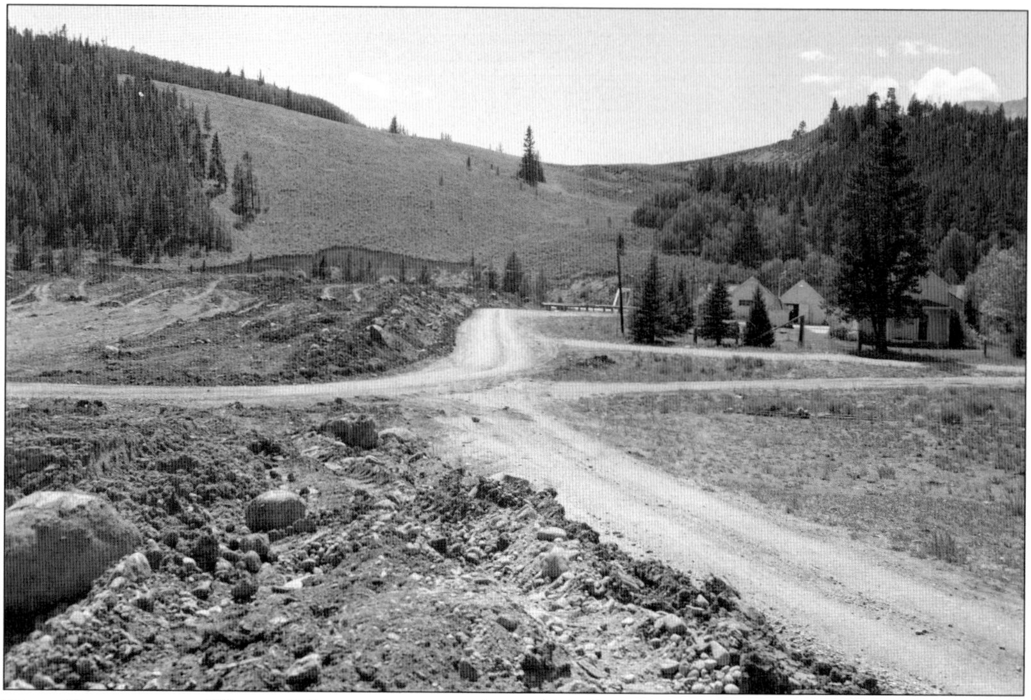

Dam Foundation Work. This is the view from 600 degrees north of the axis at Station No. 15 and No. 50, showing the toe of spoil area along the county road. This photograph is dated August 9, 1956.

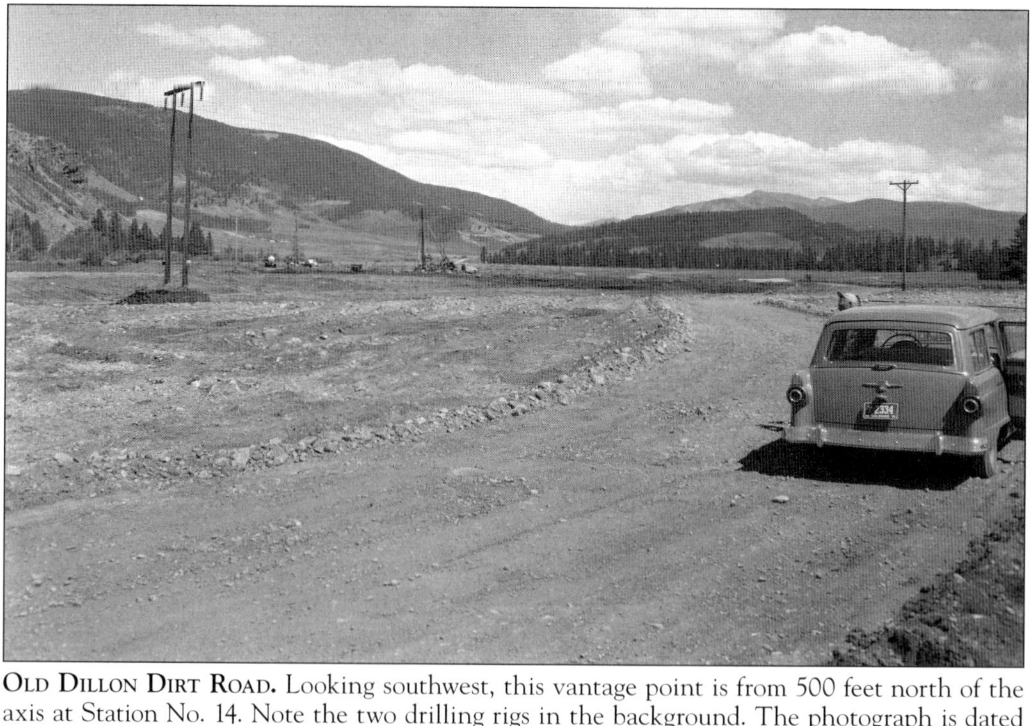

Old Dillon Dirt Road. Looking southwest, this vantage point is from 500 feet north of the axis at Station No. 14. Note the two drilling rigs in the background. The photograph is dated August 9, 1956.

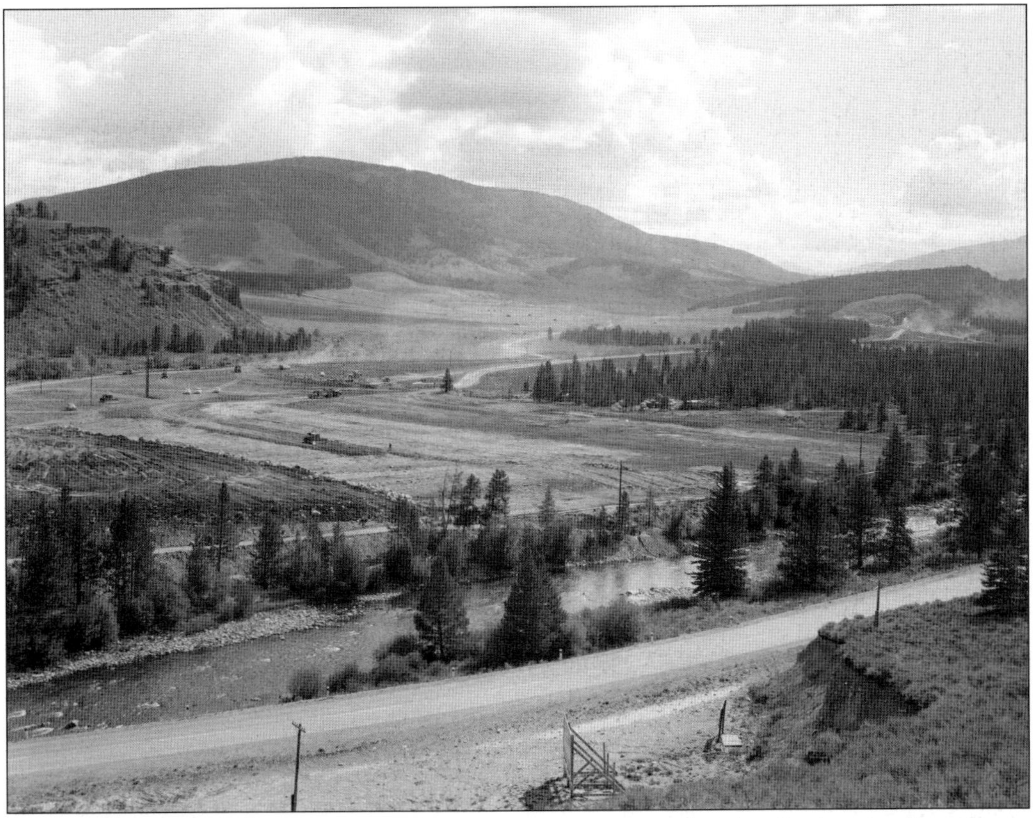

DILLON DAM SITE. Dillon Dam excavation equipment is at work redistributing the flora, fauna, random fill, and earth to accommodate the new reservoir. The point of view is east from a camera site on a hill overlooking the Blue River. This photograph was taken August 29, 1956.

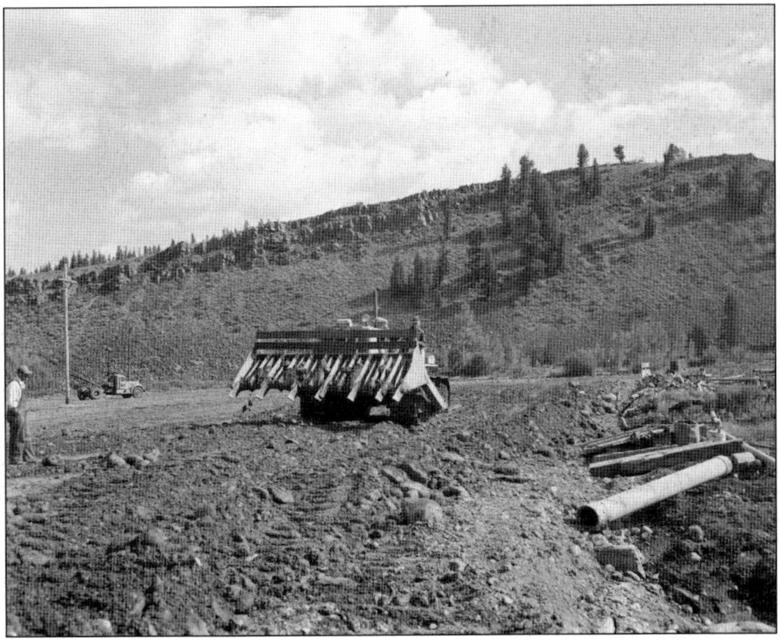

FOUNDATION. The Dillon Dam site foundation is being prepared on August 29, 1956, by utilizing a D8 cat bulldozer equipped with rock raking and scalping of oversized rock.

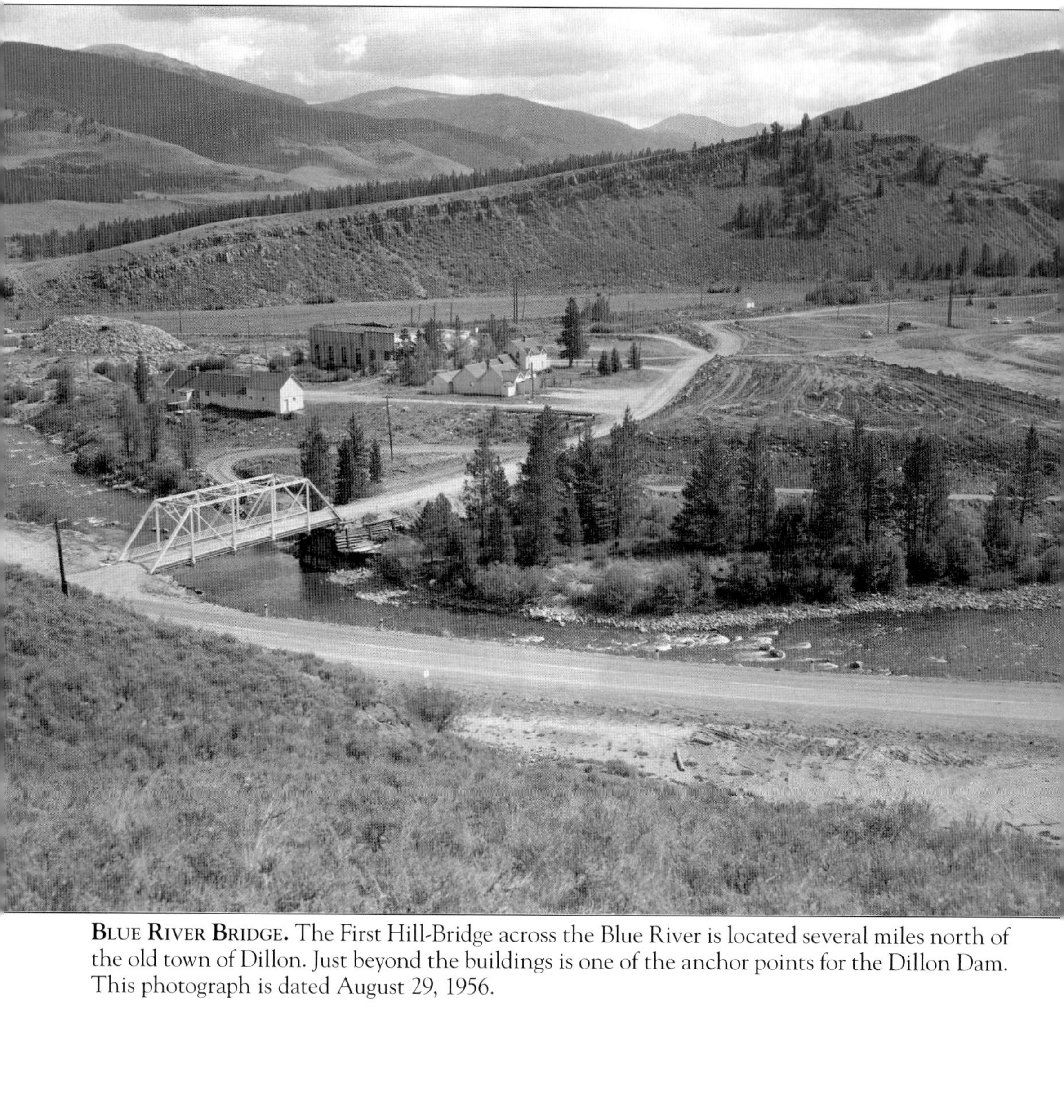

Blue River Bridge. The First Hill-Bridge across the Blue River is located several miles north of the old town of Dillon. Just beyond the buildings is one of the anchor points for the Dillon Dam. This photograph is dated August 29, 1956.

Three

Dam Outlet Works

The outlet works are all the structures and equipment used to control the release of the water from Dillon Dam. The outlet works act much like a drain in a bathtub. The outlet work tunnel, 1,700 feet in diameter, is cut into stable rock. The inlet structure houses a 15-foot, 6-inch fixed-wheel gate mounted horizontally. The tunnel carries dam water underneath the dam to the Blue River channel on the Silverthorne side of the dam. At the bottom of the control tower, as water exits the conduit, it flows into a concrete depression called a stilling basin. The purpose of the stilling basin is to calm the water before it enters the river channel.

The glory hole was designed and built by Denver Water engineers and tested by Colorado State University in Fort Collins, Colorado. The glory hole sits at an elevation of 9,017 feet and directs water down a 233-foot stainless steel shaft, which bends 90 degrees from vertical to horizontal, allowing water to descend at a rate of 15,000 cubic feet per second.

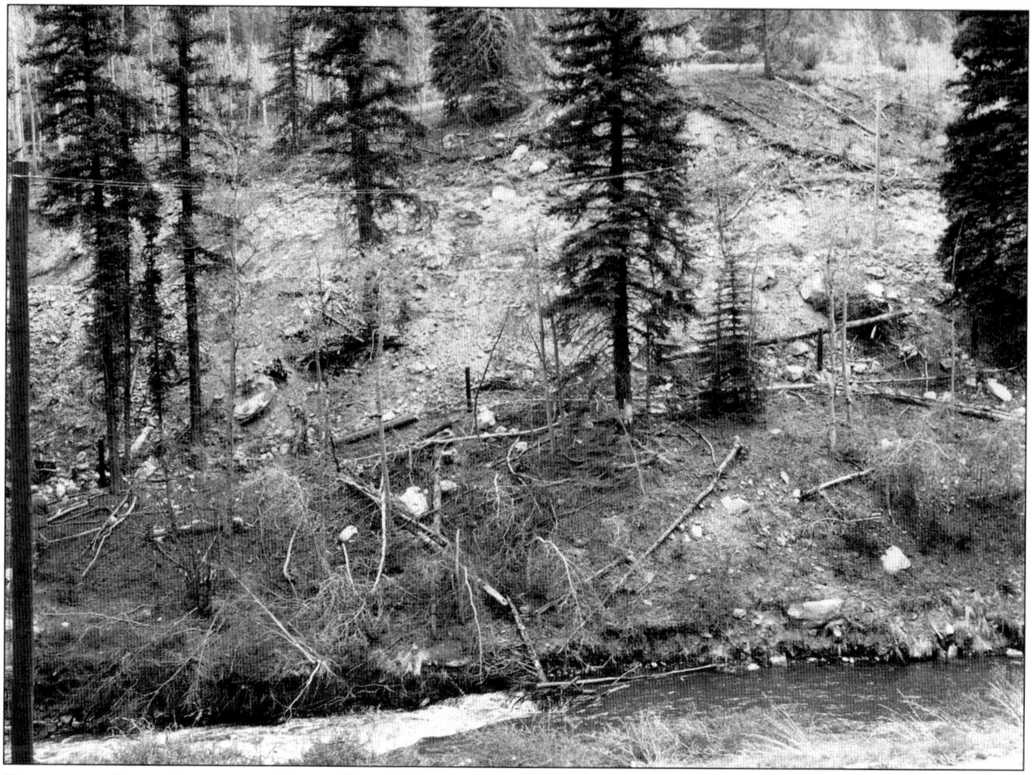

Proposed Location for East Outlet Works. This photograph, taken in June 1962, is one of many used to determine this site, which was finally selected for the East Portal of Robert Tunnel. This portal eventually allowed Dillon Dam water to be channeled into the North Fork of the South Fork of the Platte River.

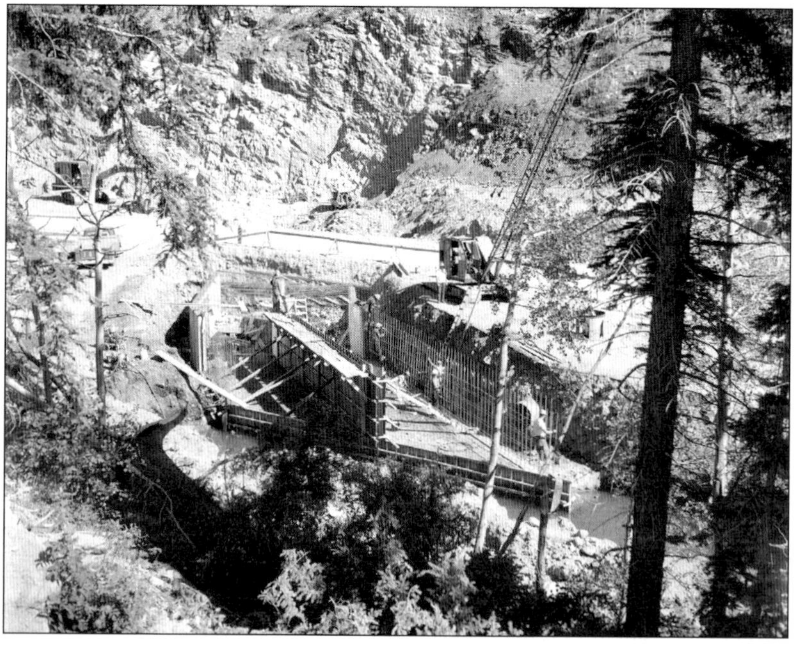

Tunnel Access Work. Work has begun on the tunnel in this photograph, dated June 1962, which looks upstream into the highway structure water crossing.

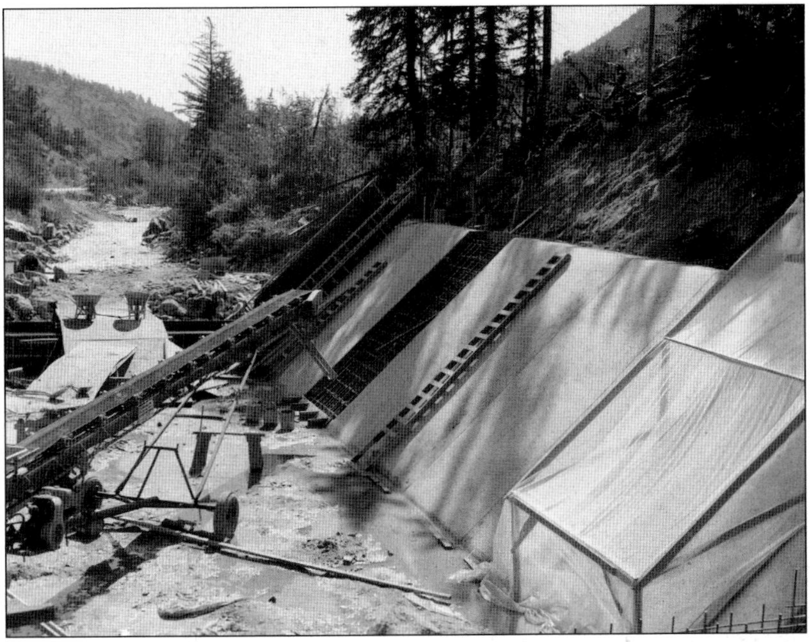

Outlet Works Project. This vantage point faces downstream through the outlet structures project, which had just begun as of June 1962.

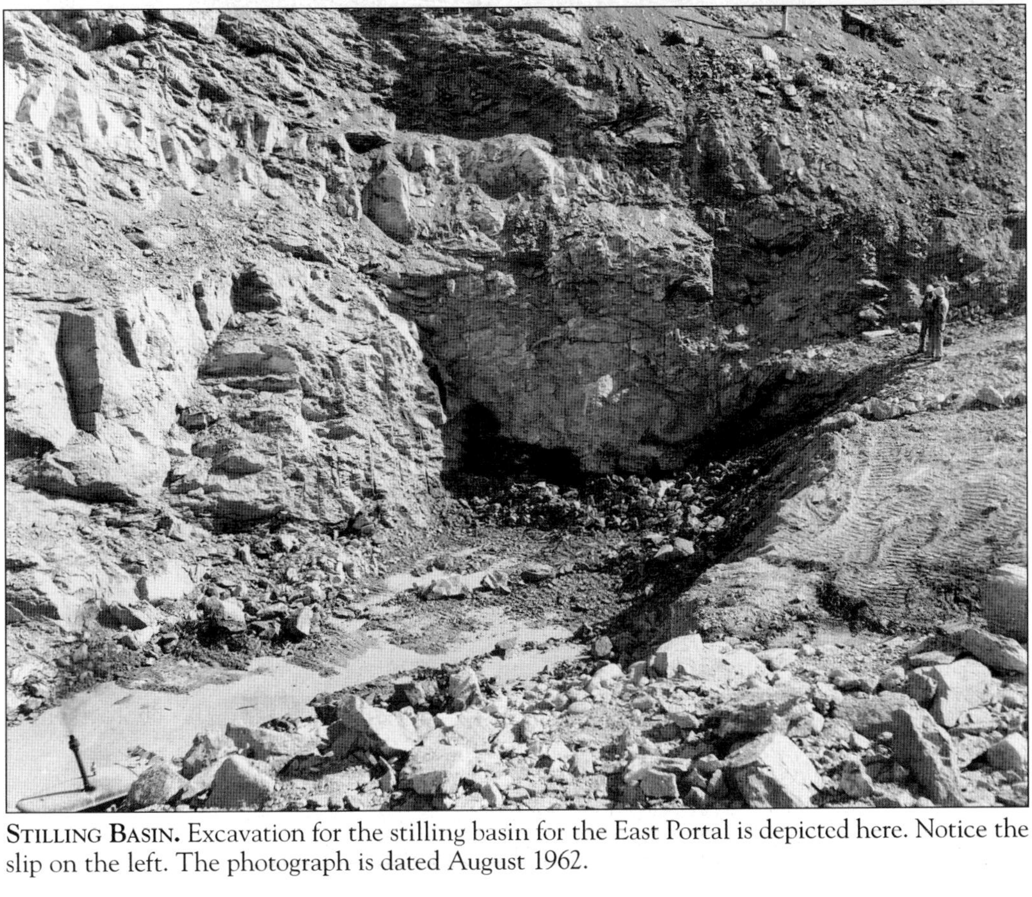

Stilling Basin. Excavation for the stilling basin for the East Portal is depicted here. Notice the slip on the left. The photograph is dated August 1962.

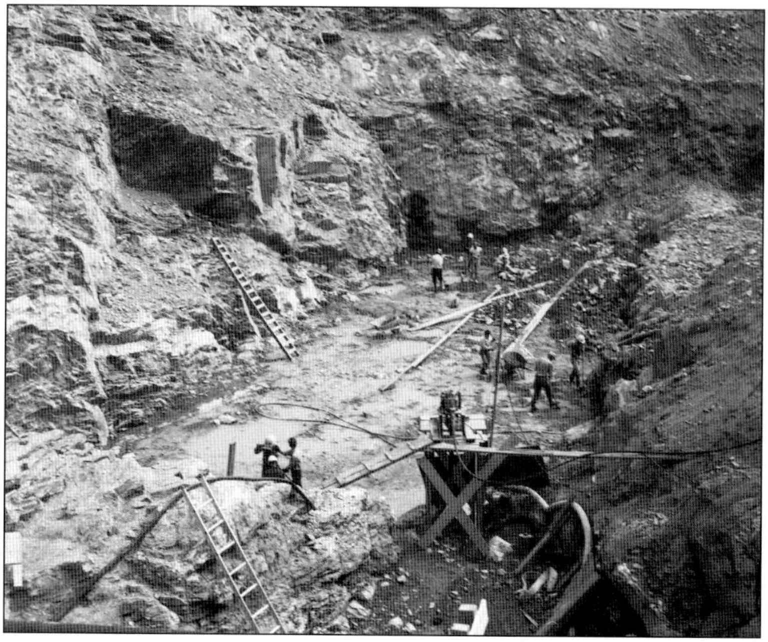

Excavation Ladder. The stilling basin excavation ladder is seen at the East Portal Outlet Works in September 1962.

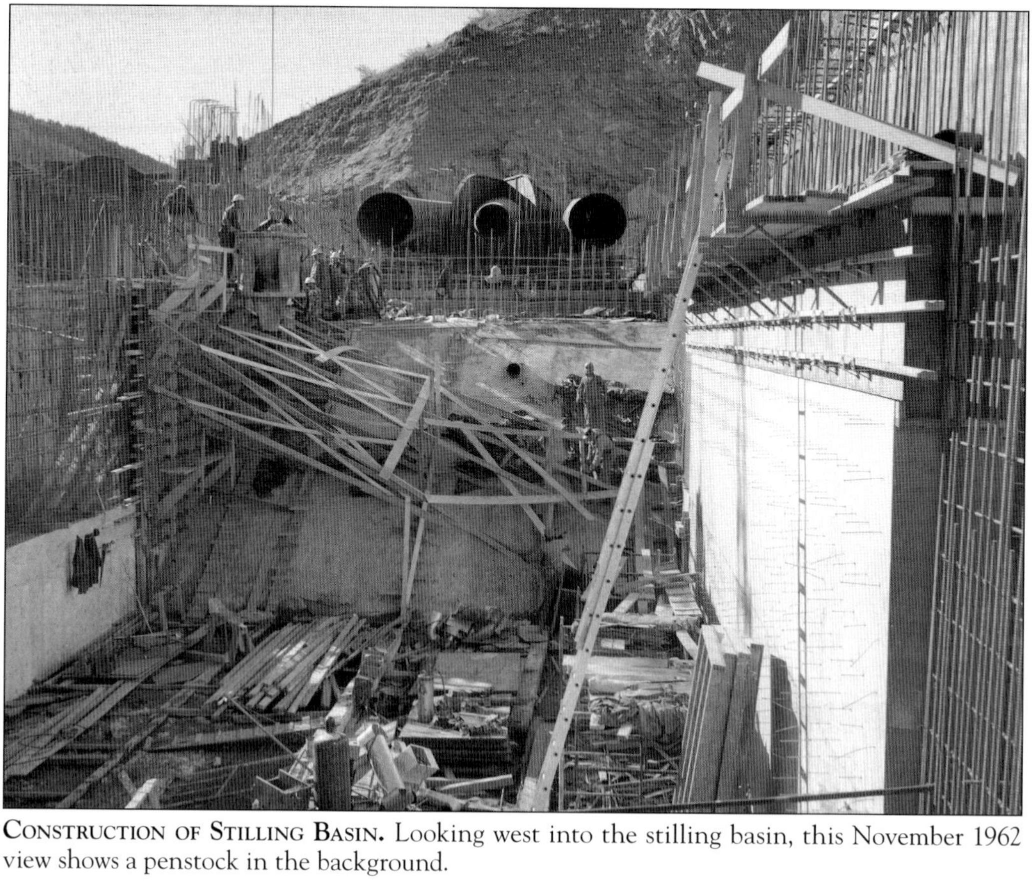

Construction of Stilling Basin. Looking west into the stilling basin, this November 1962 view shows a penstock in the background.

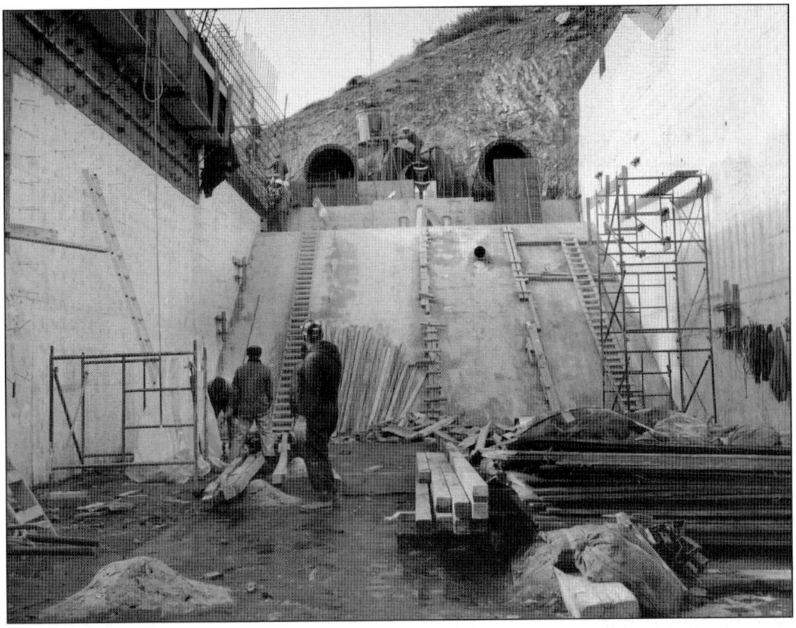

East Portal, Roberts Tunnel Outlet Works. The ready supply of the penstock at the Y-branch is plainly in view in this photograph, which was taken in November 1962.

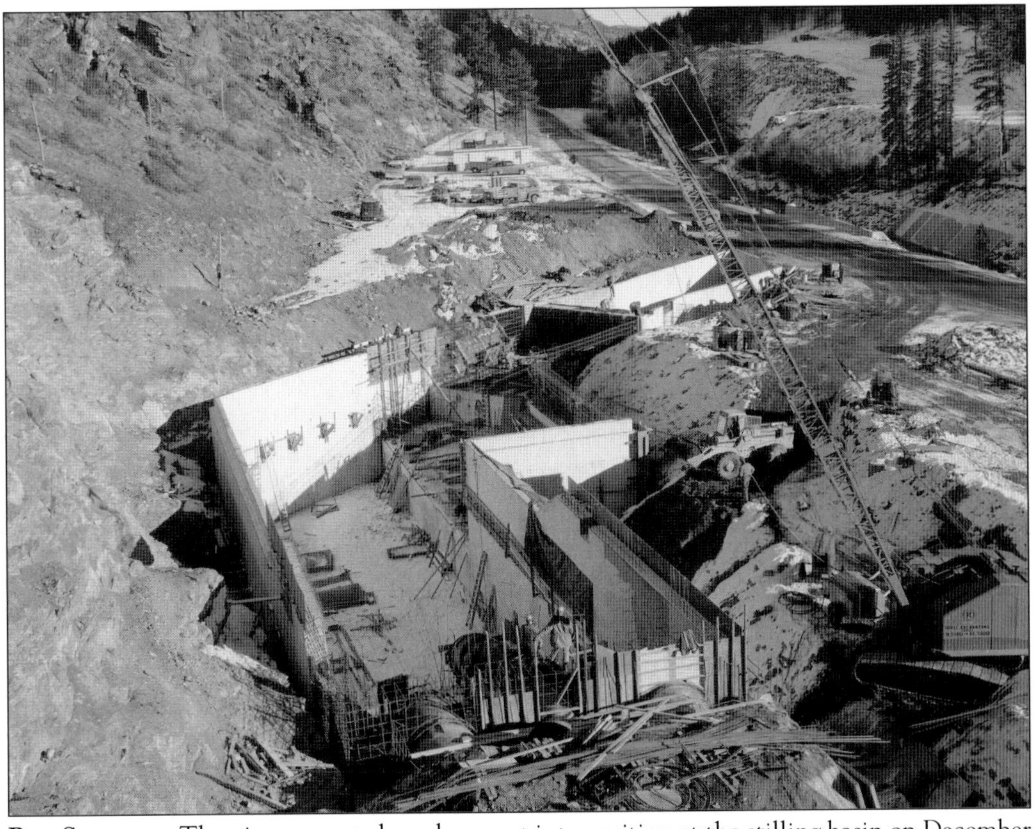

Pipe Supports. The pipe supports have been put into position at the stilling basin on December 14, 1962, at the Roberts Tunnel's East Portal Outlet Works project.

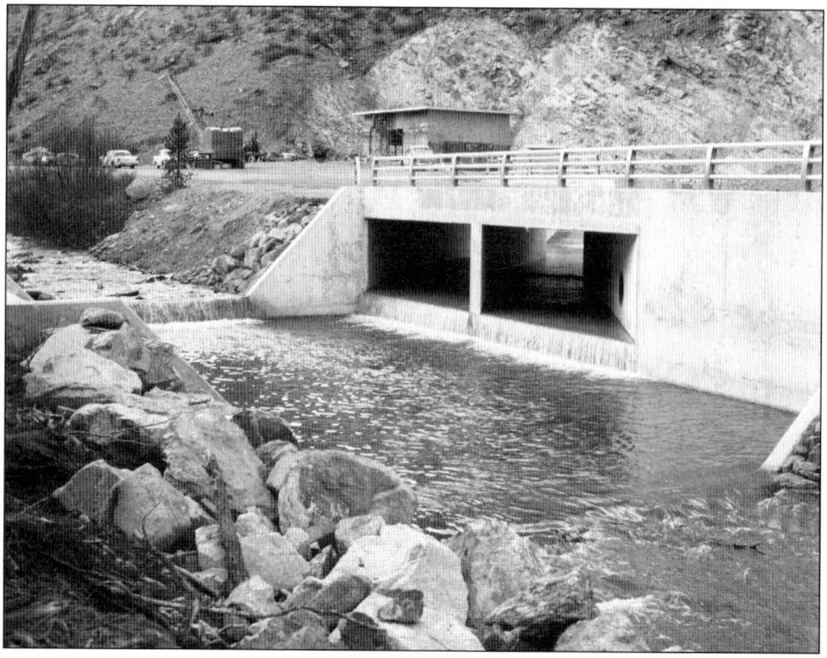

East Portal General View. A complete overview of the East Portal of the Roberts Tunnel Outlet Works is seen here on January 3, 1963.

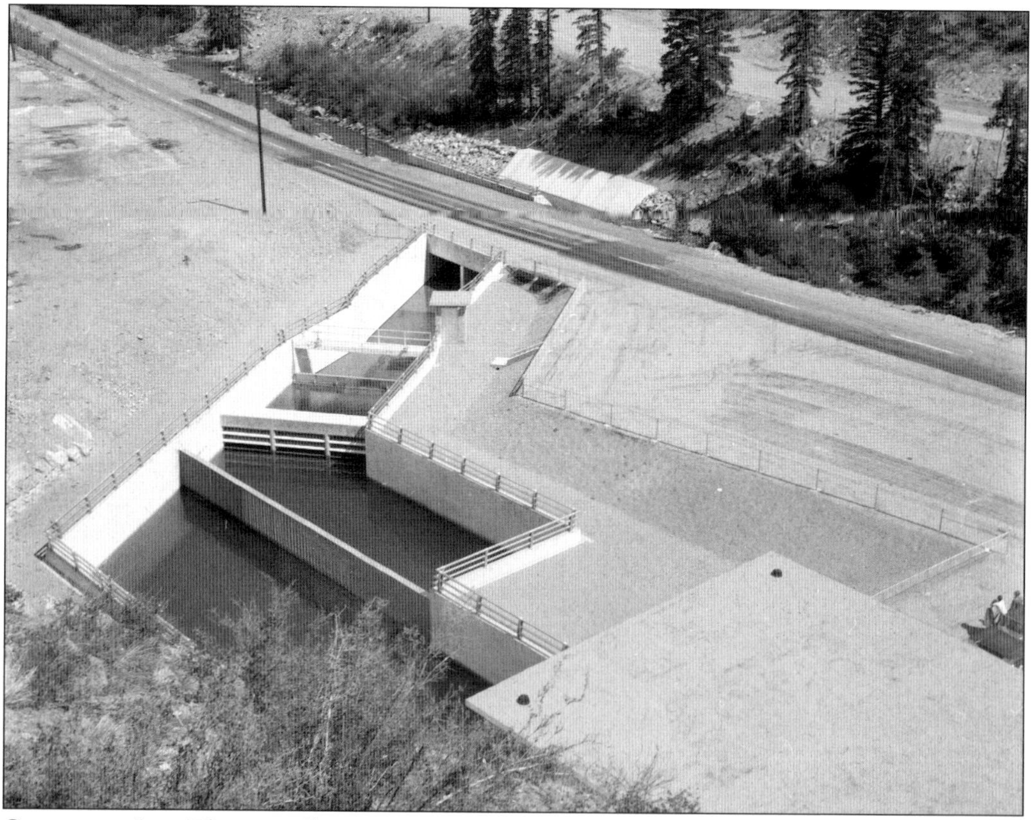

Completed Job. This overall view of the completed job on the East Portal Outlet Works was shot on July 2, 1963.

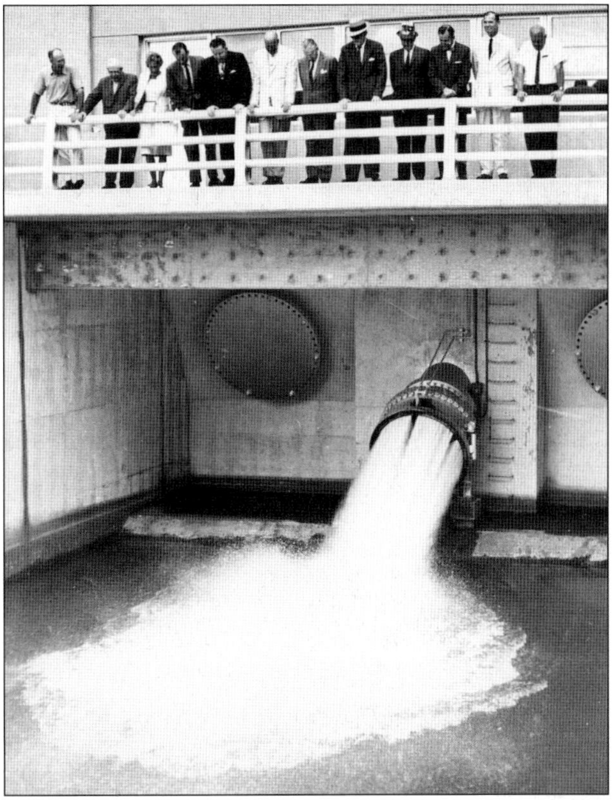

Formal Opening Ceremony. The East Portal of the Roberts Tunnel Outlet Works was formally opened on July 17, 1964. The tunnel discharged a volume of approximately 50 cubic feet of water per second into the North Fork of the South Platte River. This brought water from the western slope of the Continental Divide into Denver via the N. S. Marston Filter Plant. The dignitaries present were N. R. Petry, E. L. Mosley, Mrs. N. R. Petry, Will F. Nicholson Jr., Denver mayor Thomas G. Currigan, Hudson Moore Jr., George R. Morrison, Bill Nicholson Sr., Carl D. Brauns, G. L. Stapp, R. B. McRae, and Ted Adams.

West Side of Dam. The west side of Dillon Dam site contains the outlet works discharge area site on Blue River. This view looks south, showing the riverbed yet to be filled, on December 10, 1959.

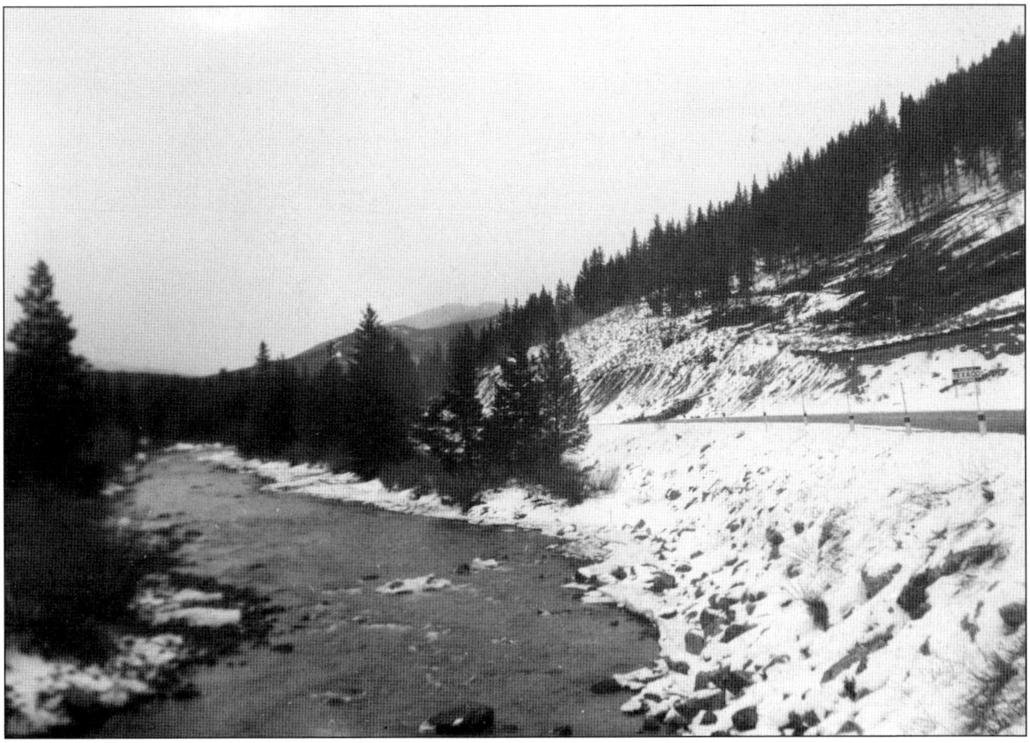

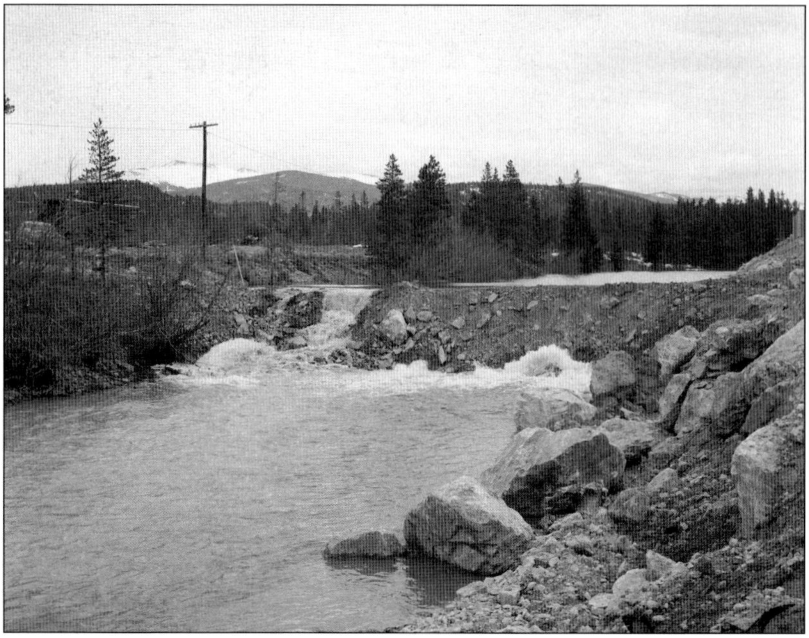

Dillon Dam Outlet. The high water in Blue River, seen from a vantage point looking south, is cutting fill on the road from the discharge excavation to the stockpile area. The photograph was taken on April 6, 1960.

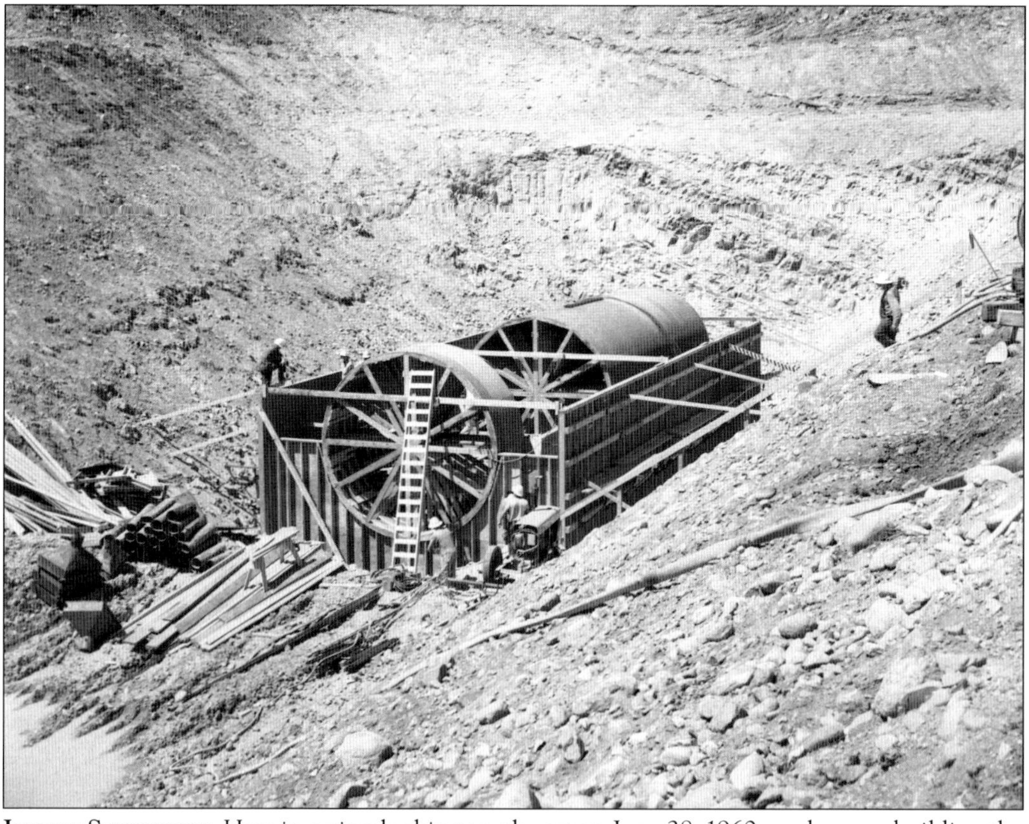

Intake Structure. Here in a view looking southwest on June 28, 1960, workers are building the forms for the intake structure at the Dillon Dam Outlet Works.

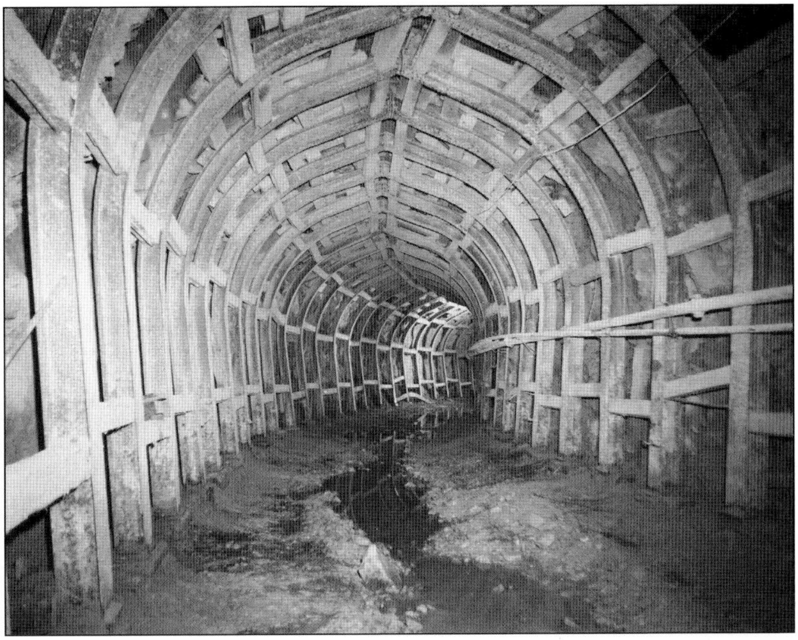

Outlet. This image looks toward the downstream portal from Station No. 11 at the Dillon Dam Outlet Works tunnel on July 1, 1960.

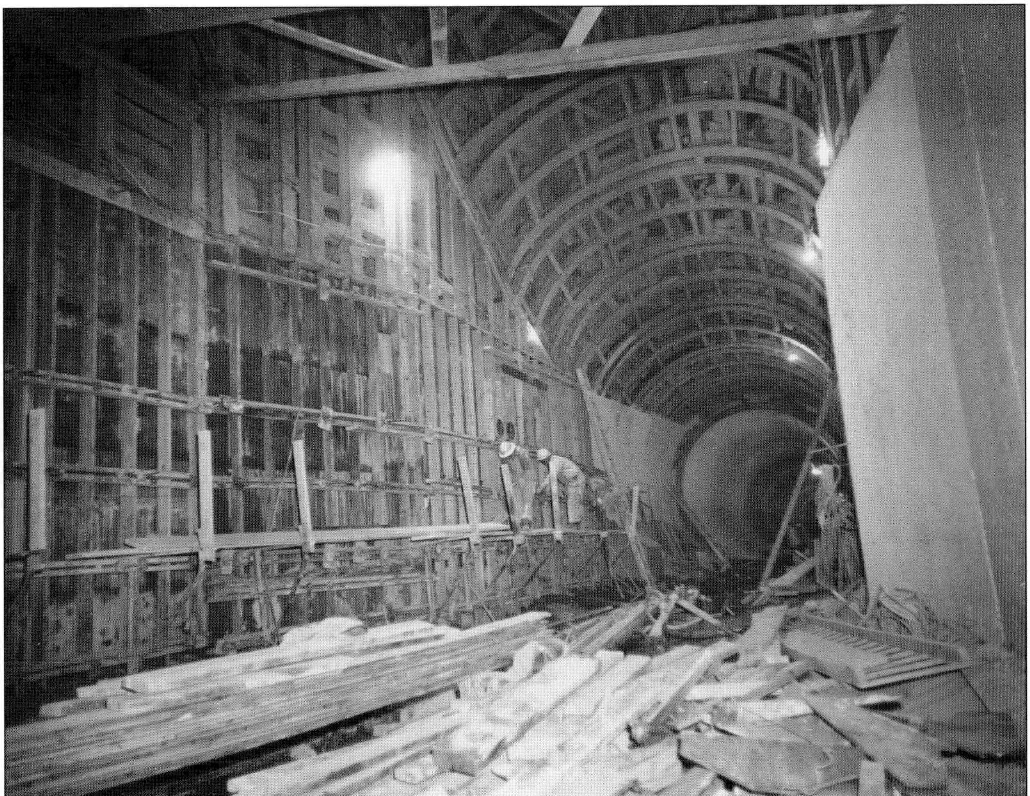

Works Tunnel. The view here is northeast in the Dillon Dam Outlet Works tunnel from Station No. 10 toward the curve on September 6, 1960.

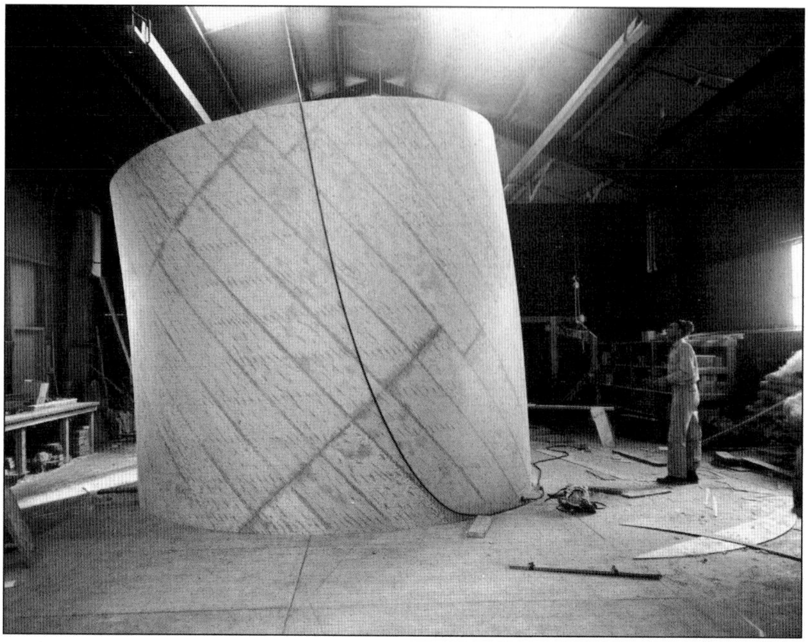

Gate Chamber. The point of view is downstream in the gate chamber. Here are people stripping the forms from first stage walls, as seen on February 17, 1961.

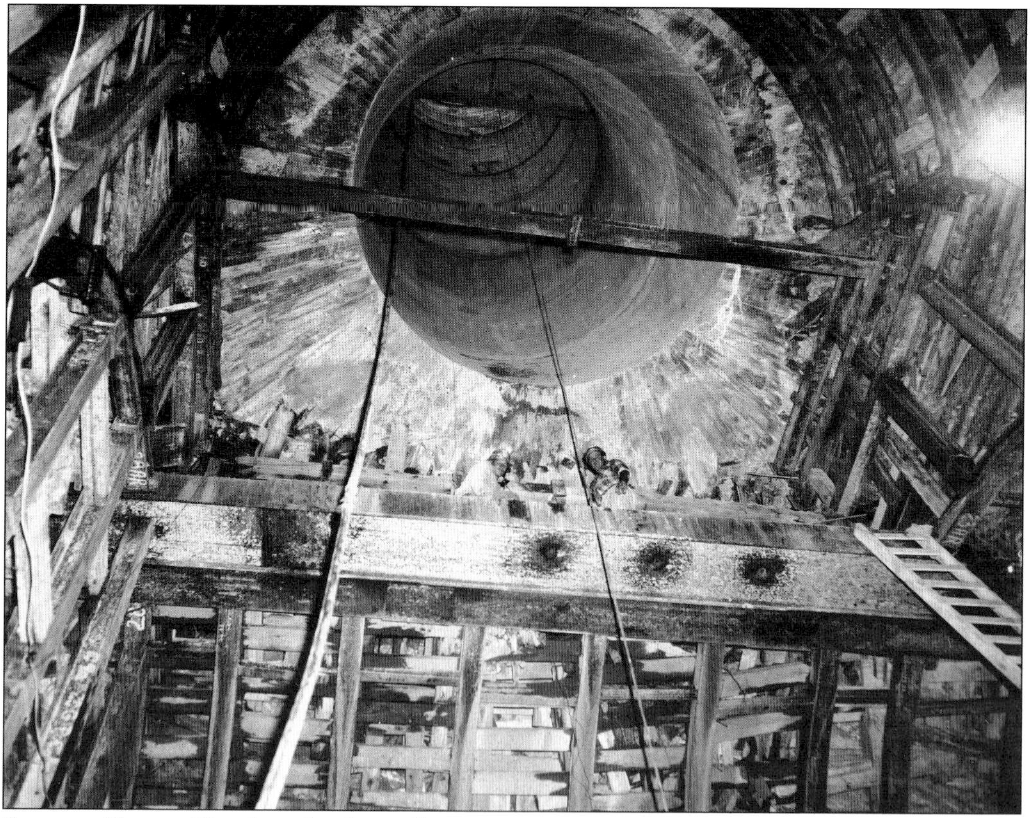

Spillway Forms. The form for the spillway curve is seen in this image, above the elevation of 8,833 feet at the Dillon Dam Outlet Works, on February 21, 1961.

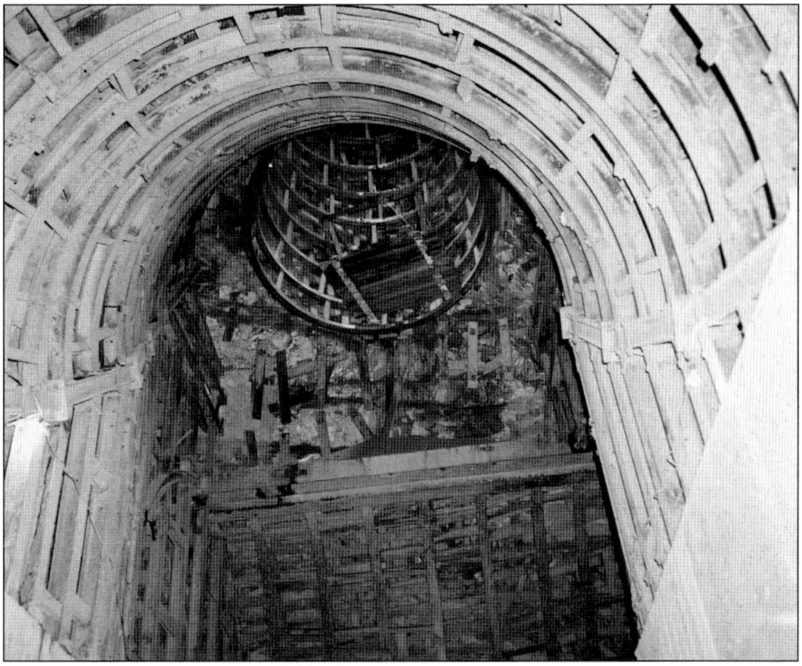

SPILLWAY SHAFT. Looking upstream at the spillway shaft in the gate chamber of the dam, this image was taken after the bulkhead under the shaft had fallen. This is at the Dillon Dam outlet works project on March 27, 1961.

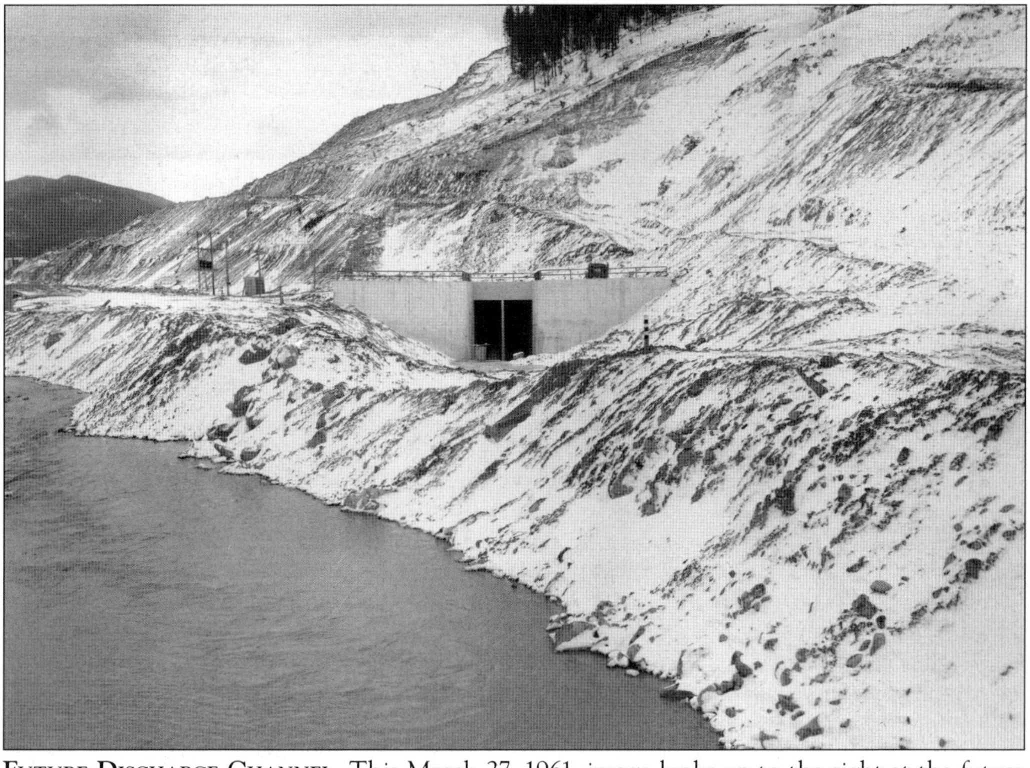

FUTURE DISCHARGE CHANNEL. This March 27, 1961, image looks up to the right at the future discharge channel that will direct water to the stilling basin from the temporary construction bridge across the Blue River.

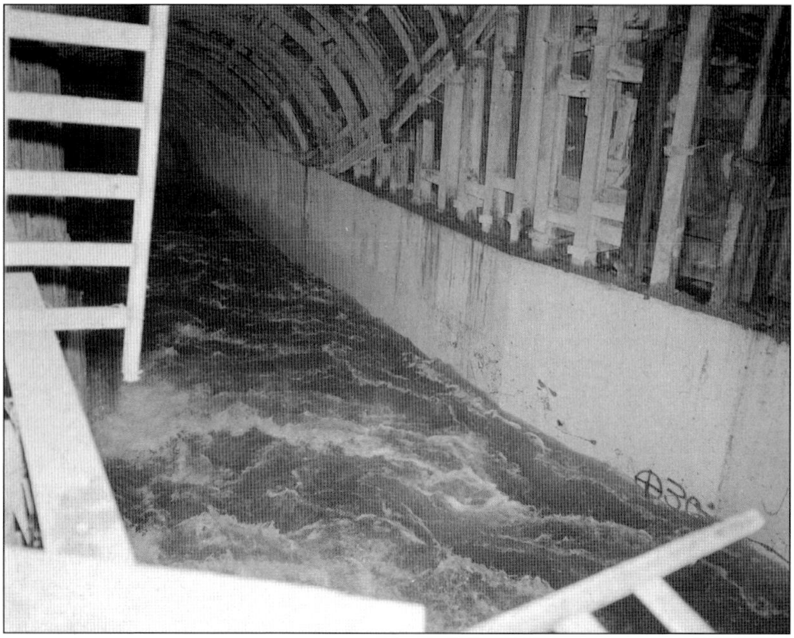

Blue River Diversion. This view downstream in the gate chamber shows the Blue River diversion at the Dillon Dam Outlet Works on June 16, 1961.

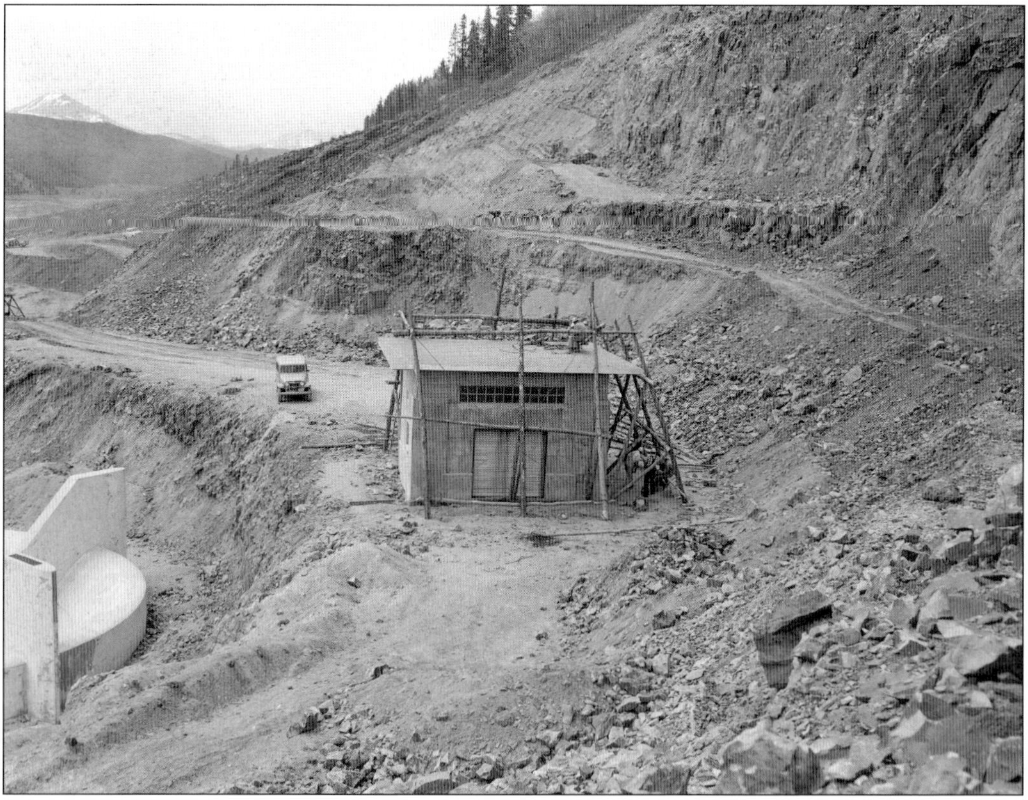

Dillon Outlet Works Control House. The protective structure was necessary at this time to keep rocks and debris from falling into the shaft. A more permanent structure was eventually constructed. The view is looking south on June 11, 1962.

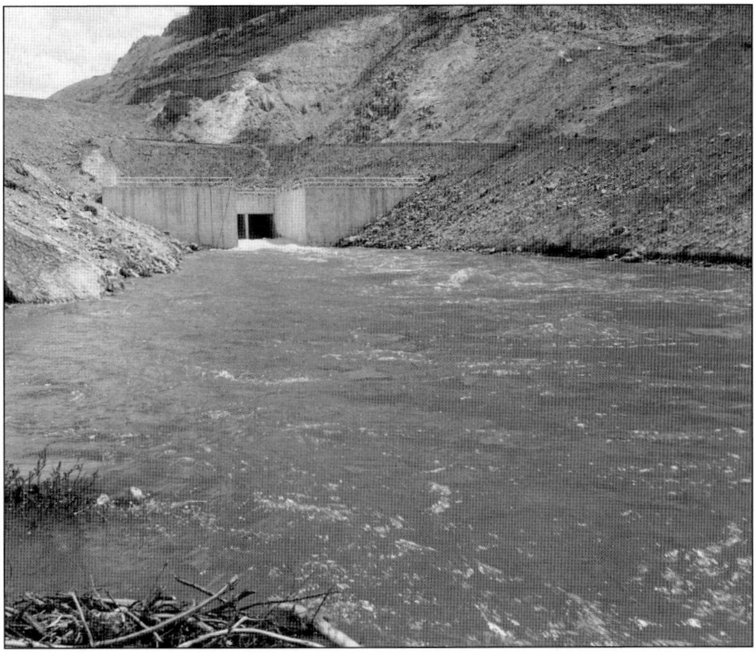

Overflow Discharge Structure. The Dillon Dam Outlet Works site discharges water when necessary and planned. It is pictured here looking south on June 13, 1962.

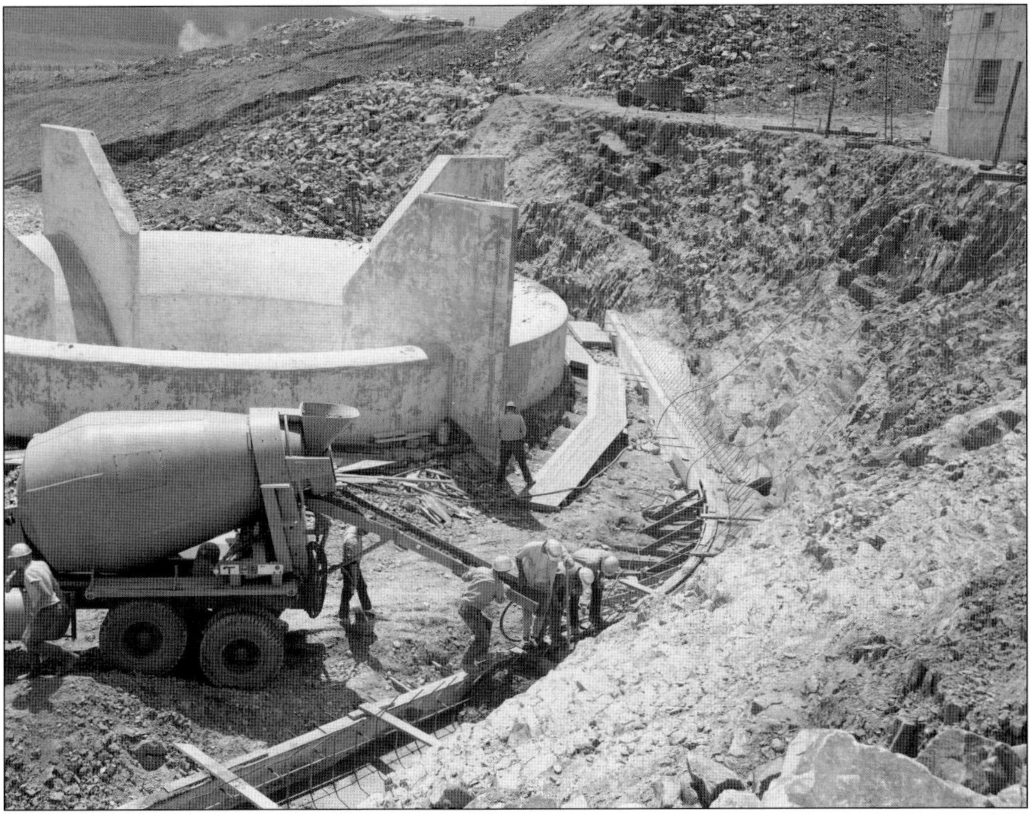

Building Concrete Wall for Overflow. Crews place concrete footing for a protective wall at the spillway approach area at the Dillon Dam on August 9, 1963.

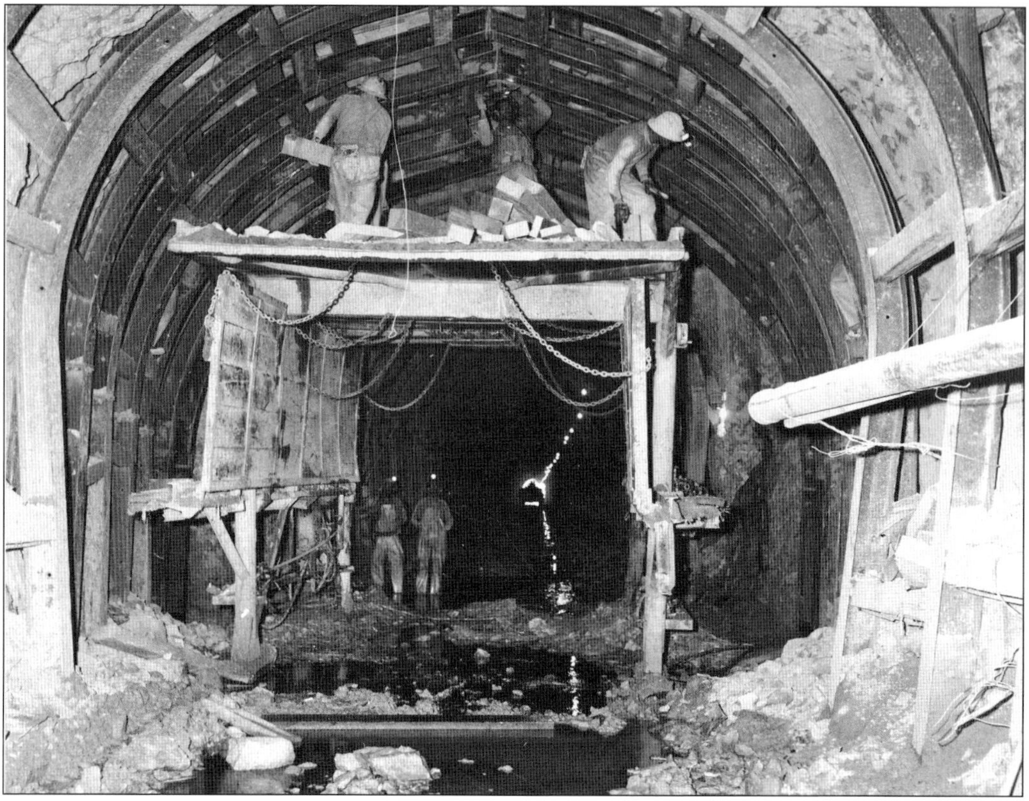

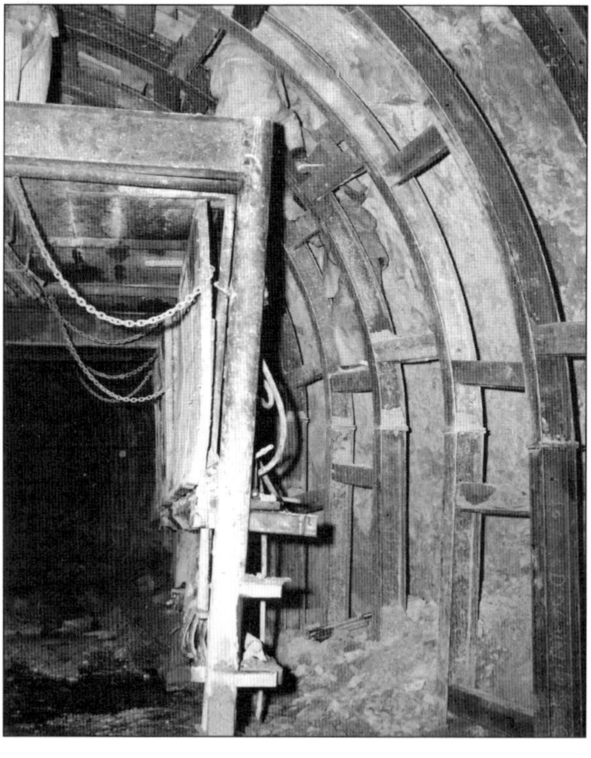

Works Gate Chamber. The Dillon Dam Outlet Works gate chamber arch is seen at Station No. 12. The view is looking upstream on September 10, 1963.

Gate Chamber at the Arch. The Dillon Dam Outlet Works is seen in this image, looking upward in the gate chamber into the spillway on September 10, 1963.

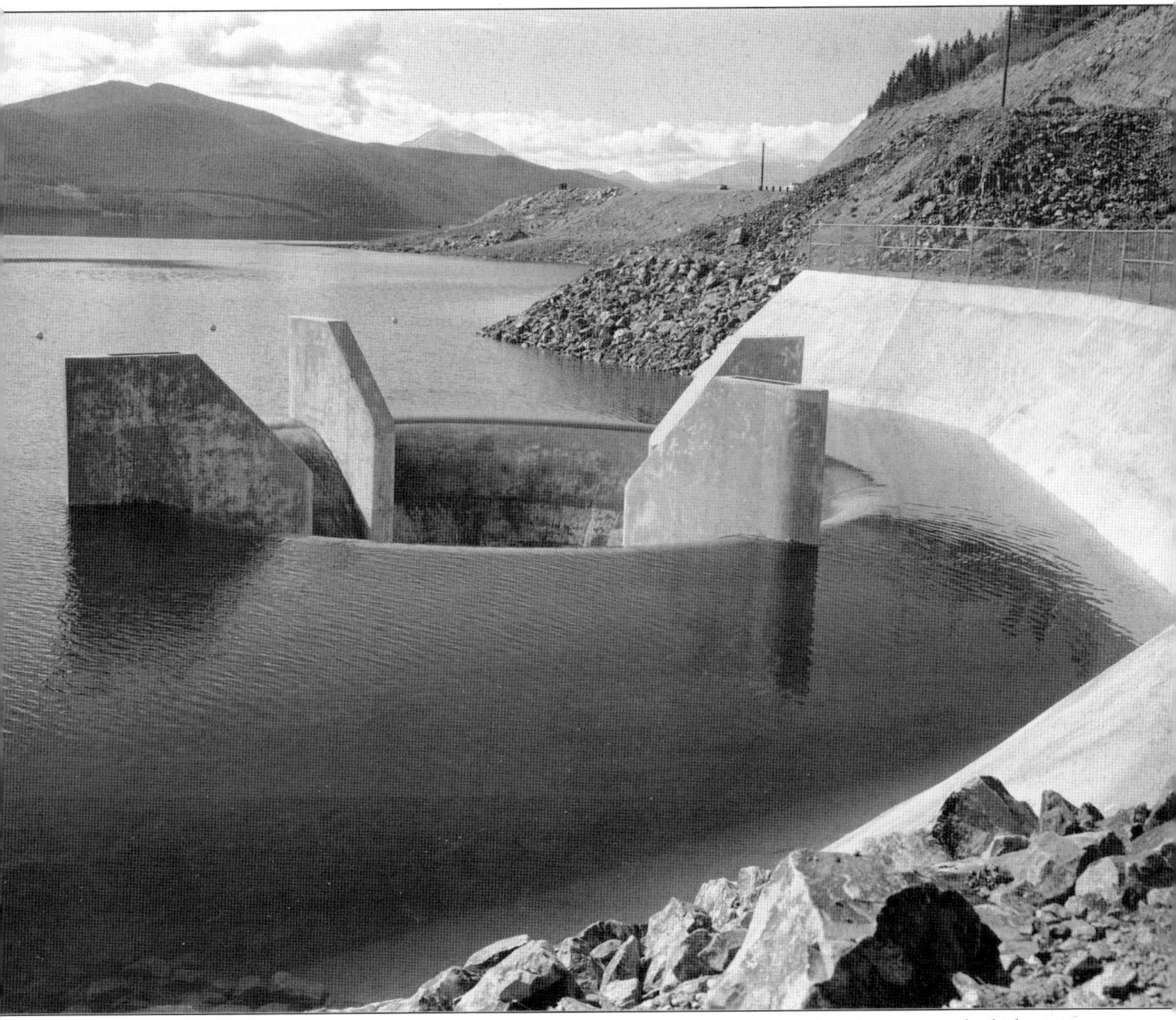

Spillway Overflow. The Dillon Dam Outlet Works spillway overflow has been popularly known as the "glory hole." Here it is during the first filling of the reservoir to capacity in August 1965.

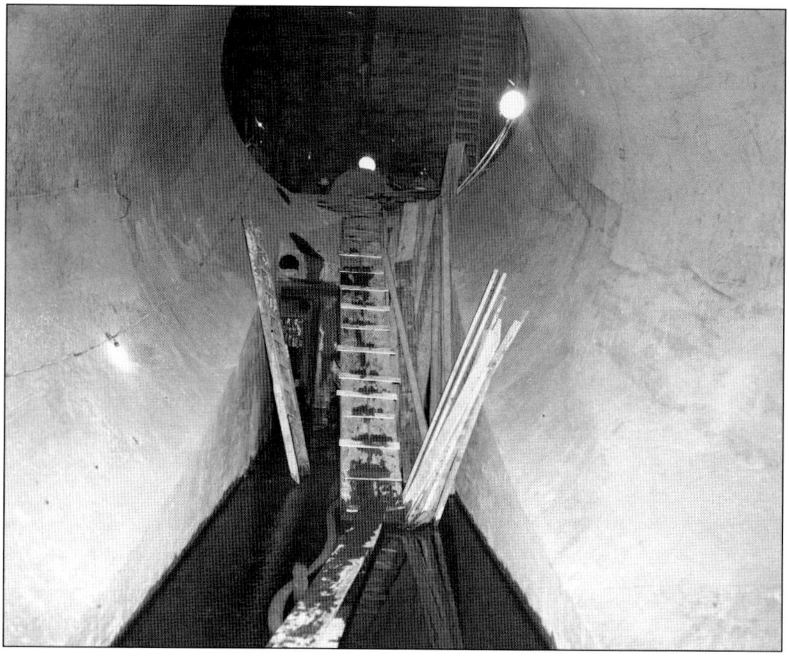

TUNNEL SUPPORTS. At the Dillon Dam Outlet Works tunnel, blocks are placed in a large over-break section at Station No. 11 on July 1, 1960.

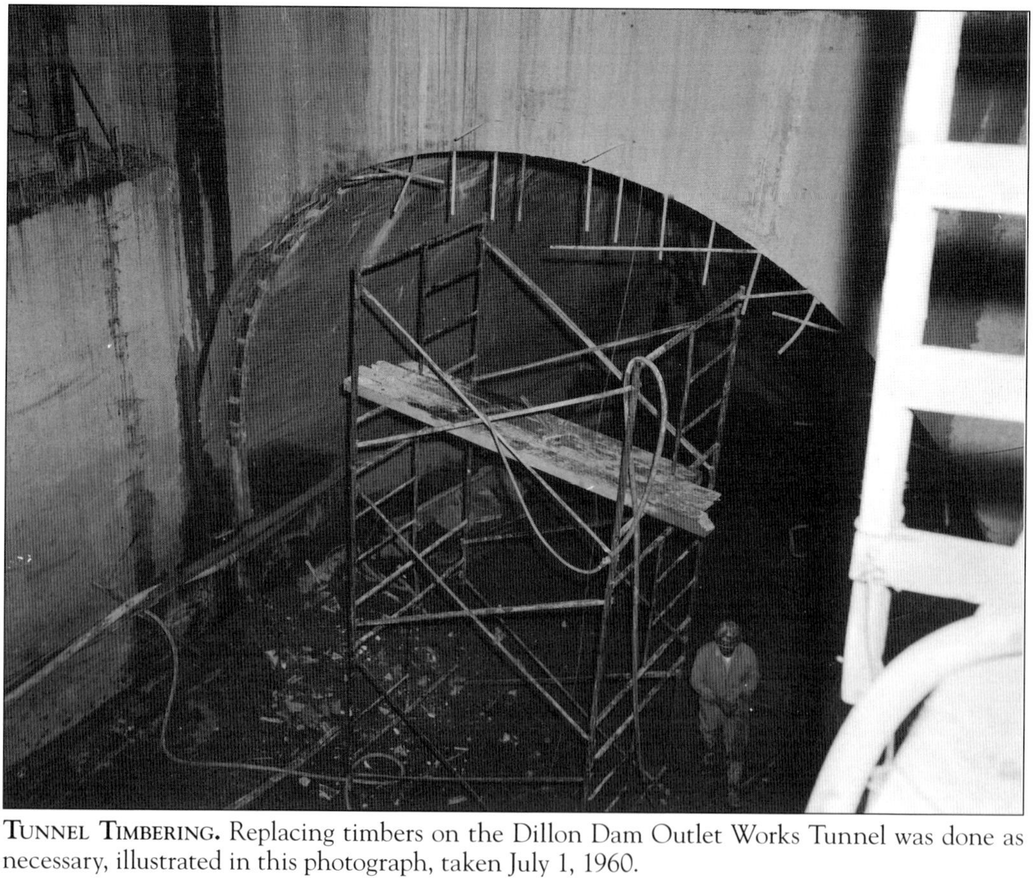

TUNNEL TIMBERING. Replacing timbers on the Dillon Dam Outlet Works Tunnel was done as necessary, illustrated in this photograph, taken July 1, 1960.

Four

THE TUNNEL

"Get that water to Denver!" Mayor Currigan reportedly yelled at one of his support staff. To do so, Denver Water designed and built, at that time, one of the longest major underground tunnels of its kind in the world utilizing the power of nature—gravity. To make certain there would be an adequate gravity flow of water, the west portal is 174.2 feet higher than the eastern portal. The gradient averages 7 feet per mile over the course of 23.3 miles in length. The inside diameter of 10 feet, 3 inches permits the tunnel to carry 1,000 cubic feet of water per second or 680 million gallons per day, assuming a water level at 9,017 feet.

Tunnel construction utilized a double-shell lining system consisting of both initial support and final lining separated by a waterproofing and drainage system. The support includes steel fiber reinforcing, or shotcrete. It also includes lattice girders, rock dowels, and other ground-stabilizing techniques. The final lining was constructed of cast-in-place reinforced concrete after the initial support and waterproofing had been placed.

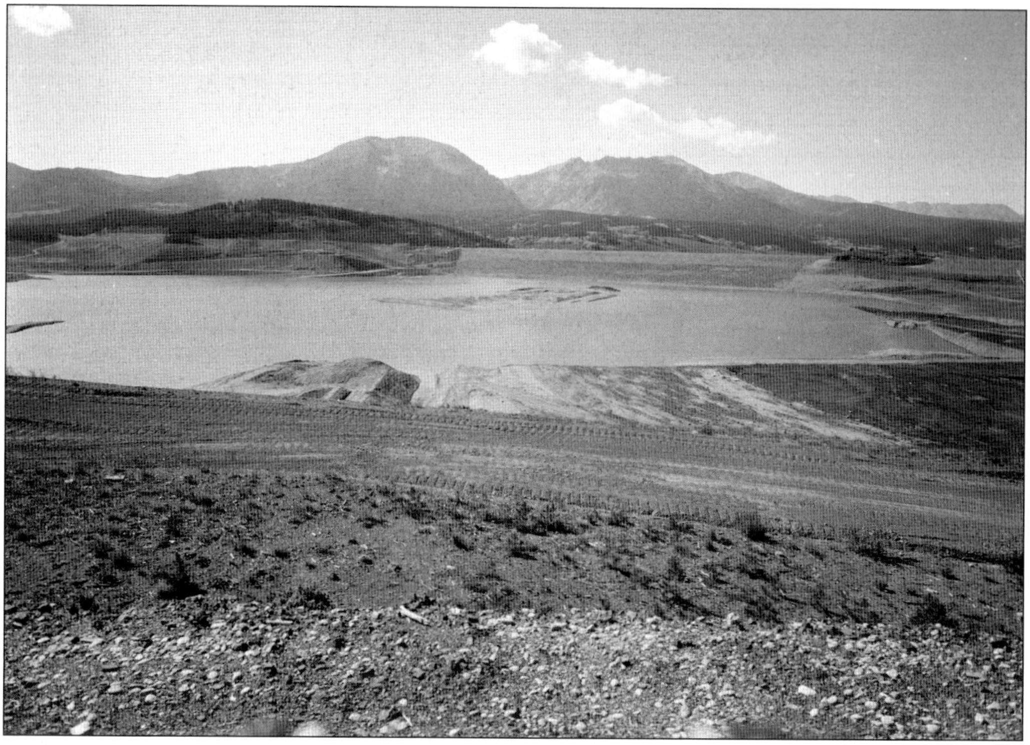

Above Roberts Tunnel. This image looks west from above the Roberts Tunnel intake at the Dillon Dam on March 4, 1963.

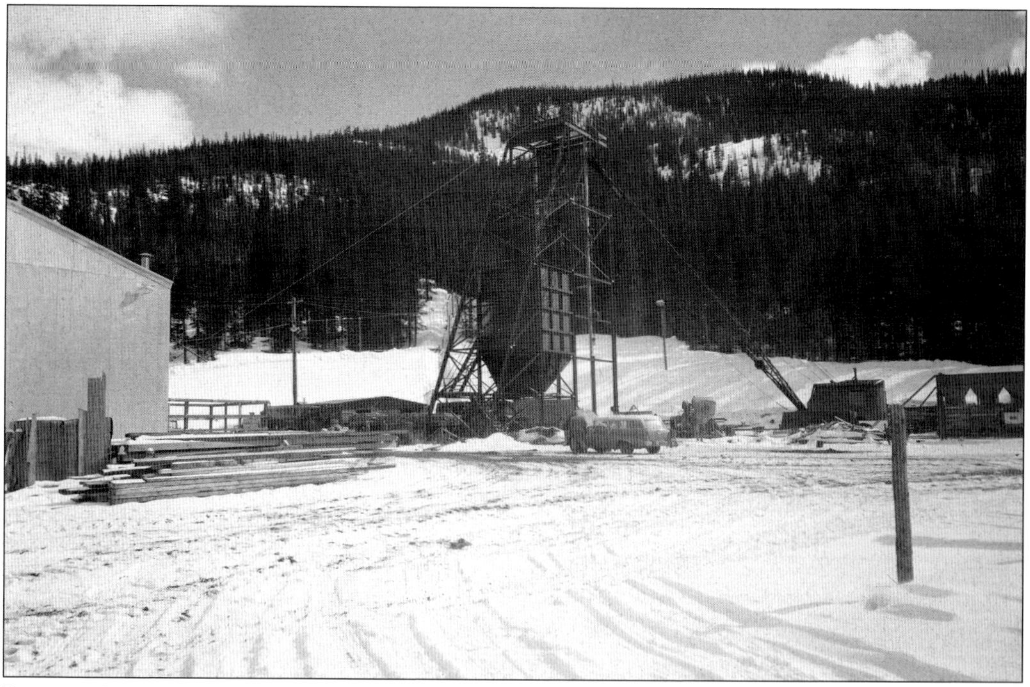

Roberts Tunnel Access Shaft. This is the access shaft hoist and frame house looking southeast on March 4, 1958.

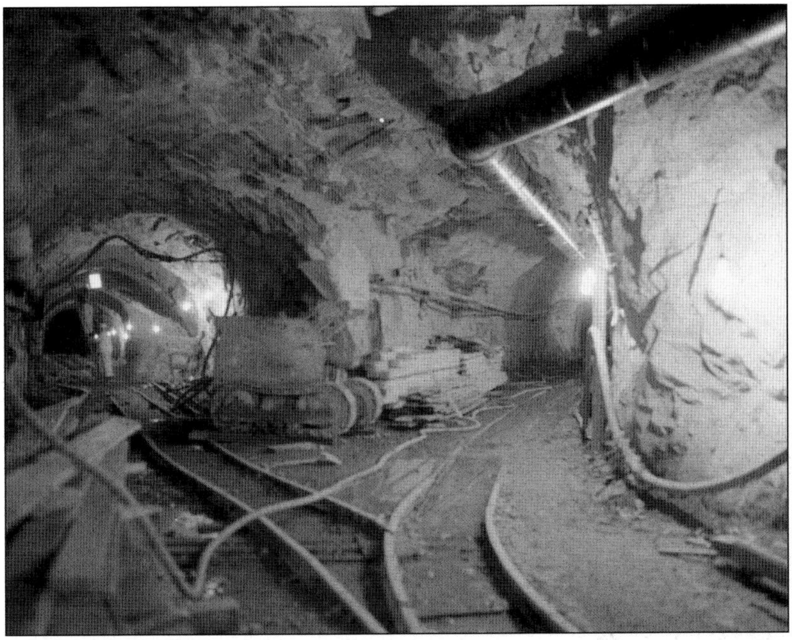

Pump Station. The access shaft in Roberts Tunnel is depicted above the heading junction with Pump Station No. 458. Note the light box in the arch of the Dillon heading. The photograph was taken on December 27, 1957.

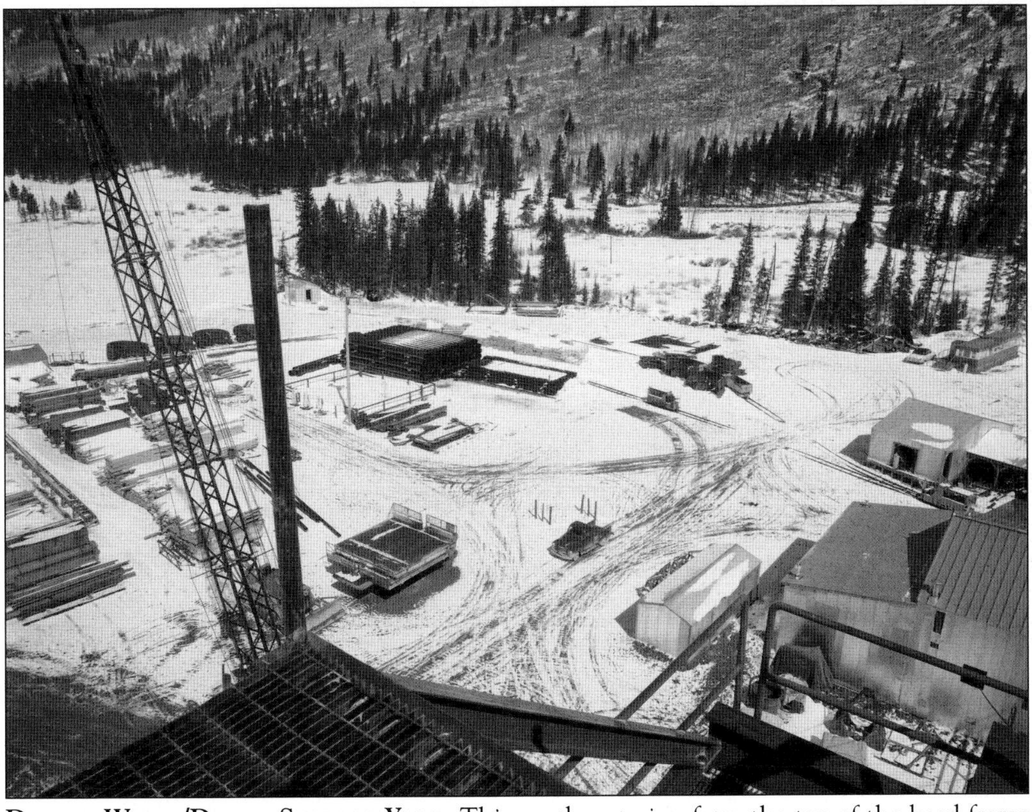

Denver Water/Dillon Storage Yard. This northwest view from the top of the head frame shows the storage yards on April 1, 1958. Notice the train tracks and train for this temporary storage division.

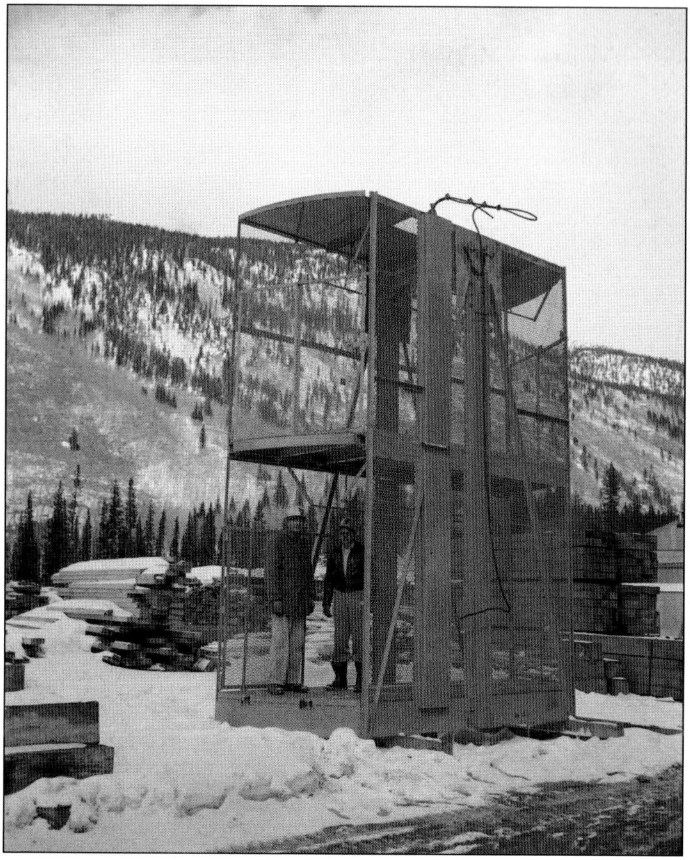

Man Trip Cage. The man trip cage at the bottom of the access shaft is visible in Roberts Tunnel. The fan and water discharge lines are at the upper right side. The view here is due west, and the date is April 12, 1958.

Access Shaft of the Dillon Heading. The Roberts Tunnel's main access shaft is pictured on April 1, 1958. It was the first supported section in the Dillon heading. The steel starts at Station No. 456.

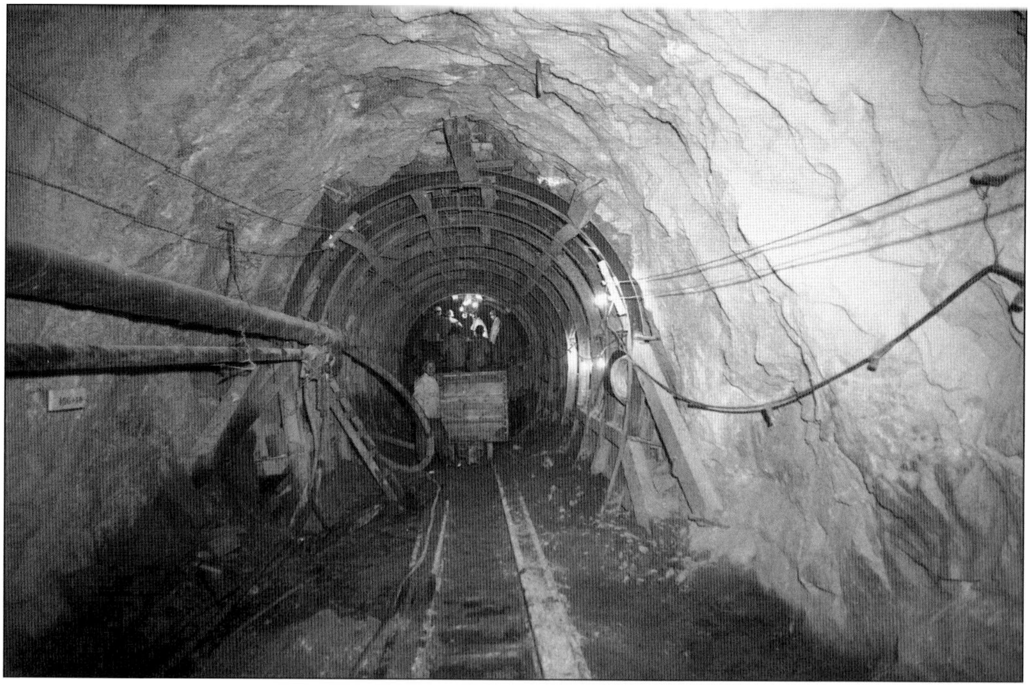

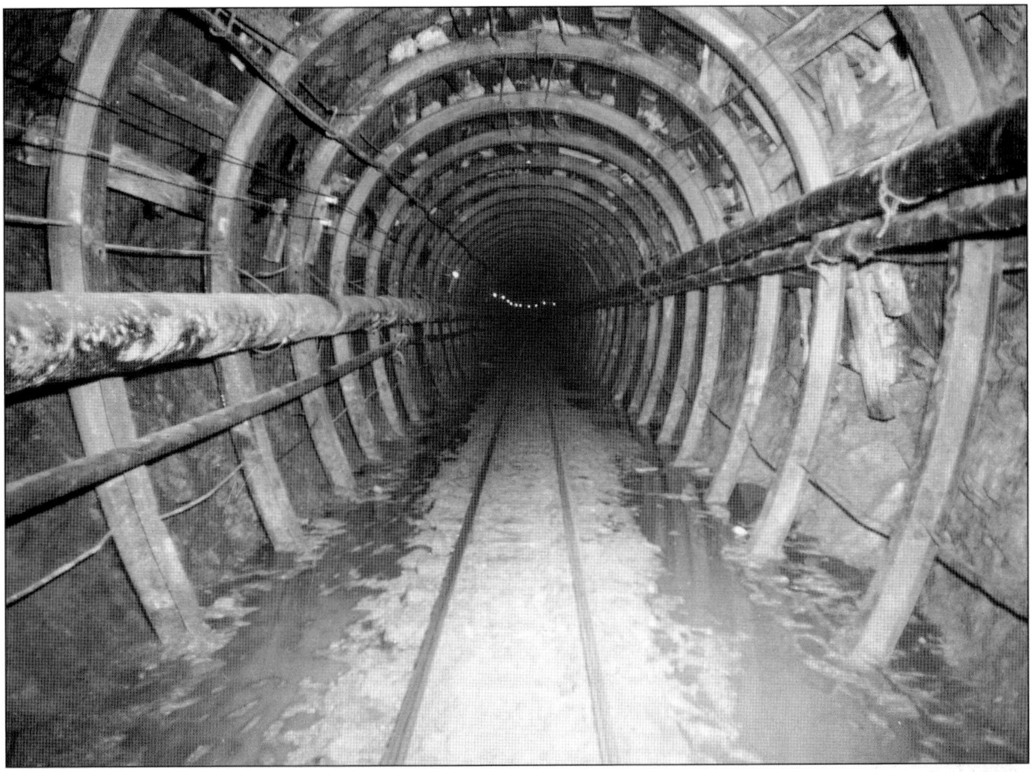

Grant Heading Access Shaft. Here is the tunnel access shaft at the Grant heading. The July 6, 1960, view is east from Station No. 466, showing the condition of the invert and the water accumulation.

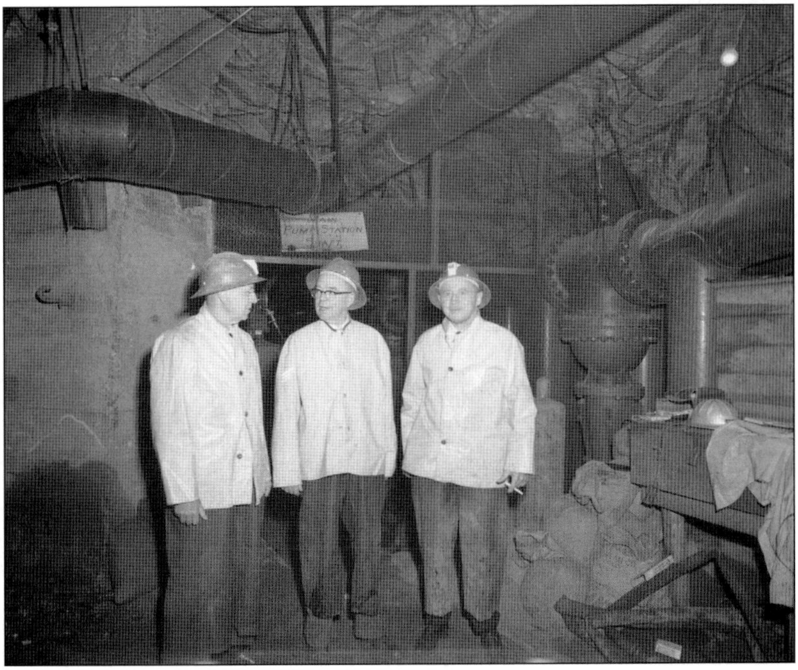

Engineers. Bob Hatcher (left), Tom Campbell (center), and Horace Tomlinson are pictured at the main pump station in the access shaft of Roberts Tunnel on July 20, 1960.

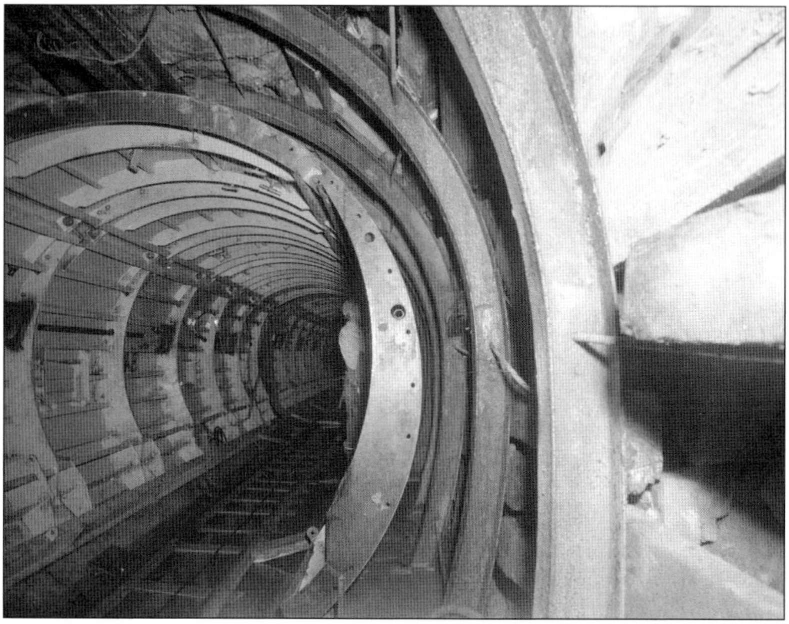

ACCESS SHAFT. The Roberts Tunnel access shaft is seen from an end view with the steel form in place. Notice the space between the forms and the steel rings. This photograph was taken on December 1, 1960.

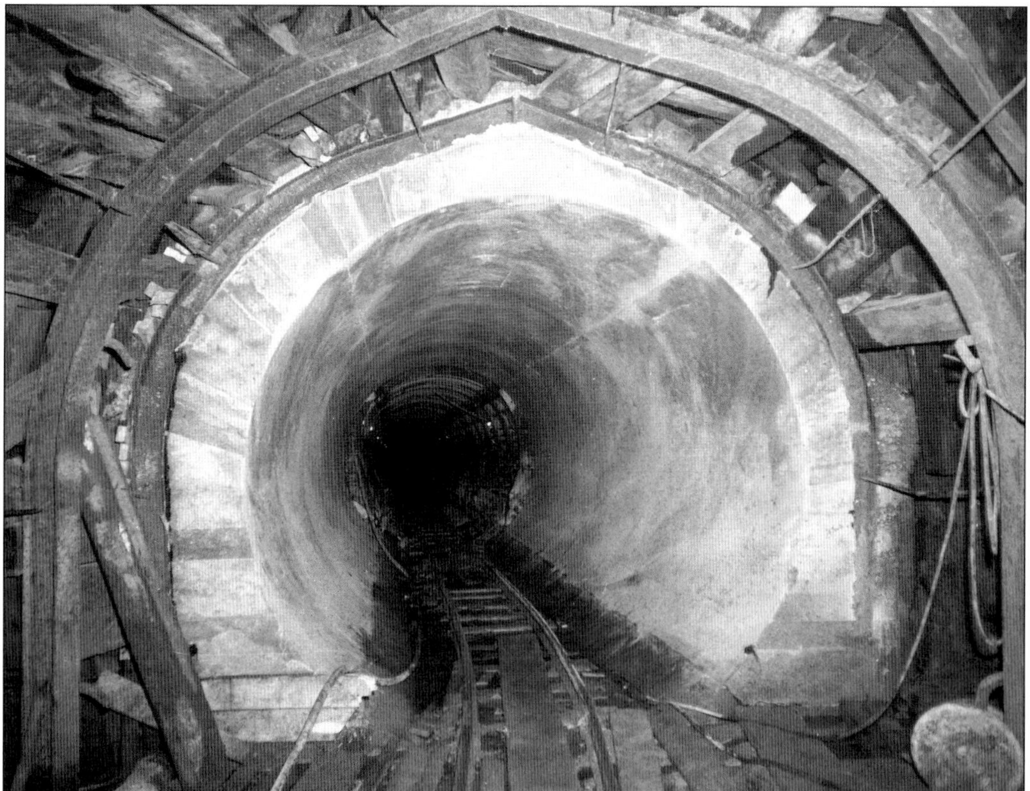

ROBERTS TUNNEL BULKHEAD. The bulkhead at angle point no. 2 is seen in this westward-looking view near the access shaft of the Grant heading of Roberts Tunnel.

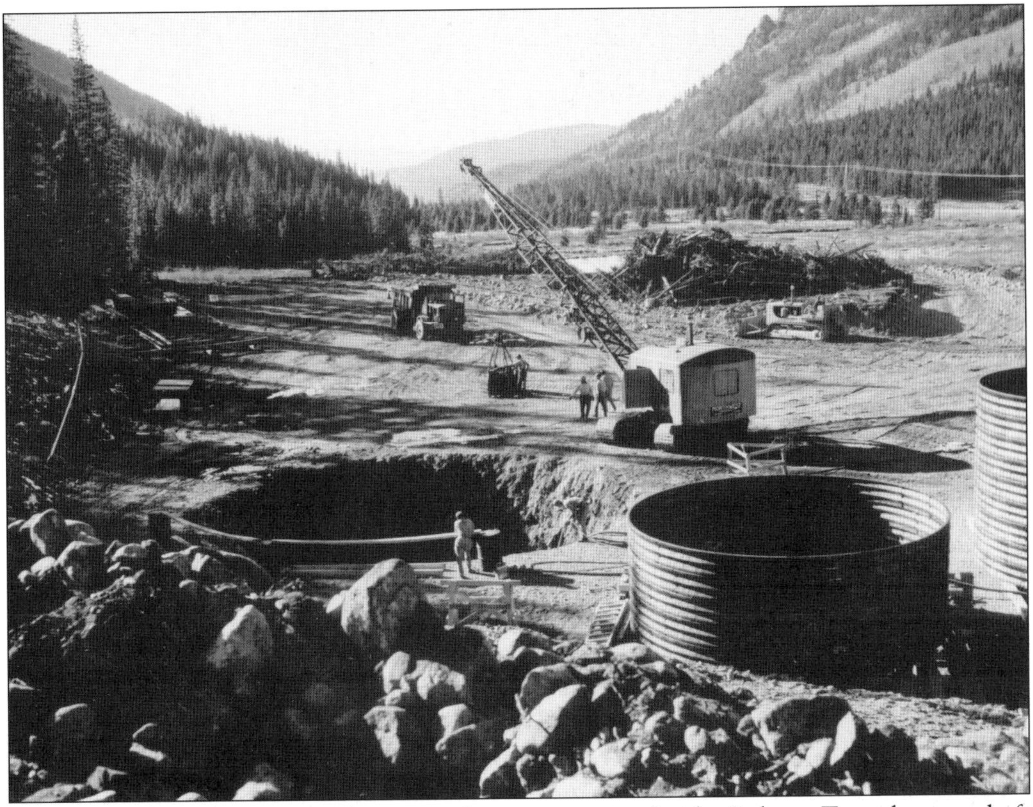

Montezuma Access Shaft. The exit and entrance point for the Roberts Tunnel access shaft are seen here. The September 5, 1956, image looks southeast toward angle point no. 2 from Montezuma Road, which is almost on the tunnel tangent.

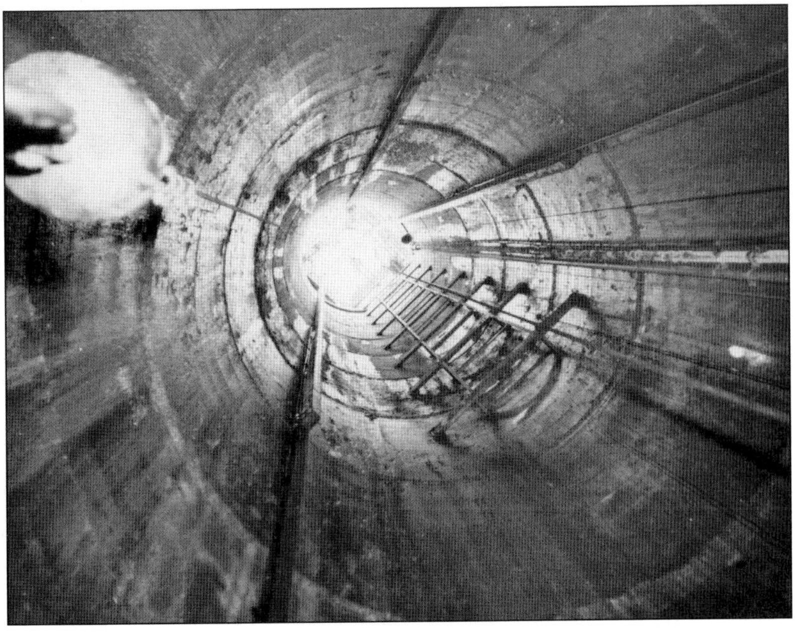

Sunlit Access. The general condition of the access shaft is depicted with the guides and structure for the manway. The view looks upward from approximately 90 feet below the collar on March 18, 1957.

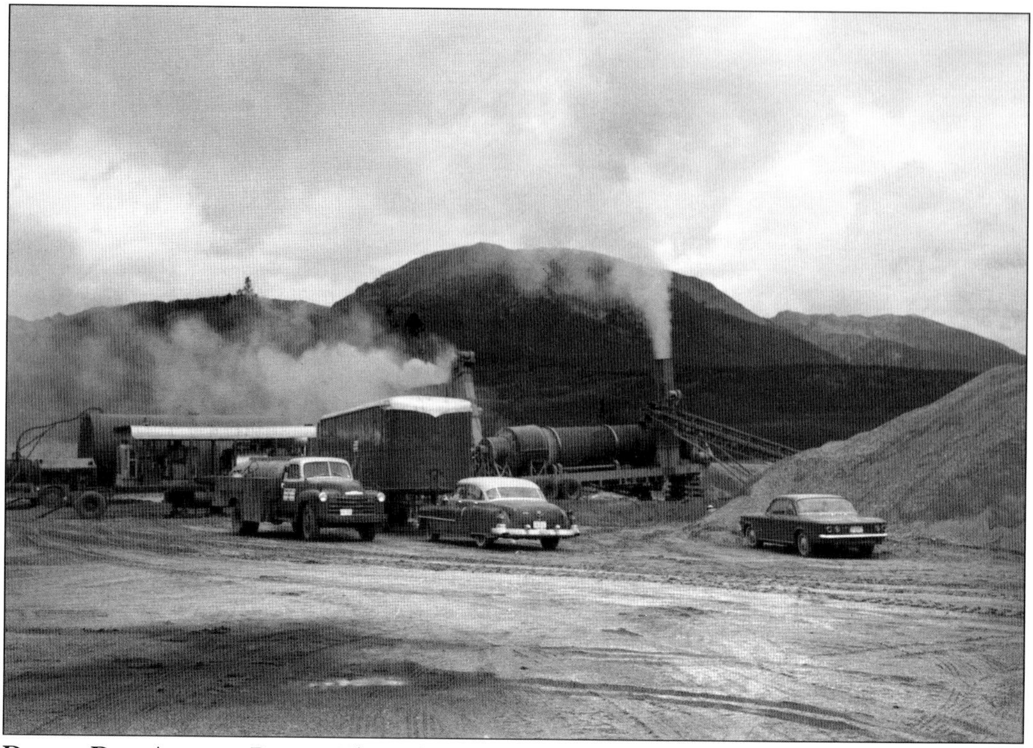

Dillon Dam Asphalt Batch. The Giberson asphalt pits are pictured on August 5, 1963.

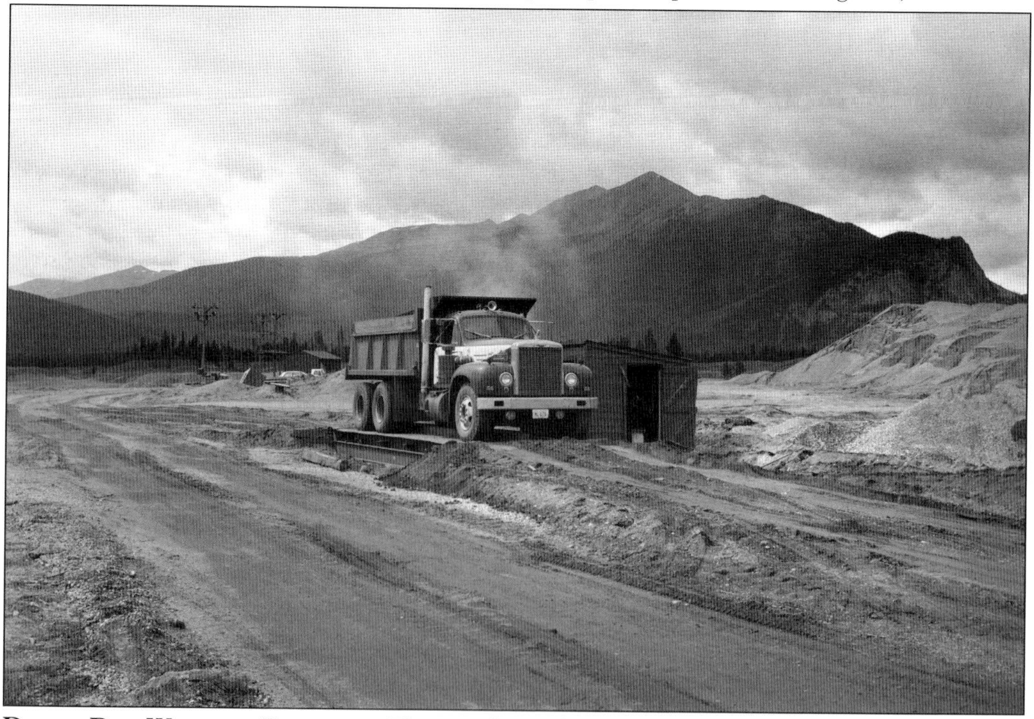

Dillon Dam Weighing Platform. This weighing platform was used for the asphalt batch plant at Giberson pits. The photograph is dated August 5, 1963.

Five

Roberts Tunnel's East Portal

Excavating Roberts Tunnel was labor intensive, an engineering problem, time consuming, and very expensive. Construction employees used horizontal drills for drilling dynamite holes, filled the holes with dynamite, and removed the shattered rock (called mucking). Subsequently, workers constructed timber and steel arch supports (lattice girders) and rock dowels used to stabilize key blocks and to strengthen the rock mass, which would also provide supplement support for the initial lining. Feeler holes were drilled to determine the amount of cement (grout) needed, and then grout was pumped in. This was the process used over and over until the tunnel was completed.

According to Sandra F. Mather's *Dillon, Denver, and the Dam*, "Forty-six holes were drilled at a time and filled with dynamite. For every twenty feet blasted deeper into the tunnel, twenty pounds or more of dynamite were required. For each 200 to 250 pounds of dynamite detonated, thirty-four cubic yards of much were created." Mucking was accomplished with air-driven, rack-mounted shovels. Rail tracks were laid 24 inches apart, and the locomotives, both diesel and electrical, pulled the cars to and from the tunnel.

Electric fans were in constant use to haul out the dust and gases created by the dynamite explosions. By reversing the fans, fresh air was brought into the tunnel.

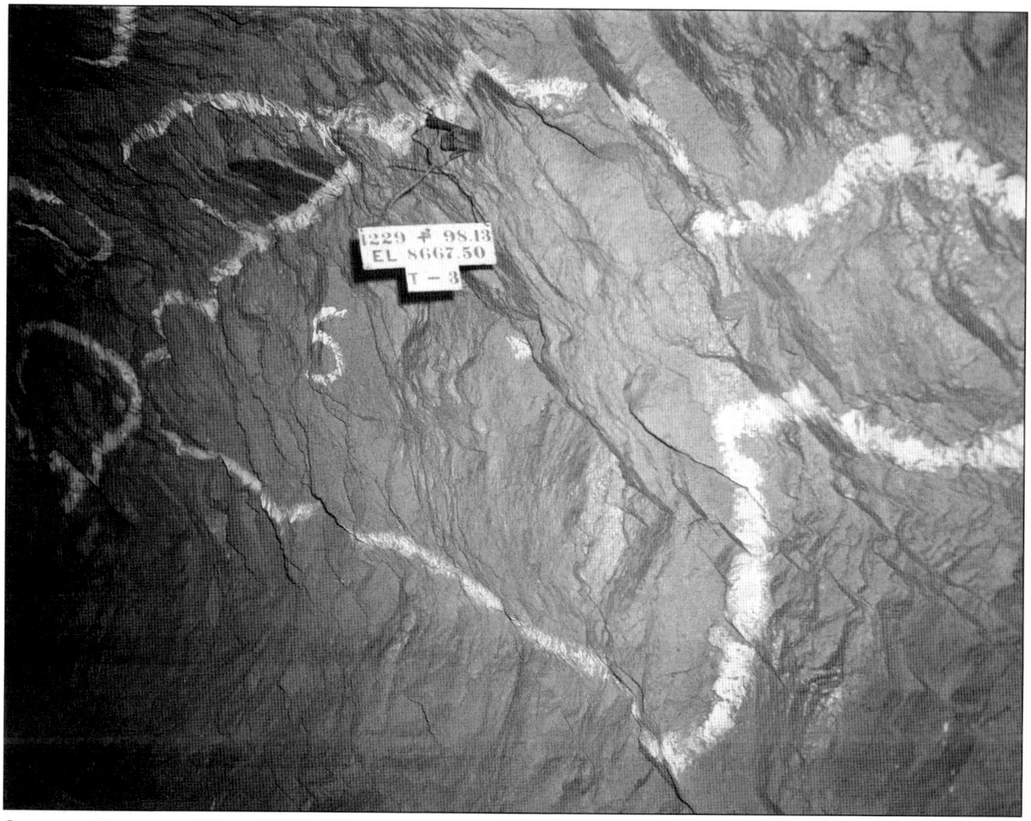

Survey Station No. 1229. This is a critical drilling strategy point. The viewer is looking northwest. The white lines are outlining the correct areas to be excavated. The photograph was taken on September 11, 1956. White lines outline the right areas to be excavated.

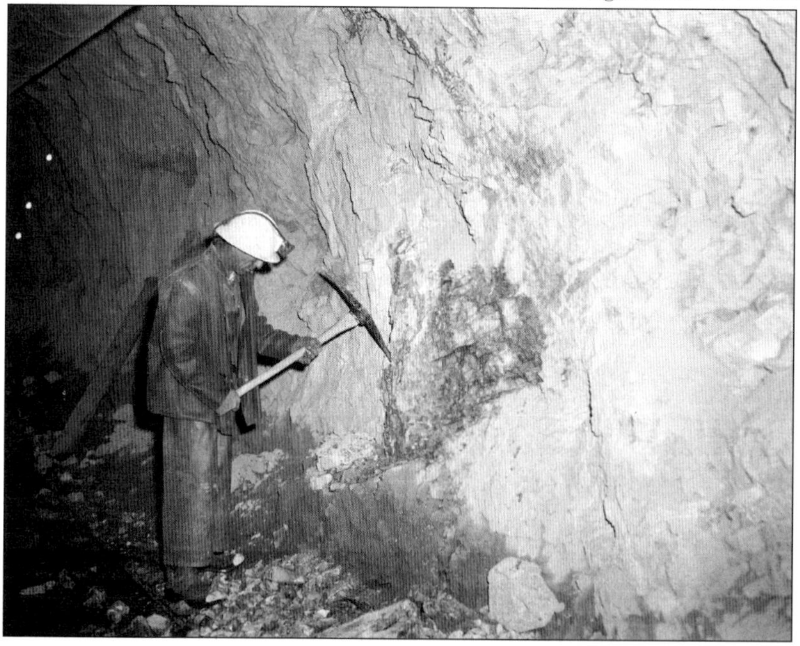

Pick and Shovel. An unidentified man uses the old miners' techniques of pick-and-shovel work at the East Portal on September 9, 1956, after the rock in the close-up image above was exposed.

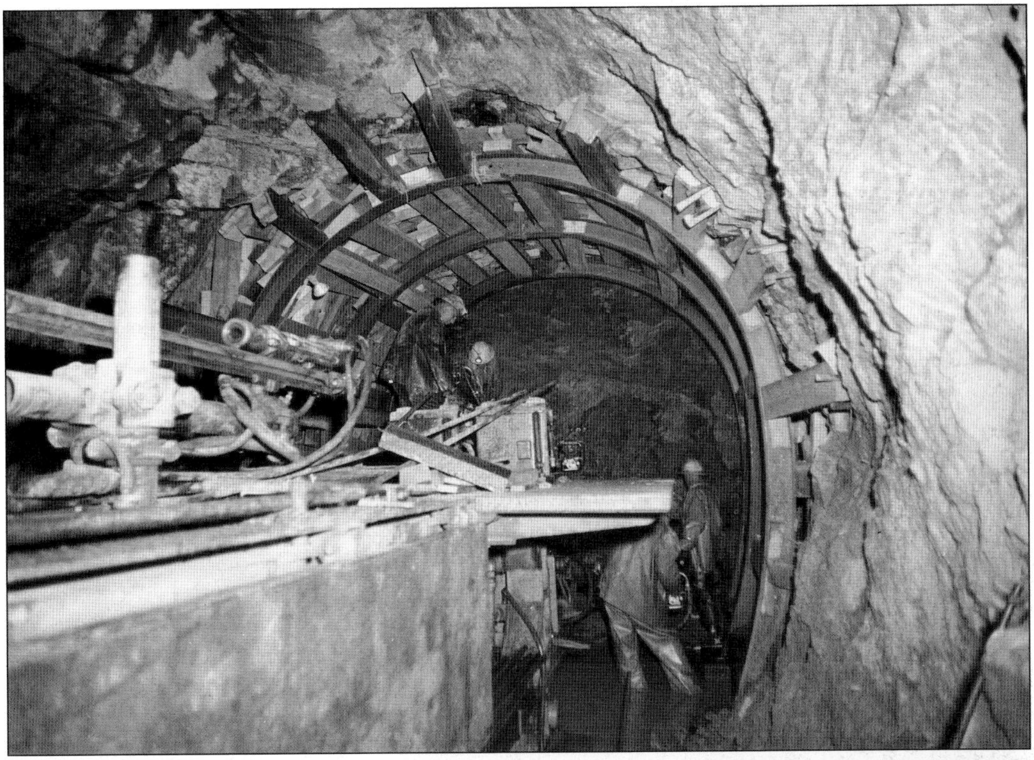

Tight Spading. At the Roberts Tunnel's East Portal, spading tights, using horizontal drilling techniques, are seen at Station No. 1189. The photograph was taken on November 13, 1956.

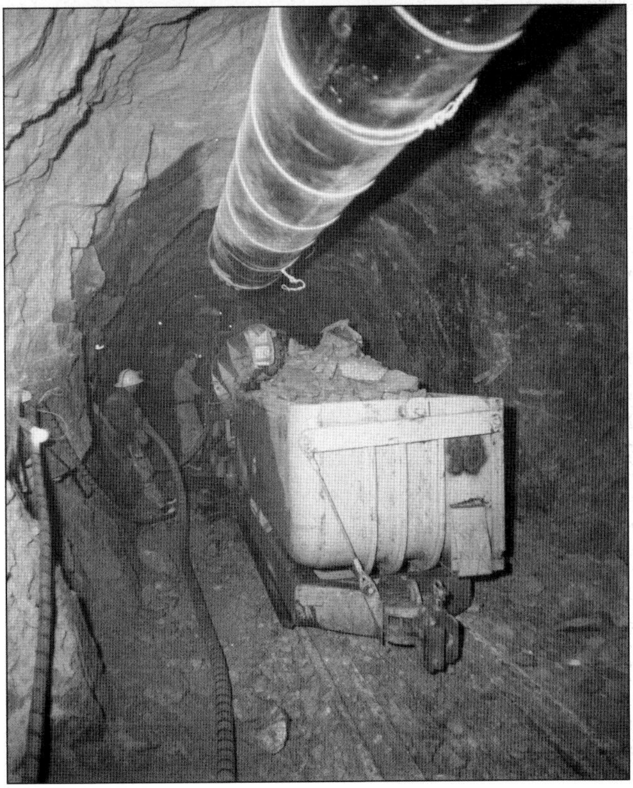

Muck Car. Workers are loading muck cars in Roberts Tunnel's East Portal with the heading at Station No. 1138. The photograph was taken on February 20, 1957.

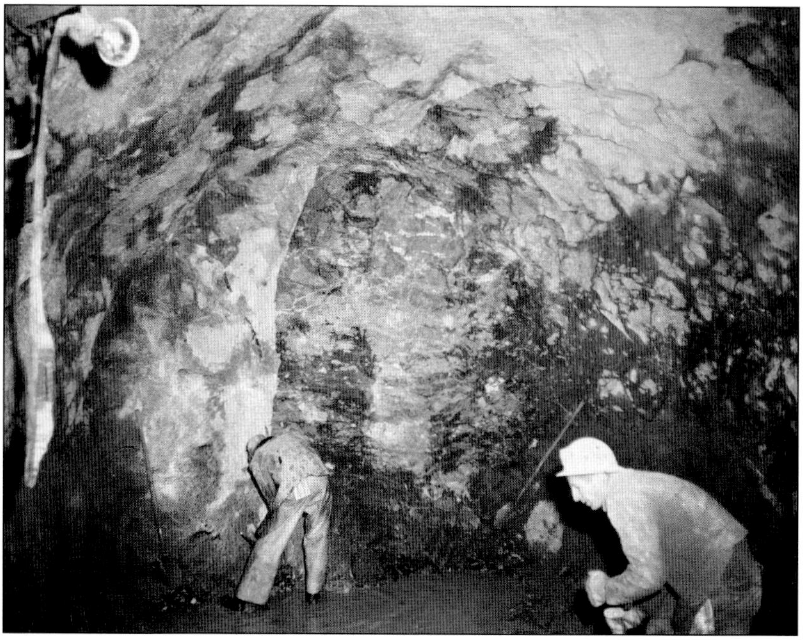

Roberts Tunnel, East Portal. The location here is the heading at Survey Station No. 1117+71. Here workmen clean up after rock spading. Notice the workman standing in water seepage and the shovel on the right side. The photograph was taken on April 15, 1957.

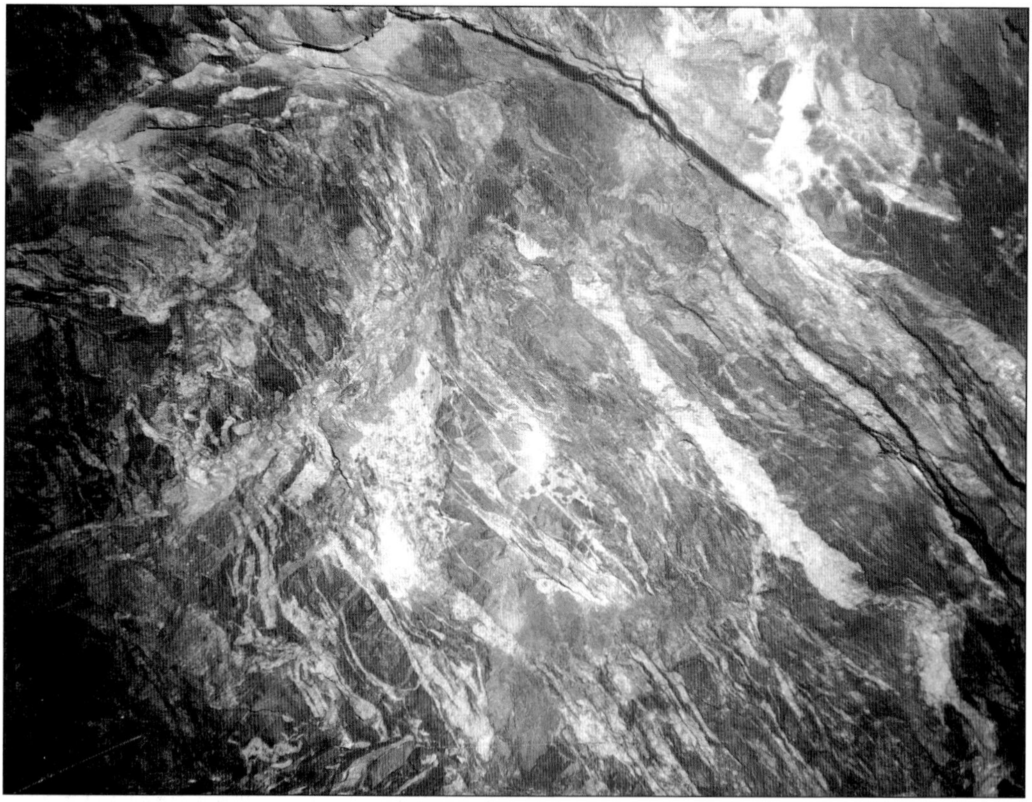

Geological Analysis. At the East Portal of Roberts Tunnel at survey Station No. 1117, the viewer is treated to a look at granite on the right half of the face of the tunnel and gneiss on the left half. The photograph was taken on June 15, 1967.

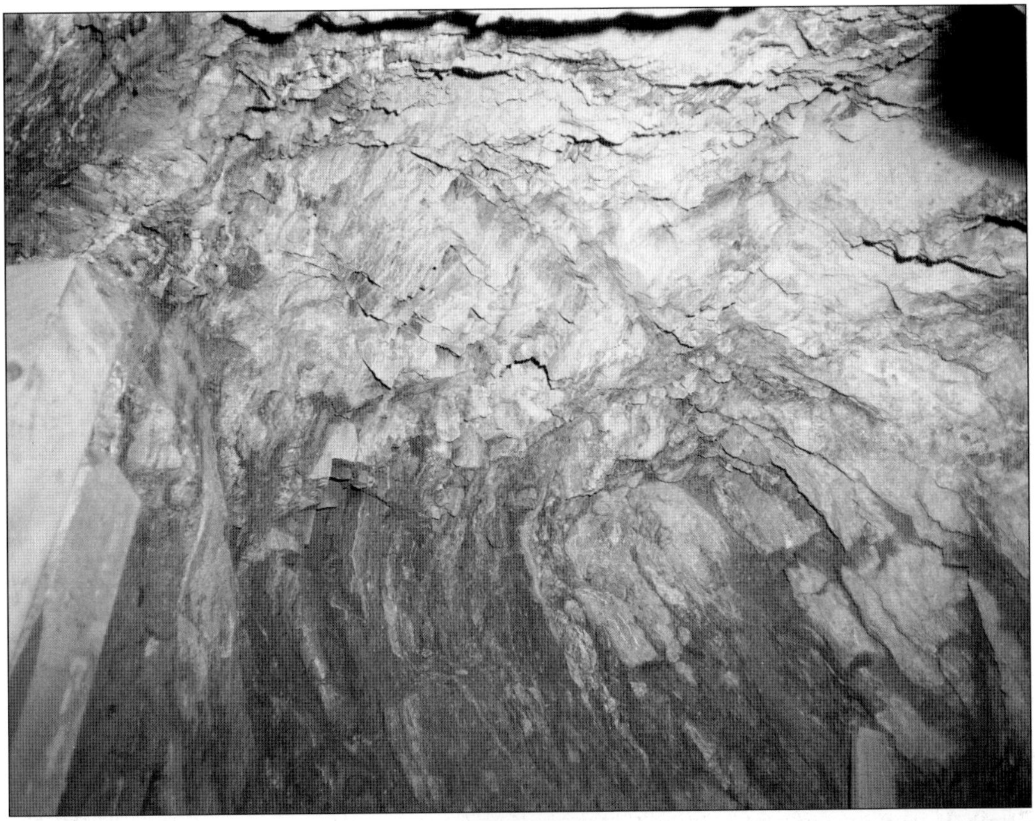

Fishing Drill. The fishing drill is depicted at Station No. 1094. The rock discovered is the usual schist and gneiss. Notice the ceiling blocking used on steel sets. The photograph was taken on June 15, 1967.

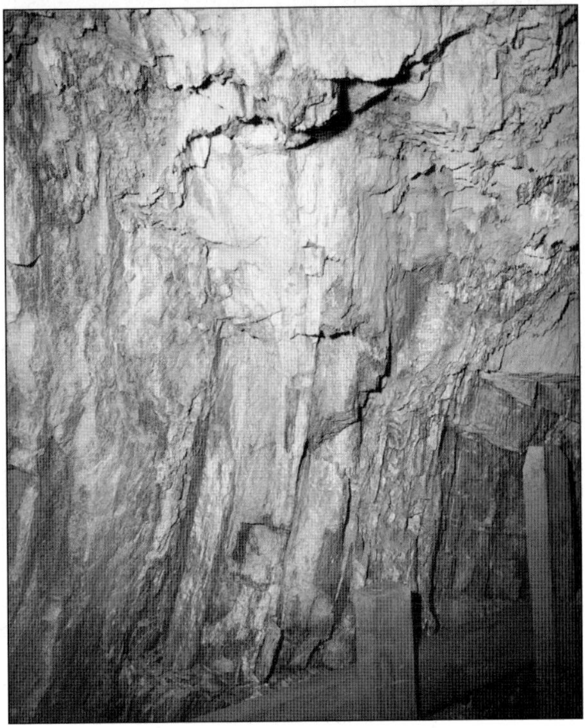

Gneiss. This is a close-up look of the heading at Station No. 1081 and its gneiss rock formation. The photograph was taken on July 16, 1957. Gneiss rock is a metamorphic rock. These rocks may have been granite, which is an igneous rock, but heat and pressure changed them.

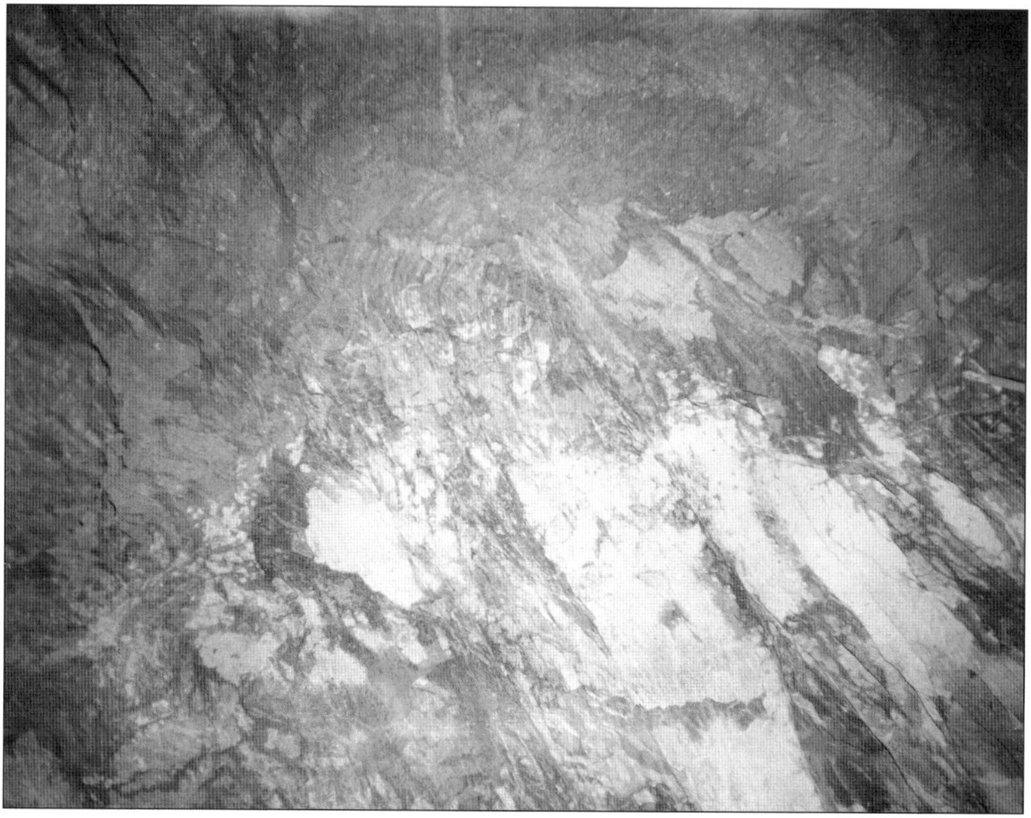

Weathered Schist Rock. Roberts Tunnel's East Portal is depicted with the top of the surge chamber raised at 325 feet. The rock is weathered schist and gneiss. Schist is another type of metamorphic rock. The westward-looking photograph was shot on February 14, 1958.

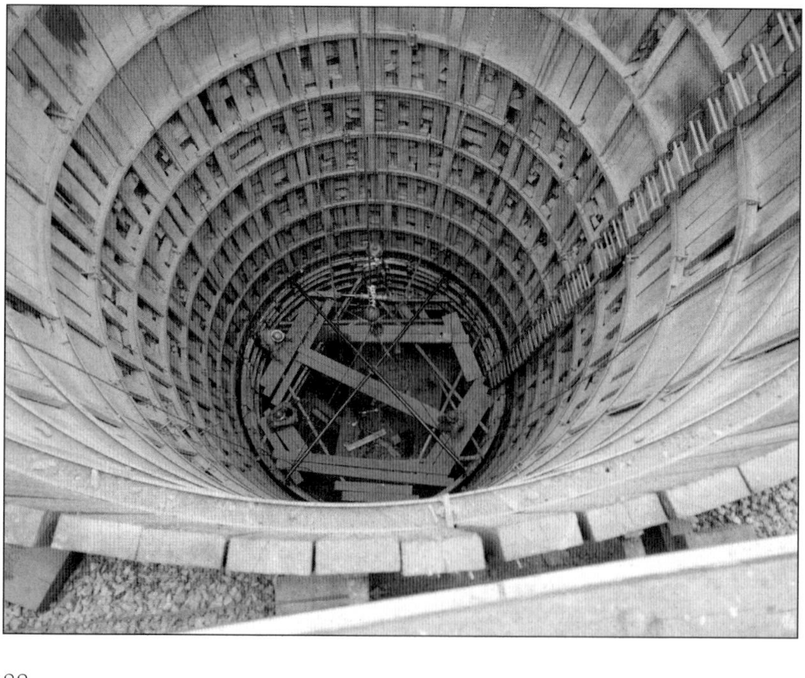

Surge Chamber. The surge chamber, when raised, tops out at 325 feet. The view is northeast on February 14, 1958.

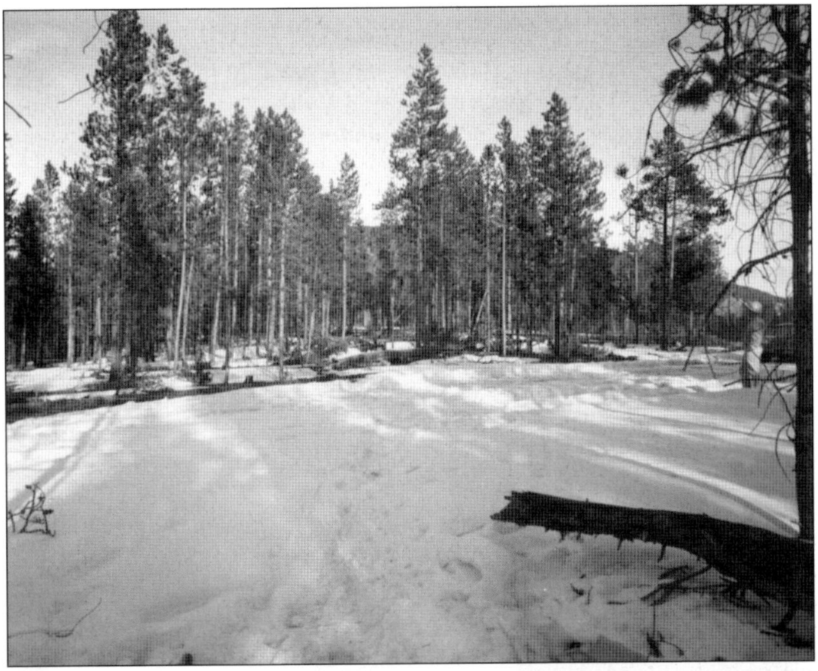

Dillon Dam Top Side View. The view near the surge chamber mentioned in the previous caption is shown here. The camera's point of view is northeast along the center line. This photograph is dated February 14, 1961.

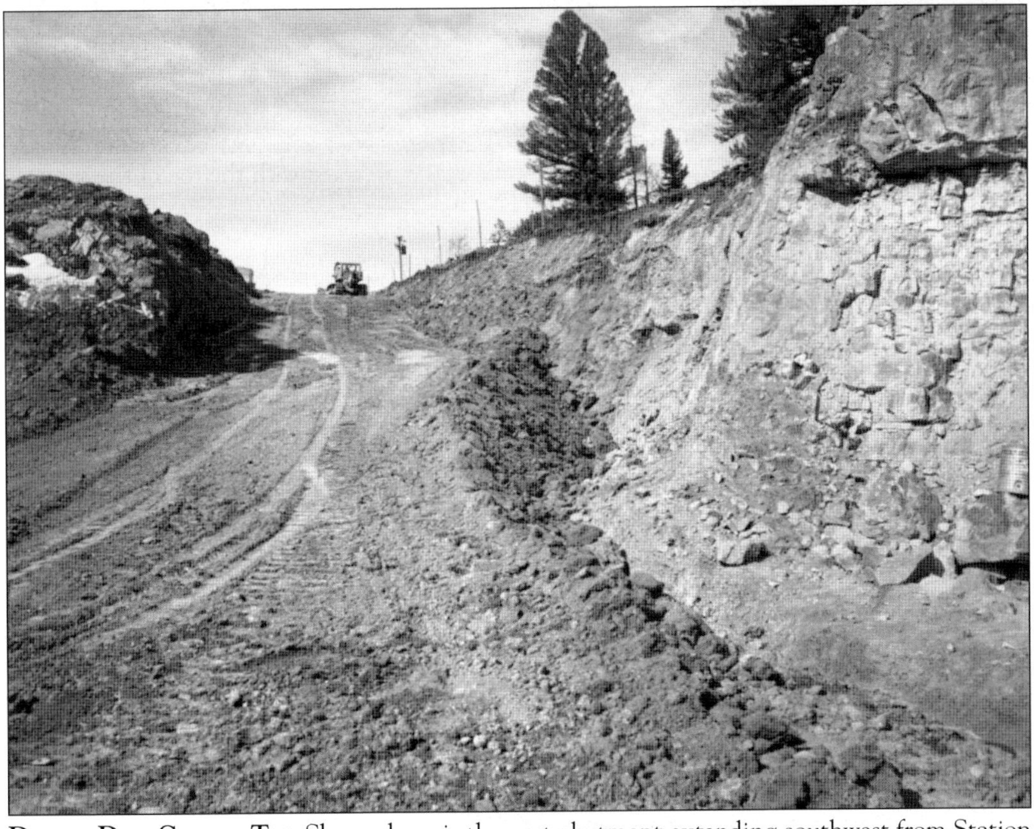

Dillon Dam Cut to Top. Shown here is the east abutment extending southwest from Station No. 32+00 in soft shale sheared between two faults. The photograph was taken April 25, 1962.

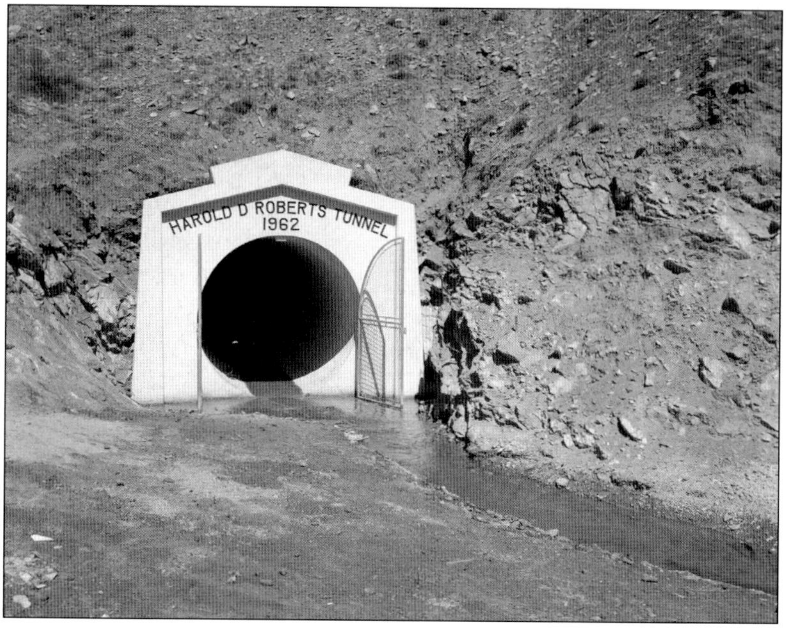

Completed Access Portal. Roberts Tunnel's East Portal boasts a completed access portal in April 1962.

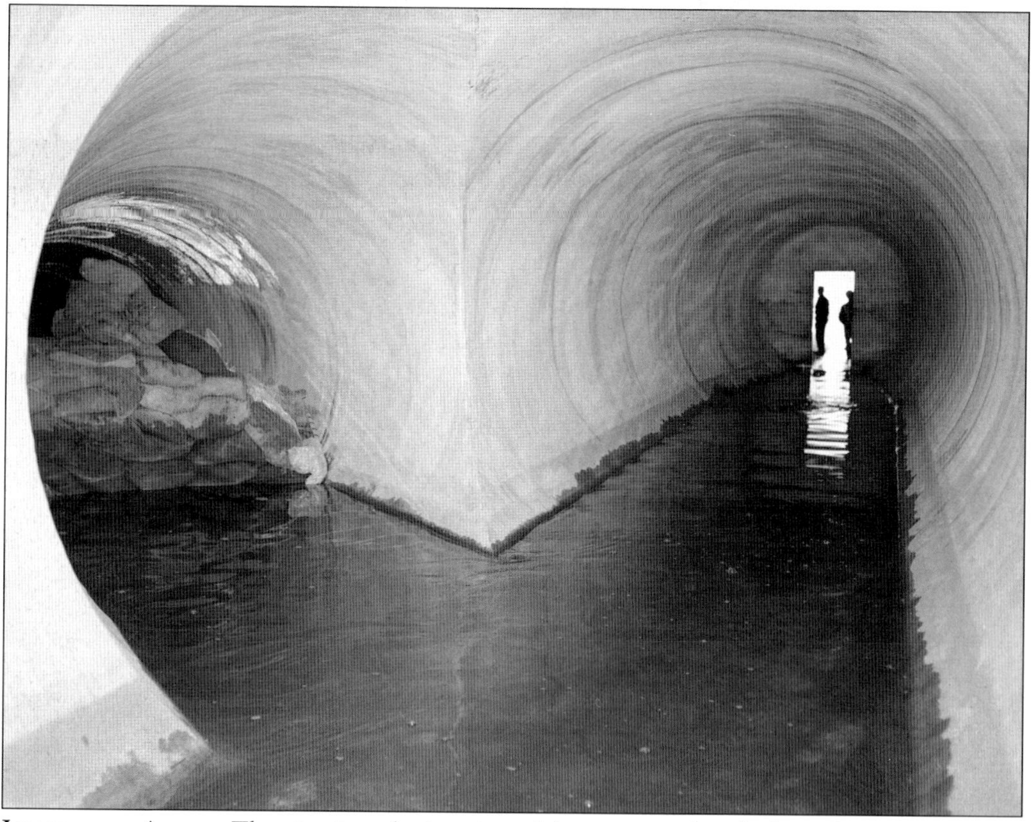

Junction of Access. The view is at the junction of the access and outlet branches of the Roberts Tunnel's East Portal on April 24, 1962.

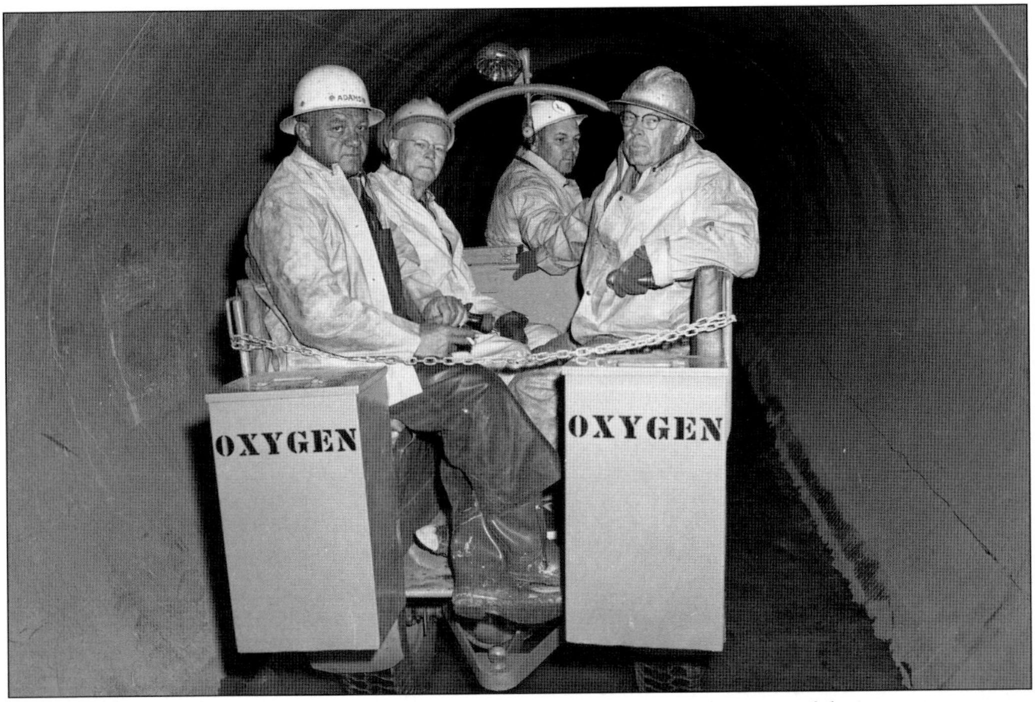

Inspection. The date of this image—April 24, 1962—is significant because of the group inspecting the completed Roberts Tunnel. The group included both political and engineering inspectors. The names were not released.

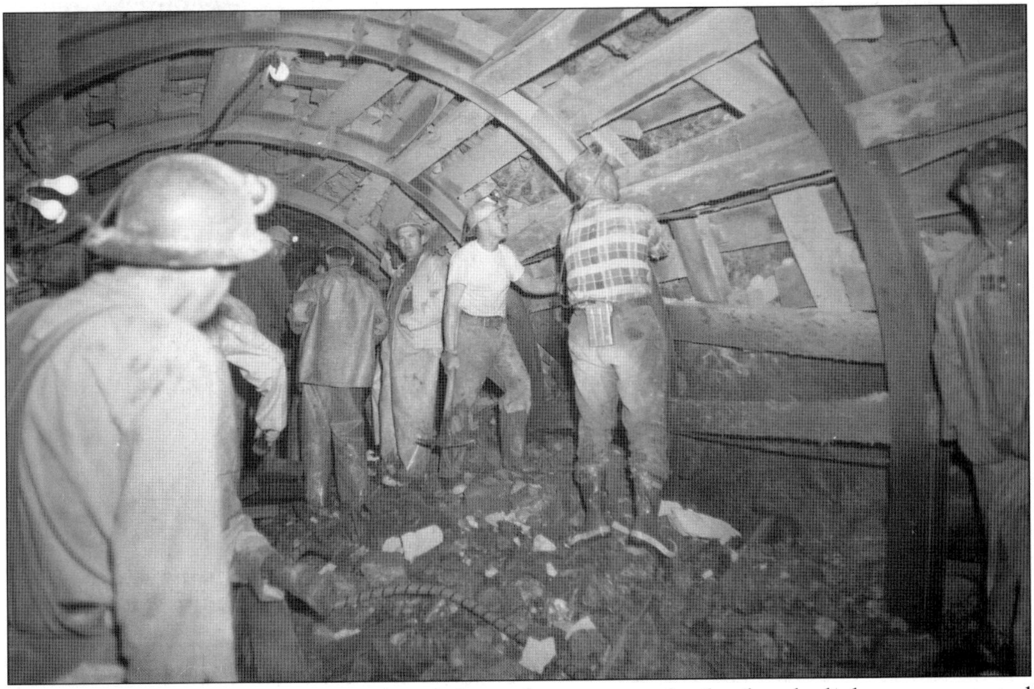

Muck Pile. Construction personnel are left standing on a muck pile after the hole was penetrated on February 24, 1960.

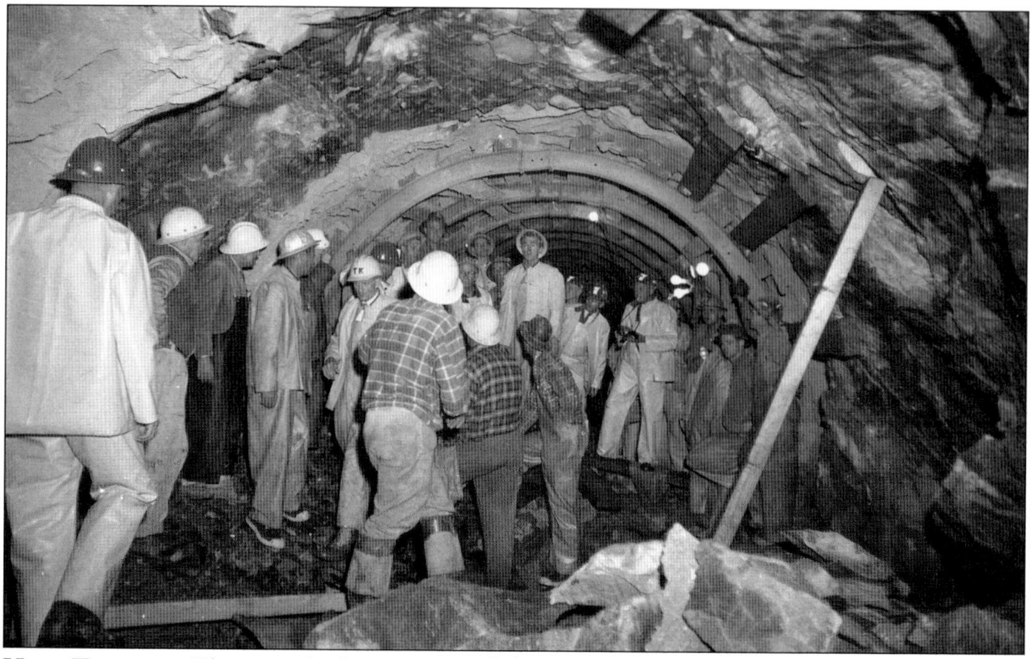

Hole Through. This view looks east toward the east portal entrance after the hole through. Note the crown bars supporting slabby (materials for crushing) ground at the top of the picture. The photograph was taken on February 24, 1960.

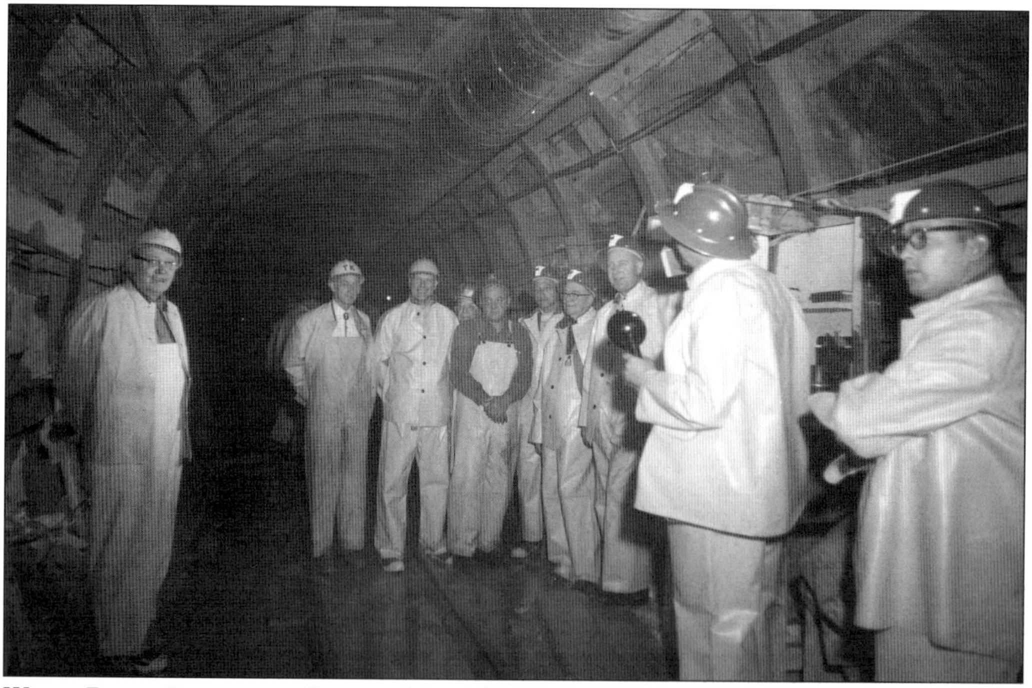

Water Board Inspectors. Personnel from the Denver Water Board and the contractor's crew are seen along with the engineers from Tipton and Kalmbach, Inc., on February 24, 1960.

Six

Roberts Tunnel's West Portal

The West Portal of Roberts Tunnel is the most admired and the most talked about portion of the project because of its positioning. The portal is located under the water of the Dillon Dam, which is on a peninsula jettisoning out into one of the deeper parts of the dam. The peninsula is covered by lodge pole pines, which carefully hide one of the control houses. There is an access road that leads to and from the control house and ties into U.S. Highway 6, which leads to an exit for Swan Mountain Road or on to Keystone and Loveland Pass.

The Roberts Tunnel's West Portal is one of the engineering marvels of the 20th century. There were no laser beam lights to point the way, nor computers to make the engineering computations faster. Some areas of tunnel excavation were so fractured it required wedges, sometimes slid from the face of excavation into the tunnel opening, where joints act as sliding planes. The situation required three-dimensional calculation: the excavated section with the height of excavation (H) and an equivalent width (W). The forces that act on the wedge are separated into driving forces that produce failure and resisting forces that provide stability. The resisting forces needed to be 1.4 times greater than the driving force.

Drilling holes in the mountainside had some expected turns and twists. Like the miners of old, the modern-day engineers encountered large amounts of unexpected water in some of the tunnels. The tunnel was driven three times under the Snake River, and many times, construction personnel were forced to bundle cement into the waterlogged rocks to stem the flow. Sometimes the water flow was so heavy it made the walls unstable, and steel ribbing was expeditiously brought in to prevent collapse. Water pumps, however, were always closely kept, and each pumped 2,500 gallons per minute. Approximately four million gallons a day were pumped into the Blue and Snake Rivers.

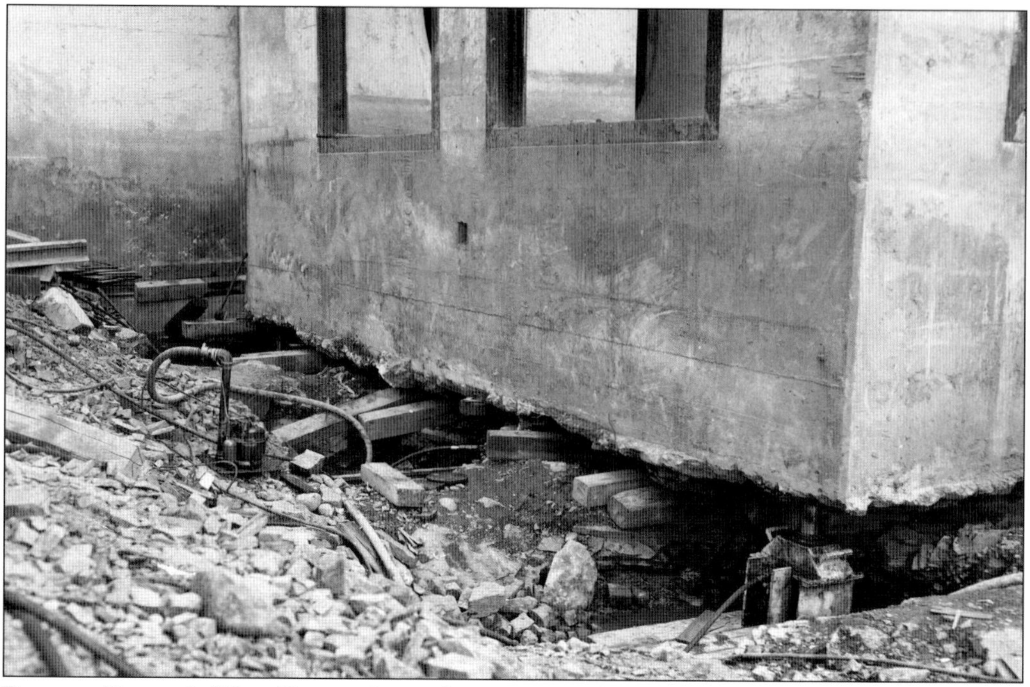

Roberts Tunnel's West Portal Inlet Structure. The West Portal's inlet structure is being raised vertically by massive hydraulic jacks. This photograph, taken on July 17, 1963, shows the second lift in the laborious process of getting the inlet into correct position.

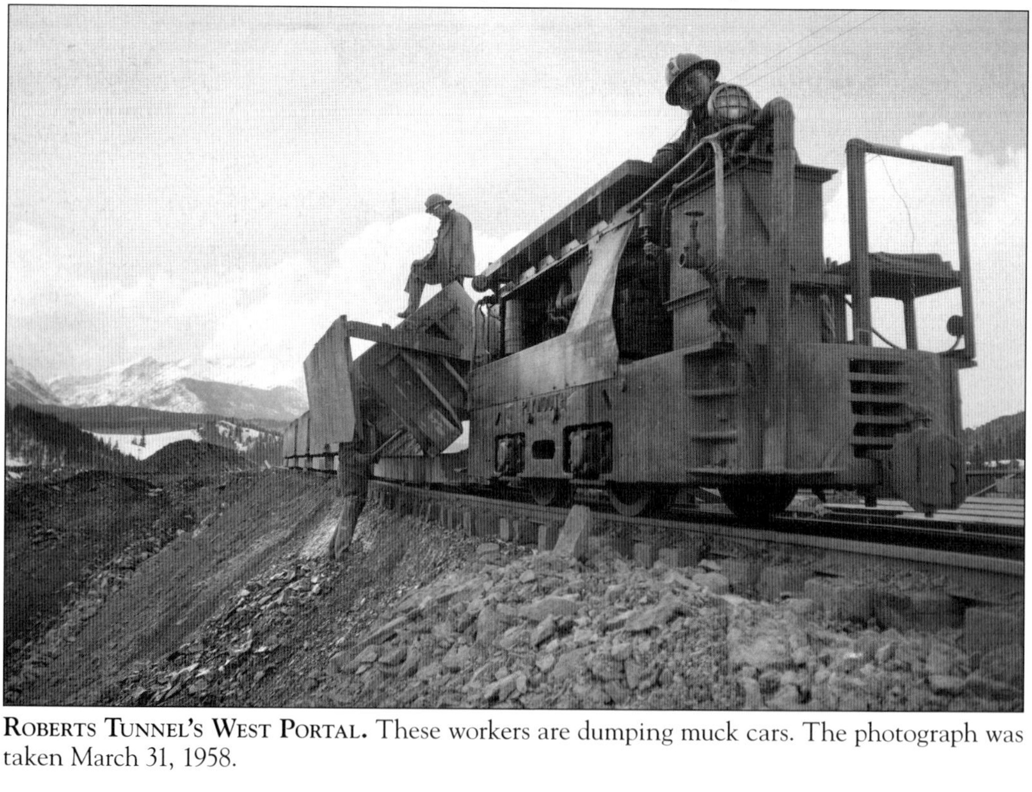

Roberts Tunnel's West Portal. These workers are dumping muck cars. The photograph was taken March 31, 1958.

WILD ELK. A wild elk is visible on the stockpile, as seen on January 29, 1961. This was a lucky camera shot taken just below the East Portal of Roberts Tunnel. The elk seen here eventually wandered away.

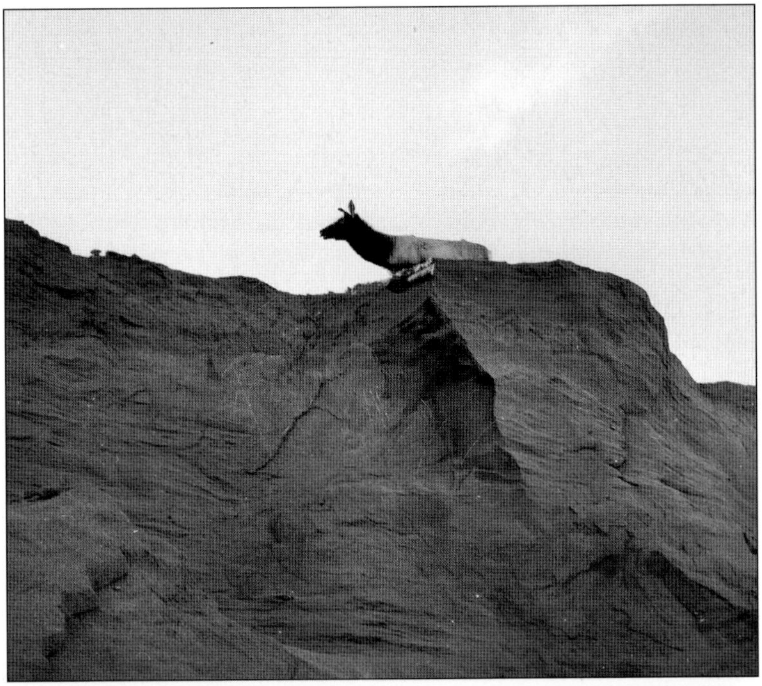

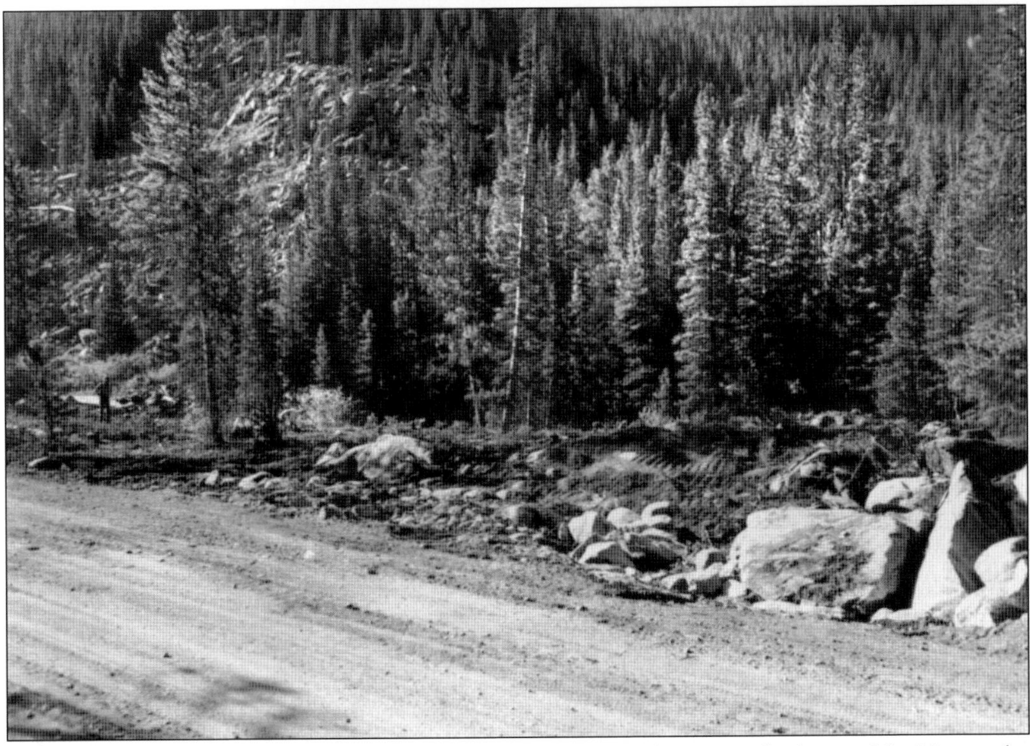

DISPOSAL AREA AT THE ROBERTS TUNNEL'S WEST PORTAL. The access shaft is visible. Notice the unidentified workman on the far left observing some excavation yet to be completed. The view faces southeast toward Angel Point No. 2 from Montezuma Road almost to the tunnel tangent. The photograph was taken September 5, 1956.

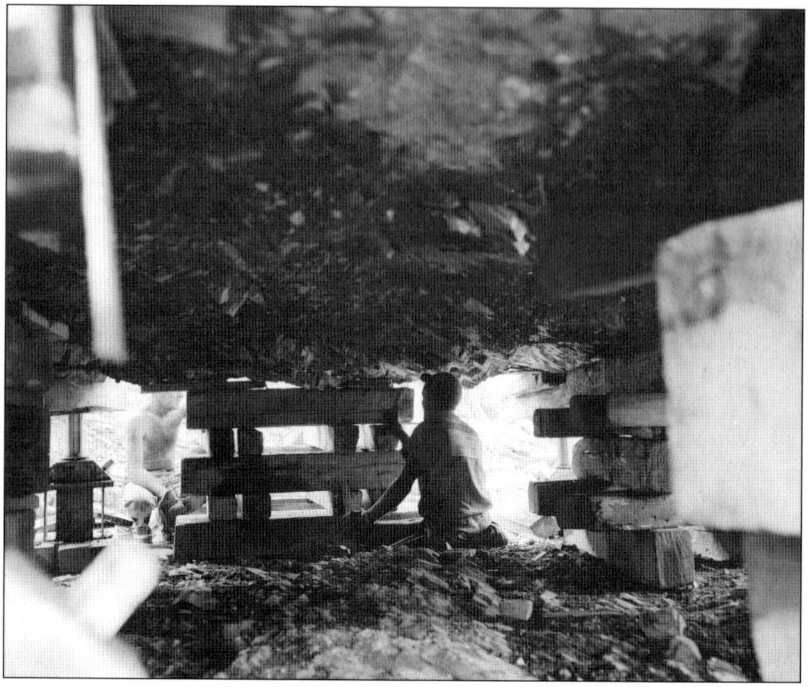

Underside Inlet Structure. The underside of the Roberts Tunnel's West Portal is seen here after its sixth vertical lift. The photograph is dated July 18, 1963.

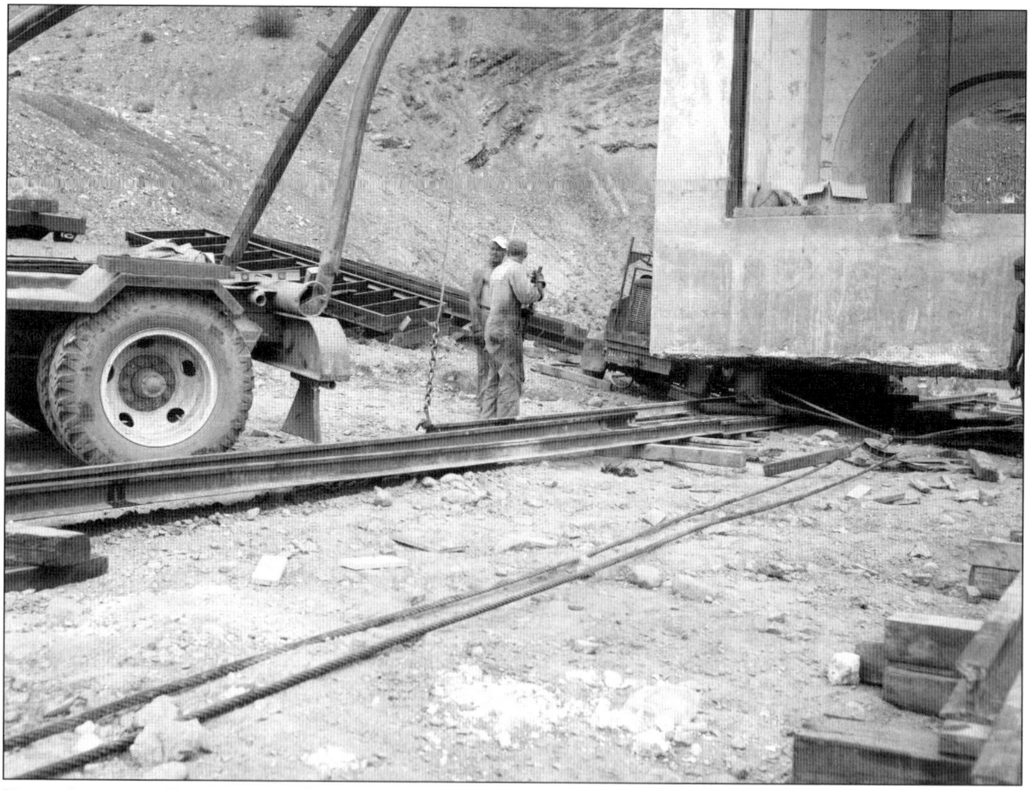

Rail Setting. Resetting rails occurred for the second horizontal move at the inlet structure of Roberts Tunnel's West Portal. The photograph is dated July 20, 1963.

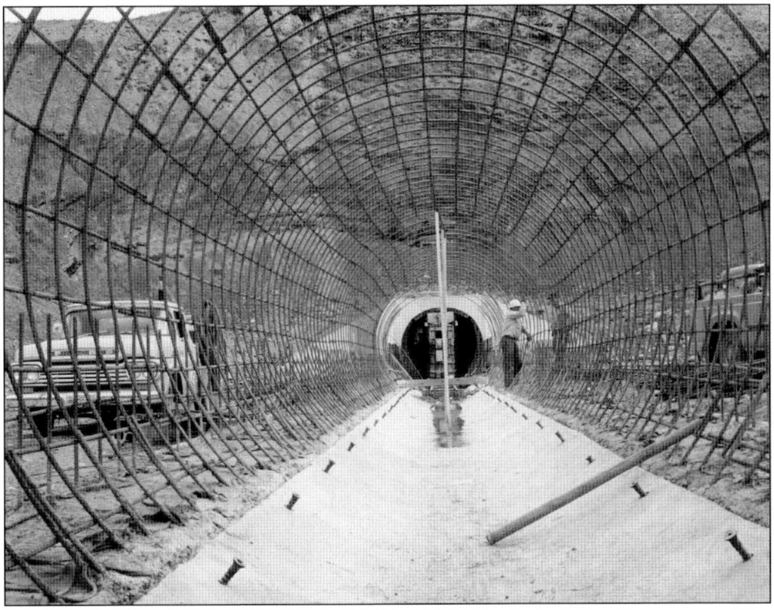

Reinforcing Steel. The intake structure shows reinforcing steel in place for the conduit arch at the Roberts Tunnel's West Portal. The photograph is dated August 9, 1963.

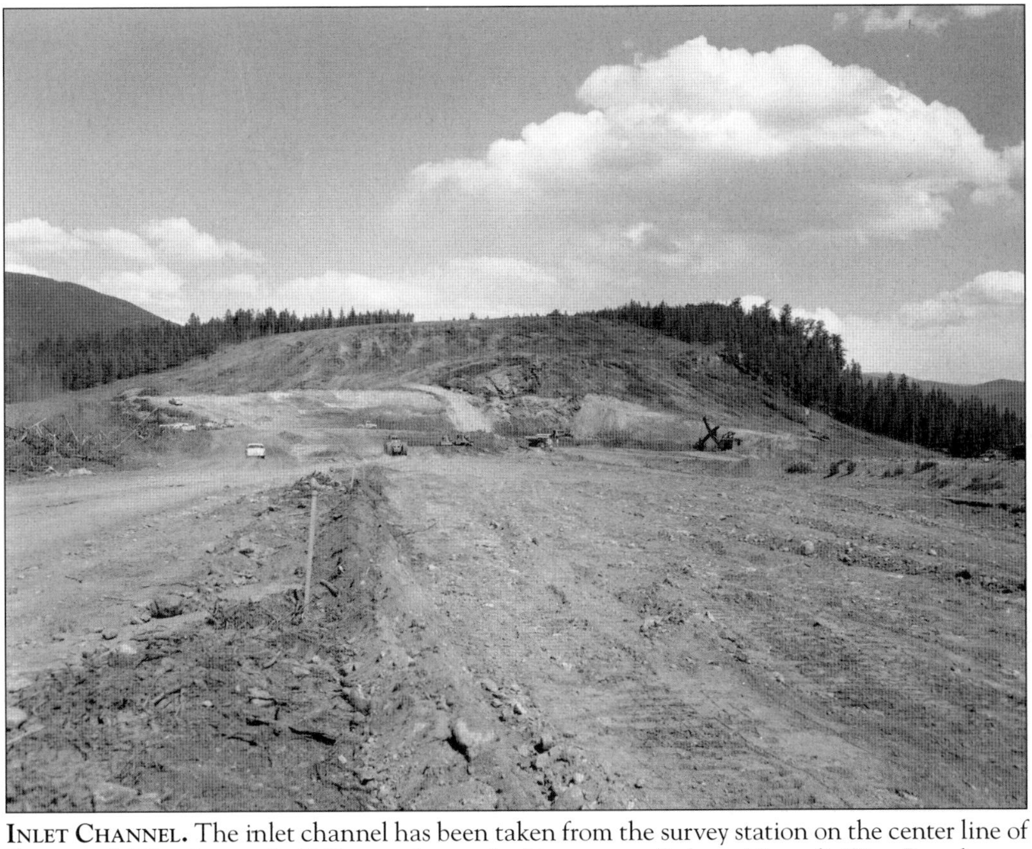

Inlet Channel. The inlet channel has been taken from the survey station on the center line of the tunnel. The August 8, 1963, view here is looking east at Roberts Tunnel's West Portal.

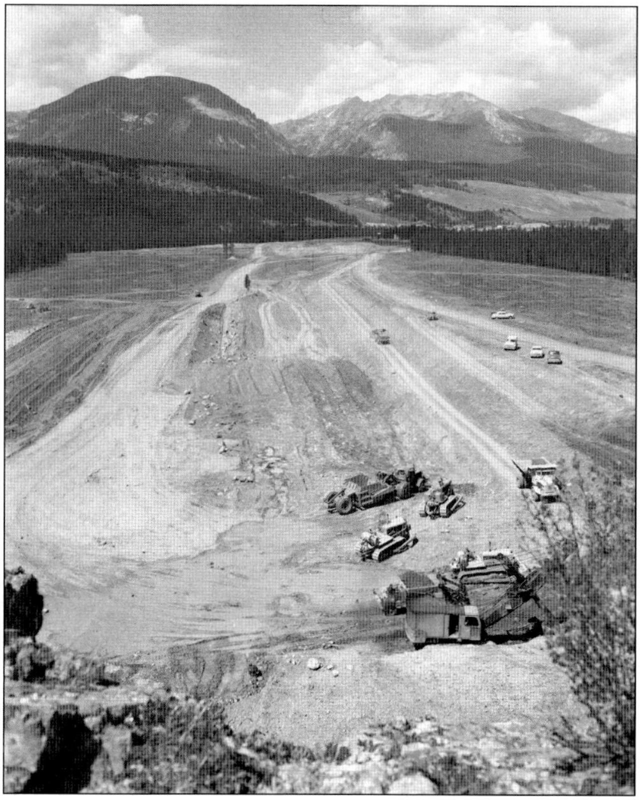

EXCAVATION. Inlet channel excavation is depicted at Roberts Tunnel's West Portal. The view is west along the center line of the tunnel taken on August 29, 1956.

ELEVATION: 8,870 FEET. Depicted are the northwest shovel and Euclid end dump at the inlet channel excavation. The photograph is dated August 29, 1956.

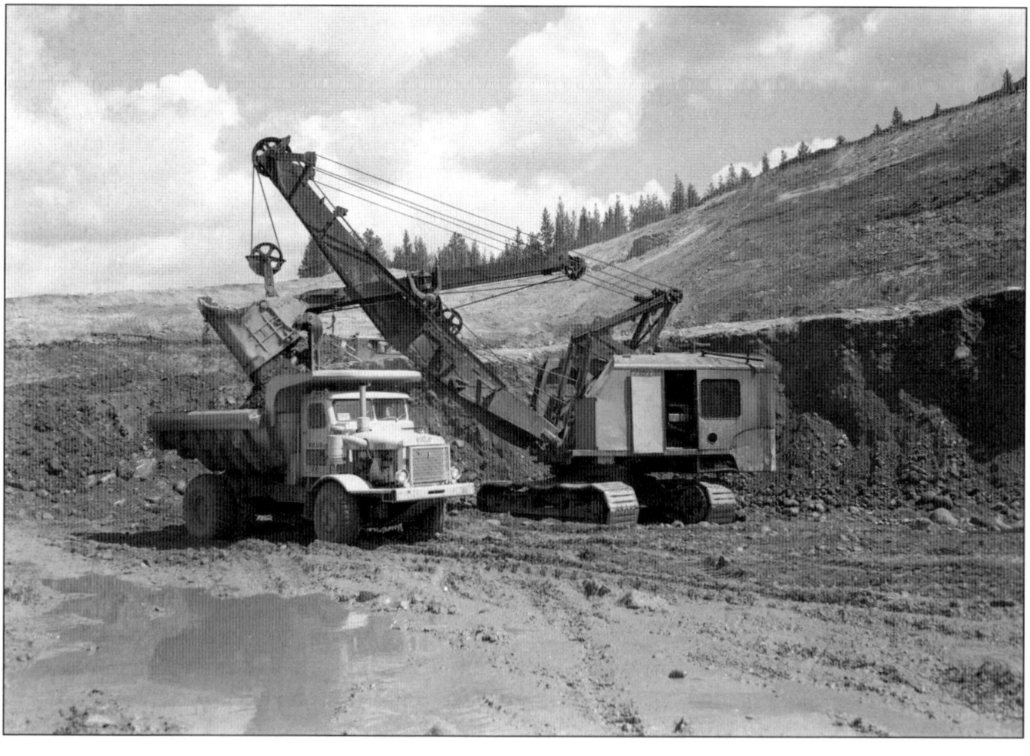

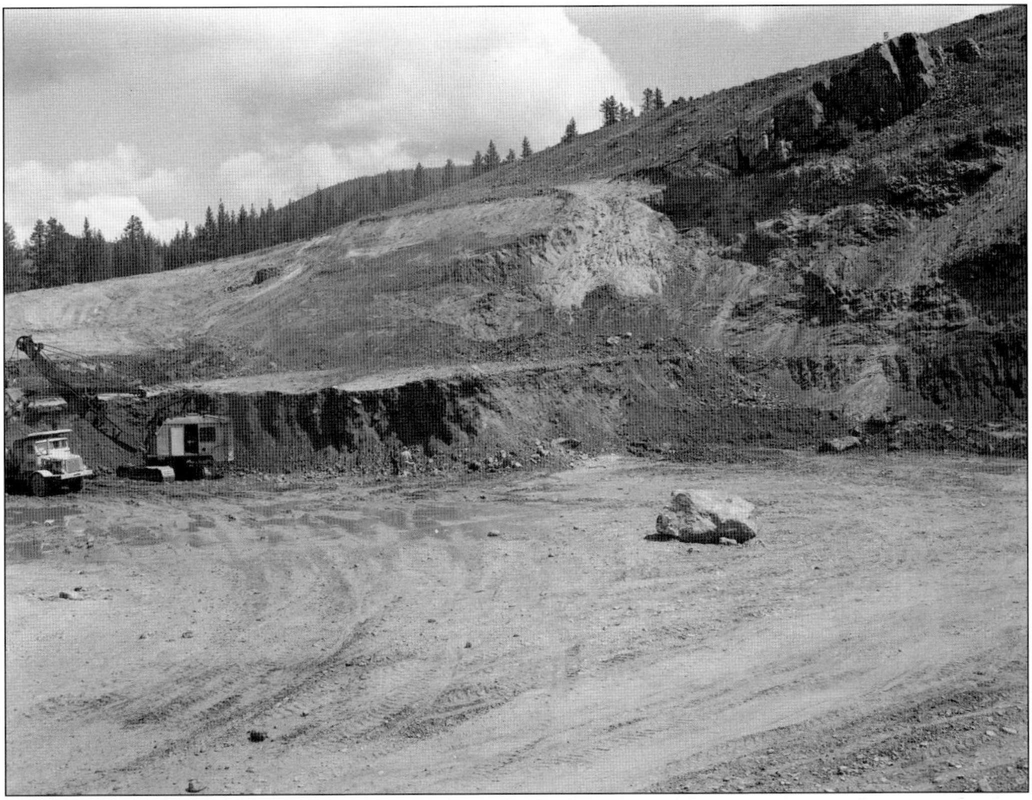

West Portal Inlet Channel. Roberts Tunnel's West Portal is seen at the inlet channel excavation. Notice the water issuing from the spring on the center line of the tunnel, where the two men are standing. The view is north from the highest berm (raised barrier) south of the tunnel line, at approximately Station No. 7, on August 9, 1956.

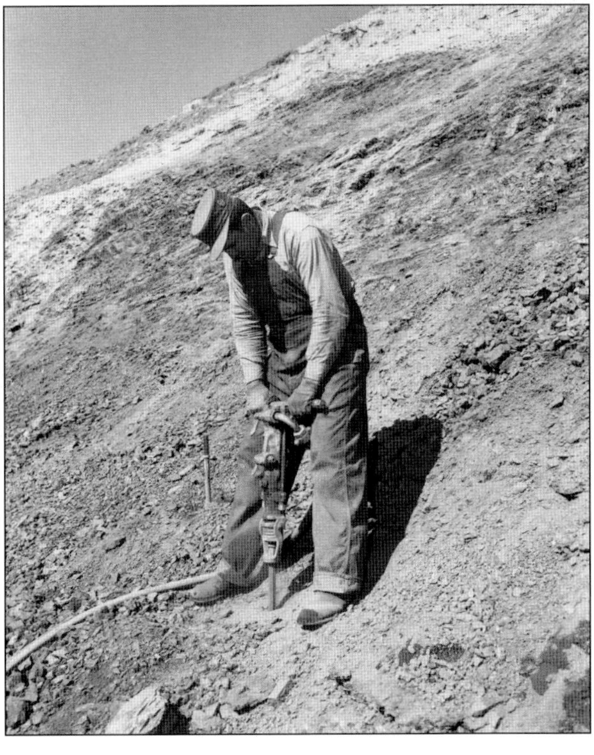

Black Shale. On the center line of the Roberts Tunnel's West Portal, drilling operations into black shale make preparations for dynamite blasting. The photograph dates from August 31, 1956.

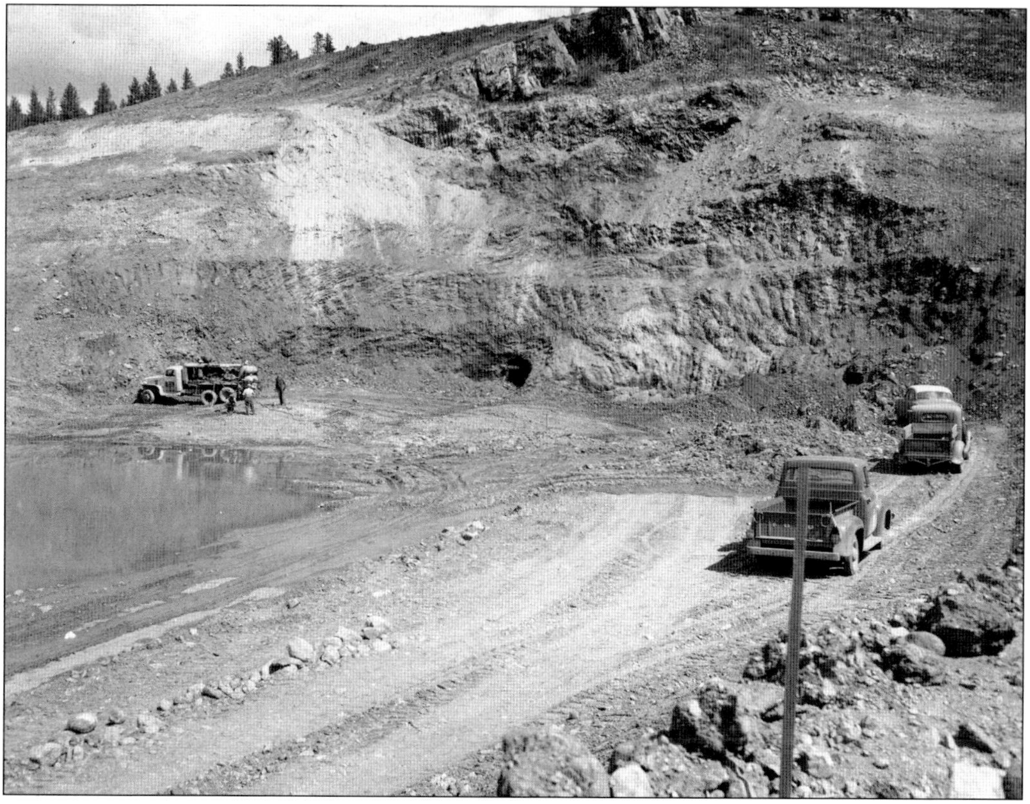

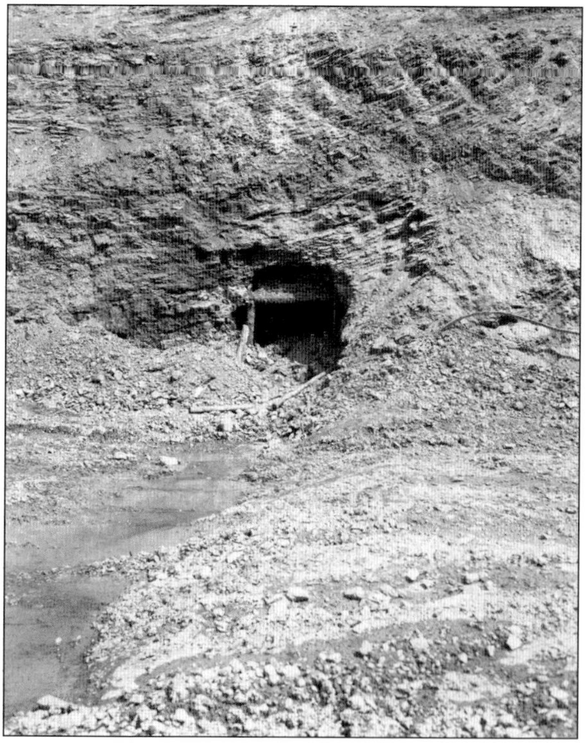

Pilot Tunnel. The pilot tunnel was uncovered at the West Portal excavation of Roberts Tunnel. Notice the water accumulation and seepage from the area around the pilot tunnel. The view looks northeast from Station No. 7, and an elevation of 8,664 feet, on September 10, 1956.

Close-up of Pilot Tunnel. This close-up look depicts the pilot tunnel of the Roberts Tunnel's West Portal. Notice the water seepage, then bedding and dipping of black shale in a Dakota formation on September 10, 1956.

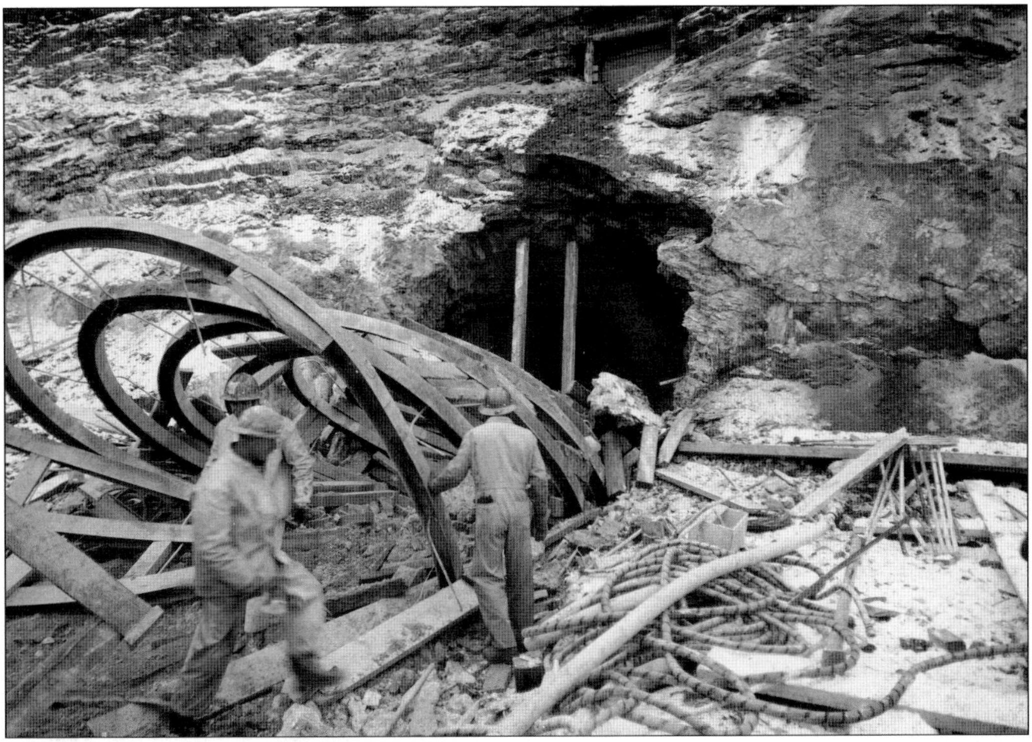

Blast Out. Steel tunnel supports are blasted out of the tunnel at the West Portal of the Roberts Tunnel. Holes were loaded in a fault, and the concussion transmitted by the gouge set the entire round off without delay. The photograph date was November 15, 1956.

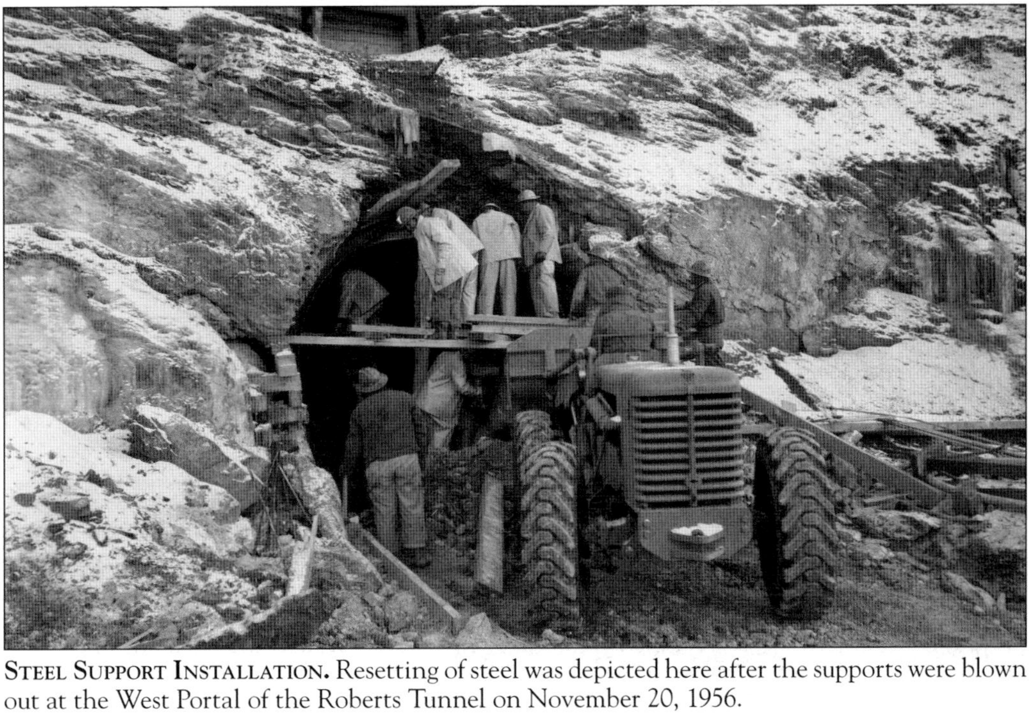

Steel Support Installation. Resetting of steel was depicted here after the supports were blown out at the West Portal of the Roberts Tunnel on November 20, 1956.

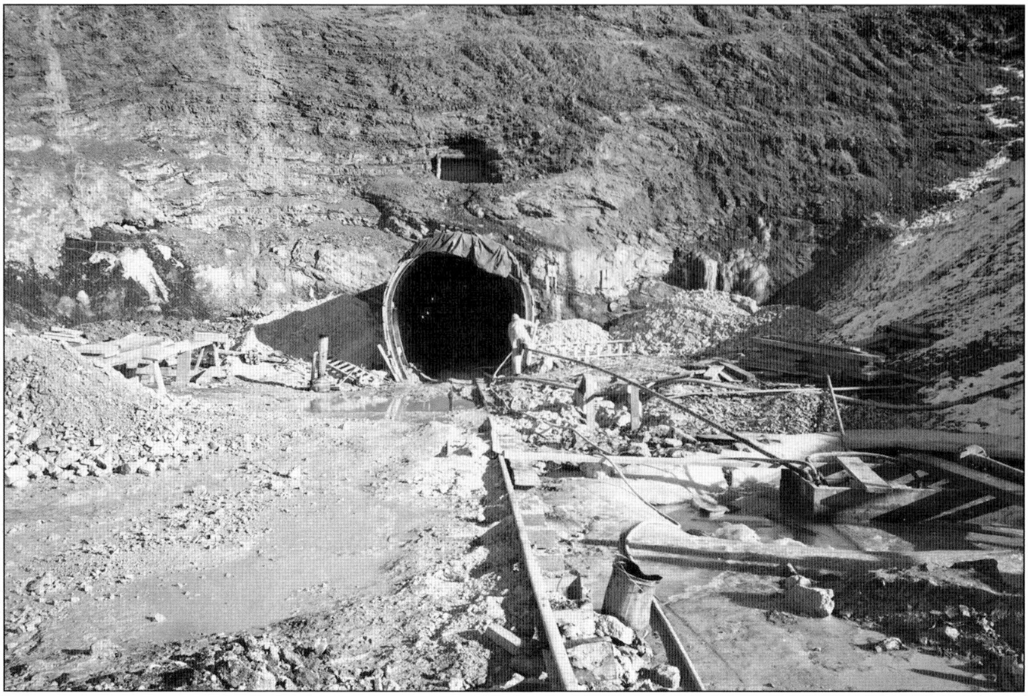

Centered Views. The reader is able to look straight into the West Portal from Survey Station No. 9 on November 28, 1956.

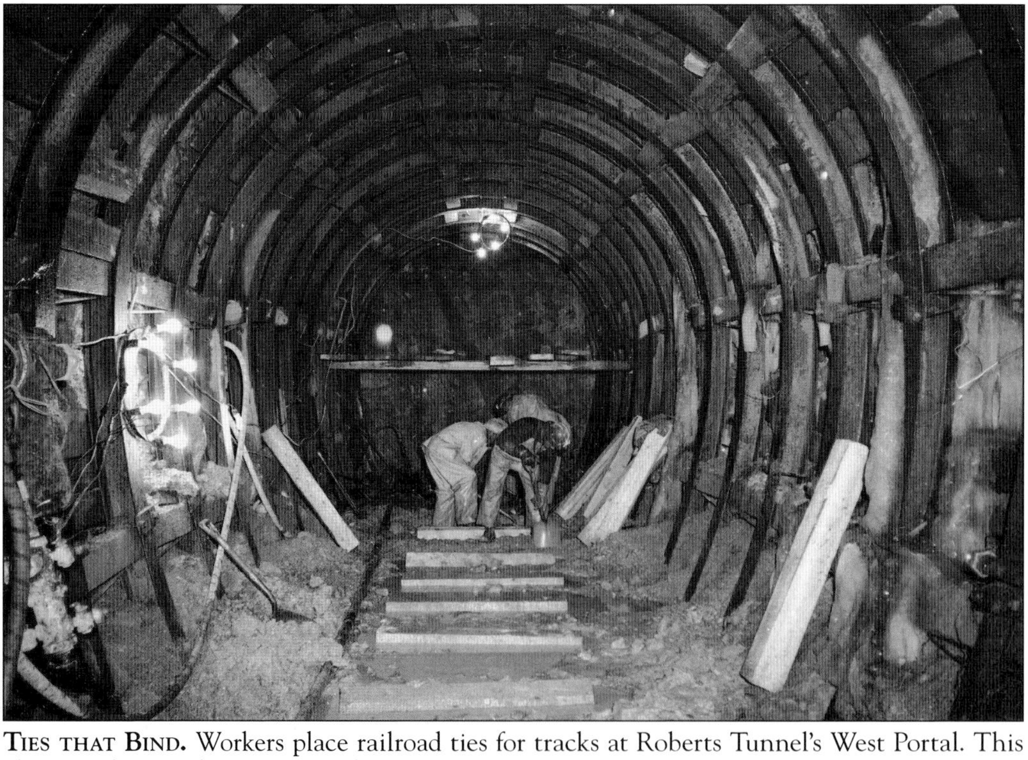

Ties that Bind. Workers place railroad ties for tracks at Roberts Tunnel's West Portal. This photograph was taken on December 5, 1956.

Hole Drilling. Necessary holes were drilled at the West Portal of the Roberts Tunnel. Workmen used the popular jack-leg, manufactured by Ingersoll-Rand. The photograph is dated December 11, 1956.

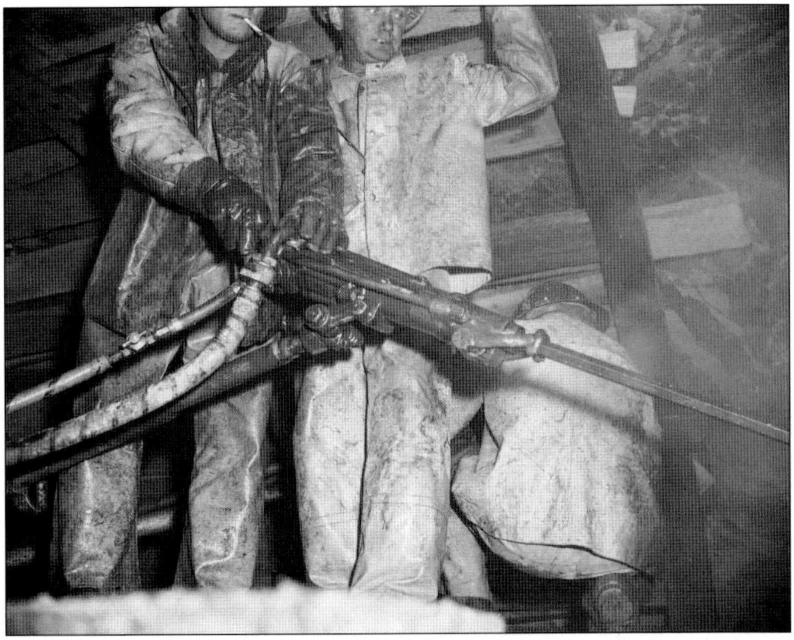

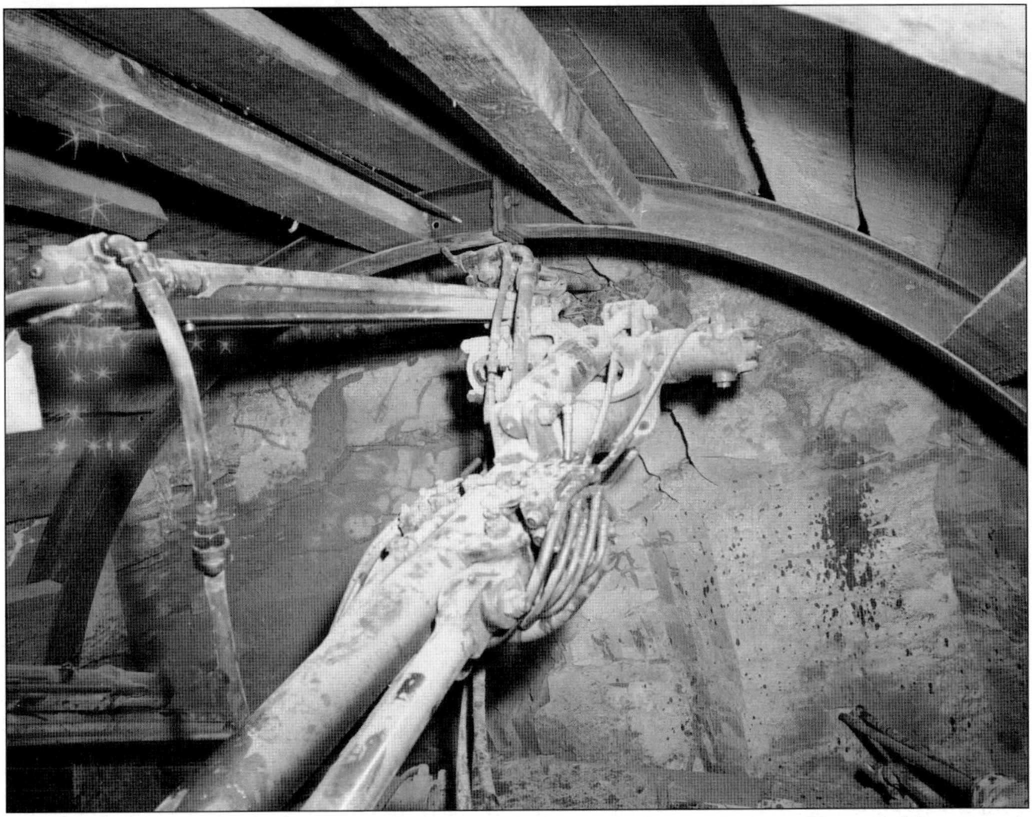

Jib Drill. This undated close-up depicts a drill jib set for drilling at Roberts Tunnel's West Portal. The heading is at Survey Station No. 10.

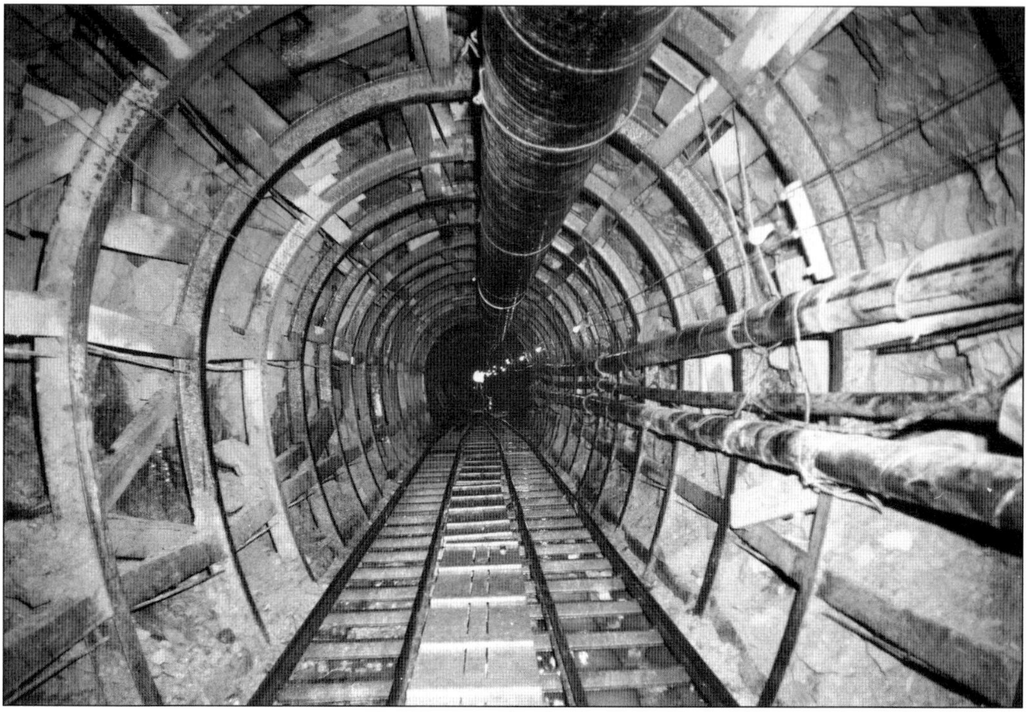

Steel Section. The California switch is seen here in the steel section of Roberts Tunnel's West Portal. The view is from Survey Station No. 11 in this photograph dated March 2, 1957.

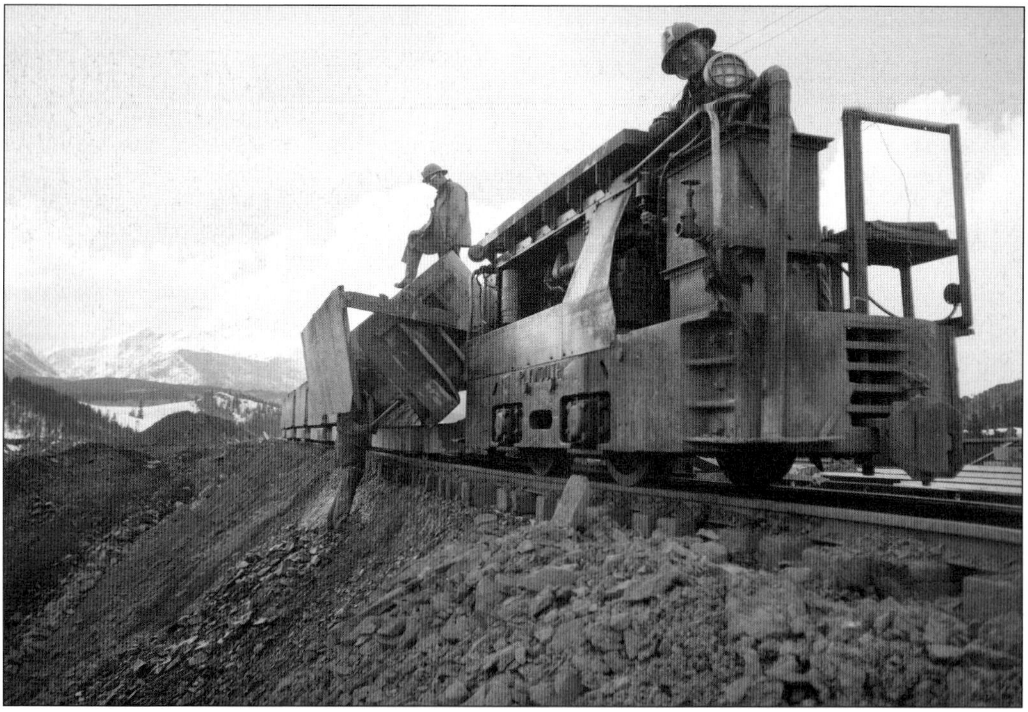

Muck Cars. Dumping muck cars is seen here at the West Portal of Roberts Tunnel on March 31, 1958.

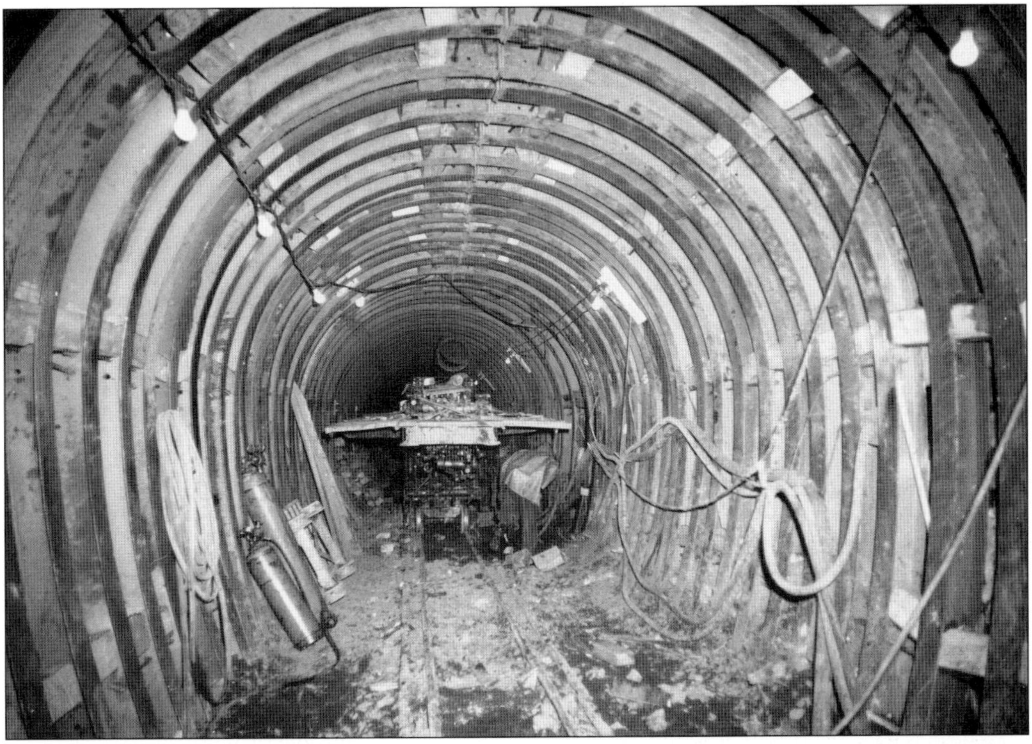

Sectional Views. A section of the West Portal of Roberts Tunnel is pictured where jump sets and struts were placed. The view is looking out from Survey Station No. 179 on June 13, 1958.

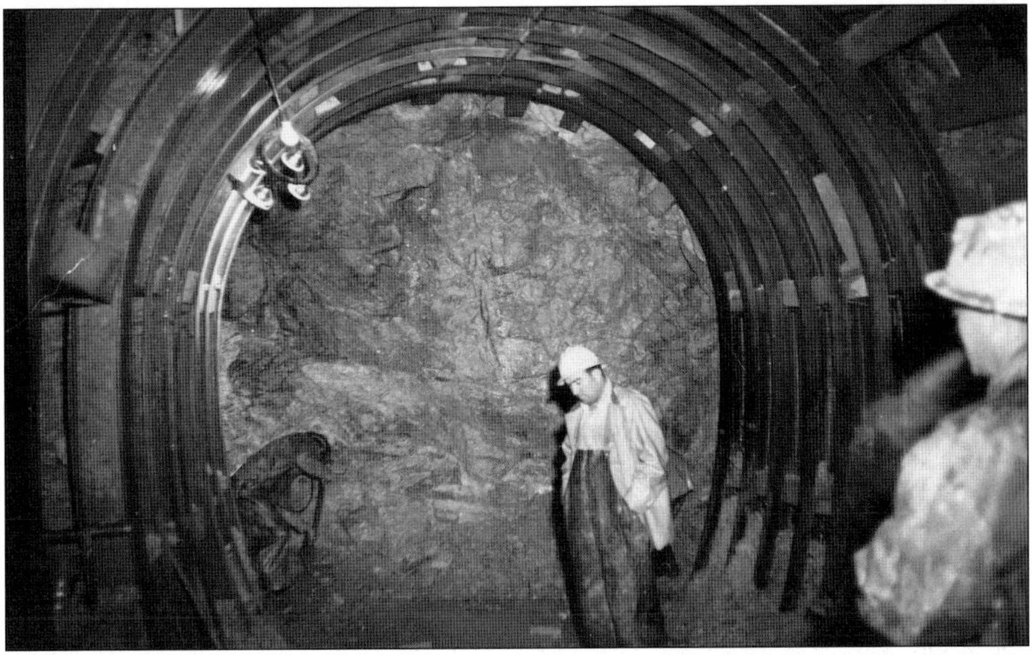

Sheared Quartz. Located near the heading at Station No. 183 of Roberts Tunnel's West Portal is this sheared quartz-biotite gneiss. It is found in abundance in the area. The photograph is dated August 1, 1958.

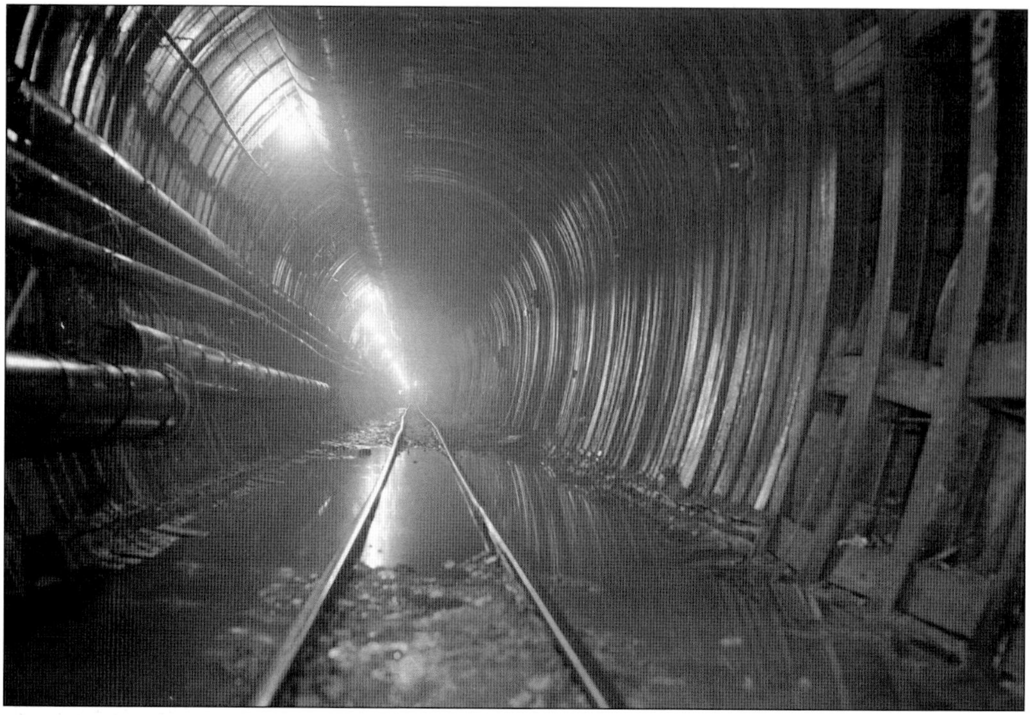

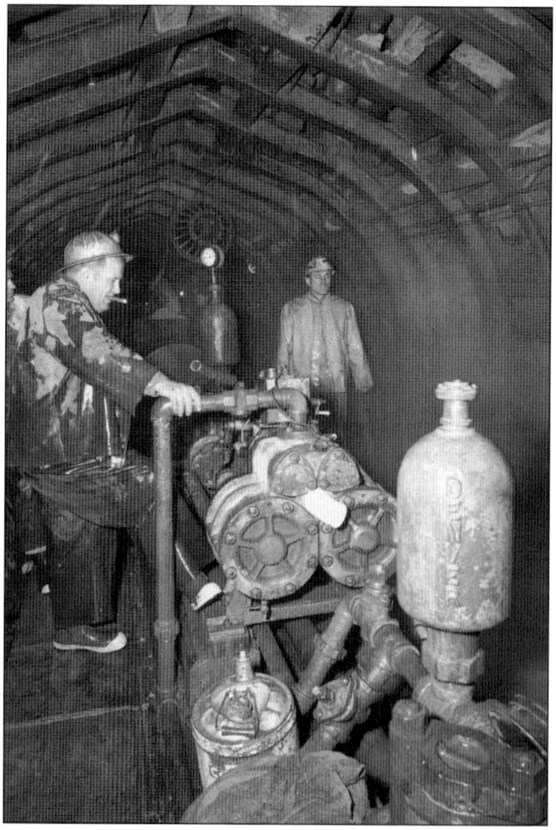

Steel Struts. The solid steel and strutted section of the West Portal of Roberts Tunnel is seen from the east from Station No. 199 on November 28, 1958.

Grouting Station. At the grouting station of Roberts Tunnel's West Portal, a Gardner Denver grouting pump is being used. The photograph is dated February 20, 1959.

EXCESS WATER. Water is accumulating at 1,200 gallons per minute from flow encountered from test holes. This view at Station No. 257 is dated August 18, 1959.

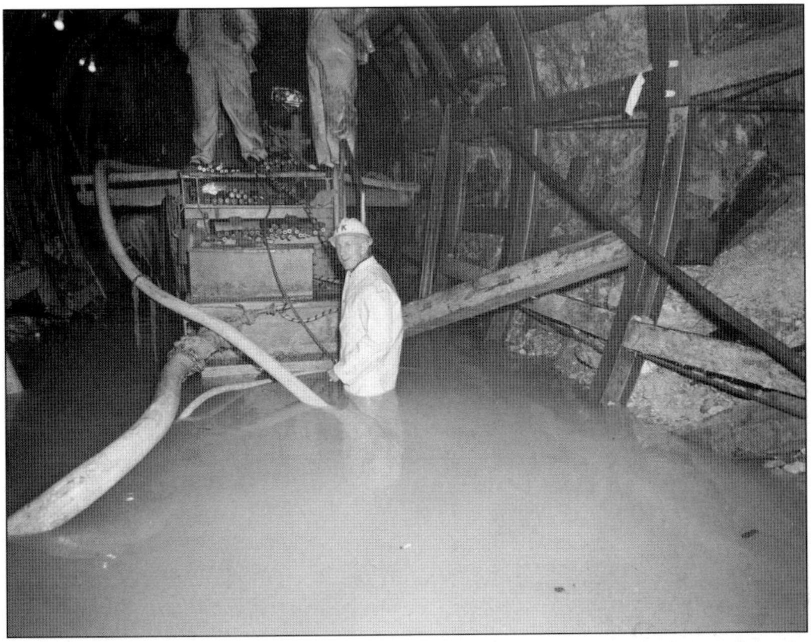

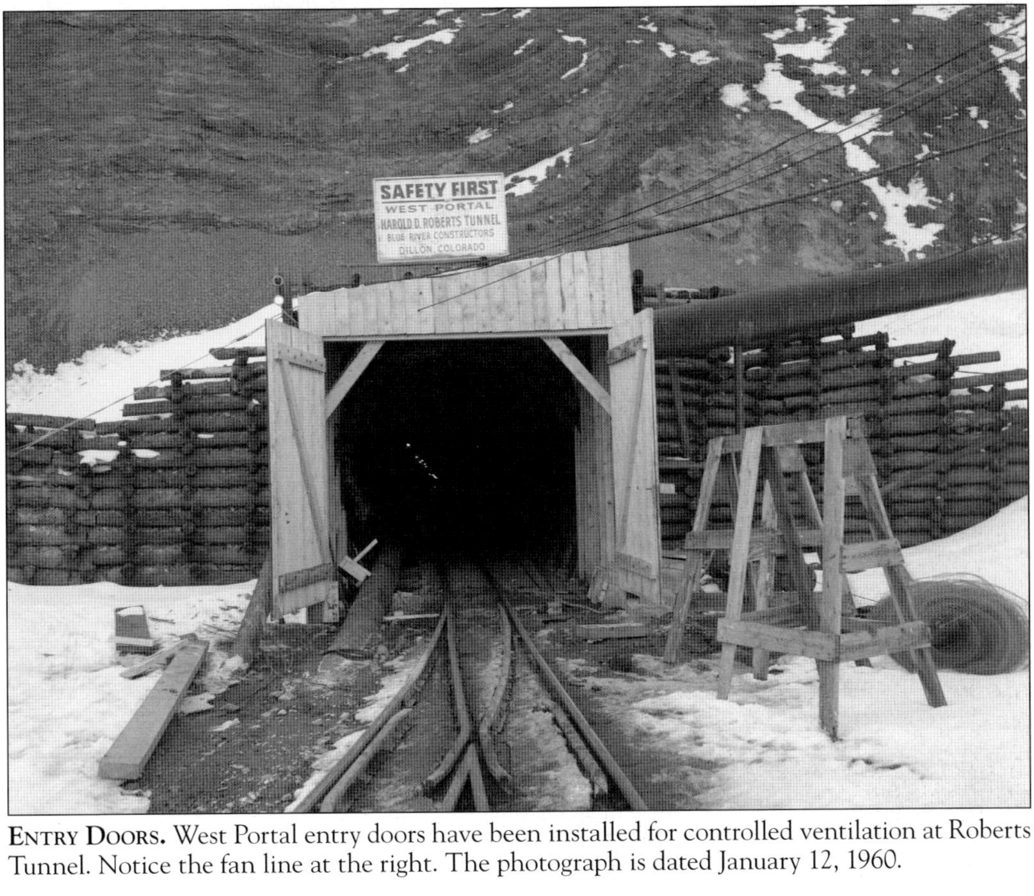

ENTRY DOORS. West Portal entry doors have been installed for controlled ventilation at Roberts Tunnel. Notice the fan line at the right. The photograph is dated January 12, 1960.

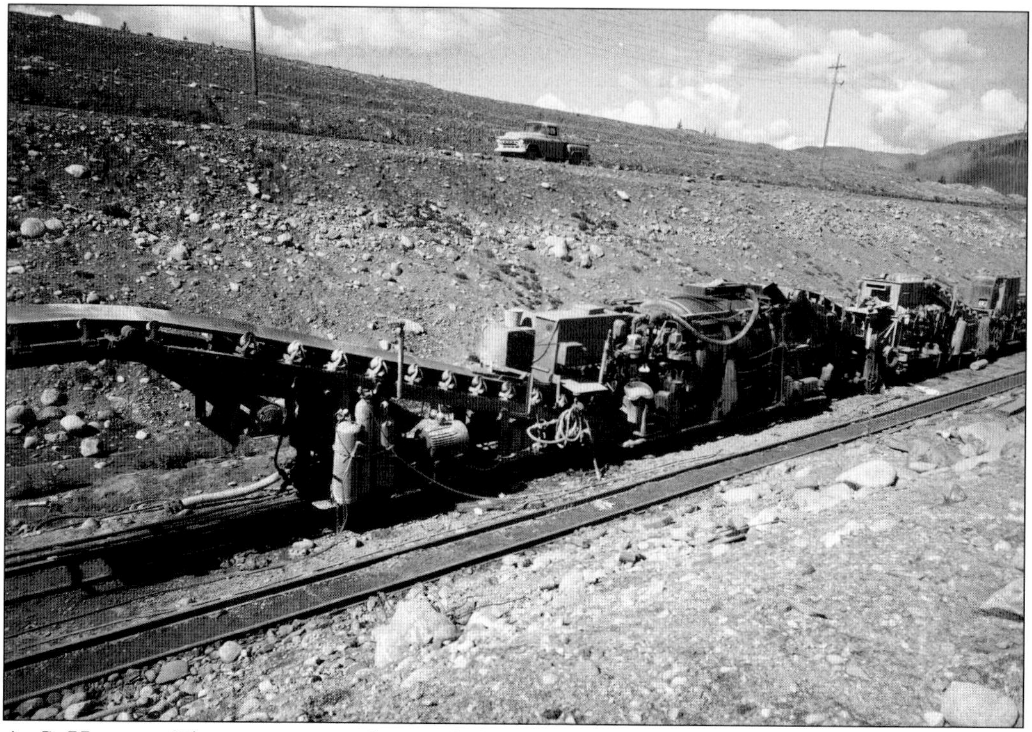

A. S. Horner. This concrete rig shows a belt and mixer in the foreground at Roberts Tunnel's West Portal. A. S. Horner Construction Company was at work on August 15, 1961.

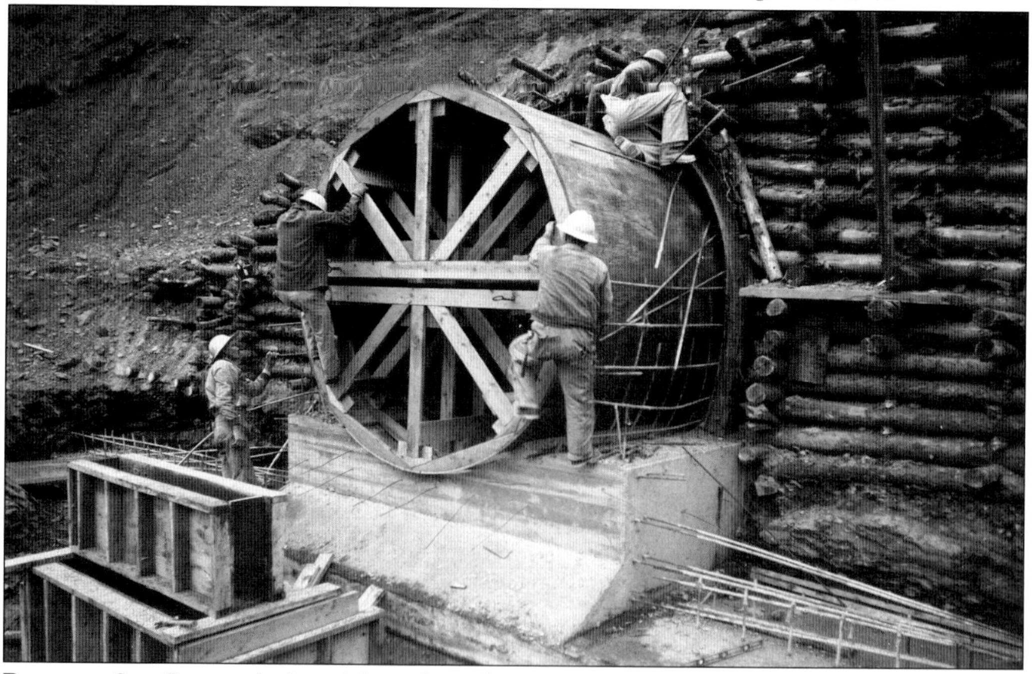

Barrel is Set. Setting the barrel form through a wing wall section at the West Portal of Roberts Tunnel was accomplished by workmen of A. S. Horner Construction Company. The photograph is dated August 15, 1961.

Emergency Exits. The view into the Roberts Tunnel's West Portal here is at the area near the emergency gate shaft in November 1961, just a few days prior to testing of the gate.

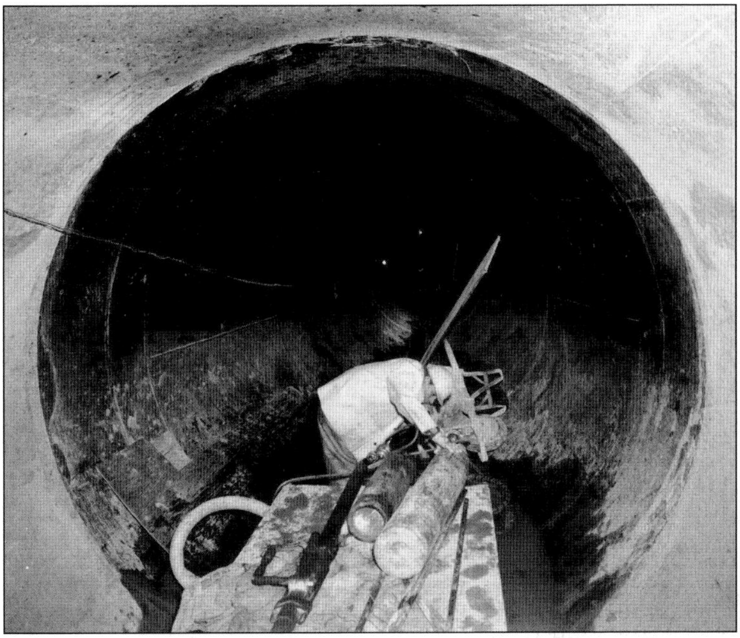

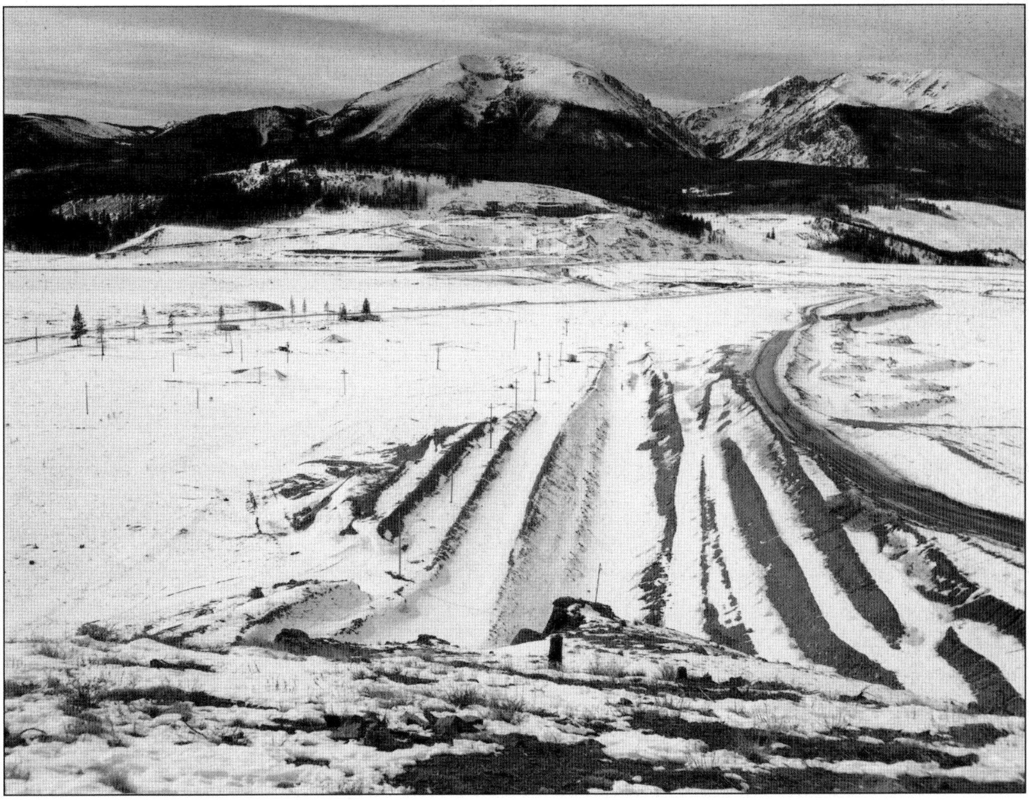

Construction Facilities Removed. This westward view from above is at the inlet channel after the removal of construction facilities at the West Portal of Roberts Tunnel. The photograph is dated April 1962.

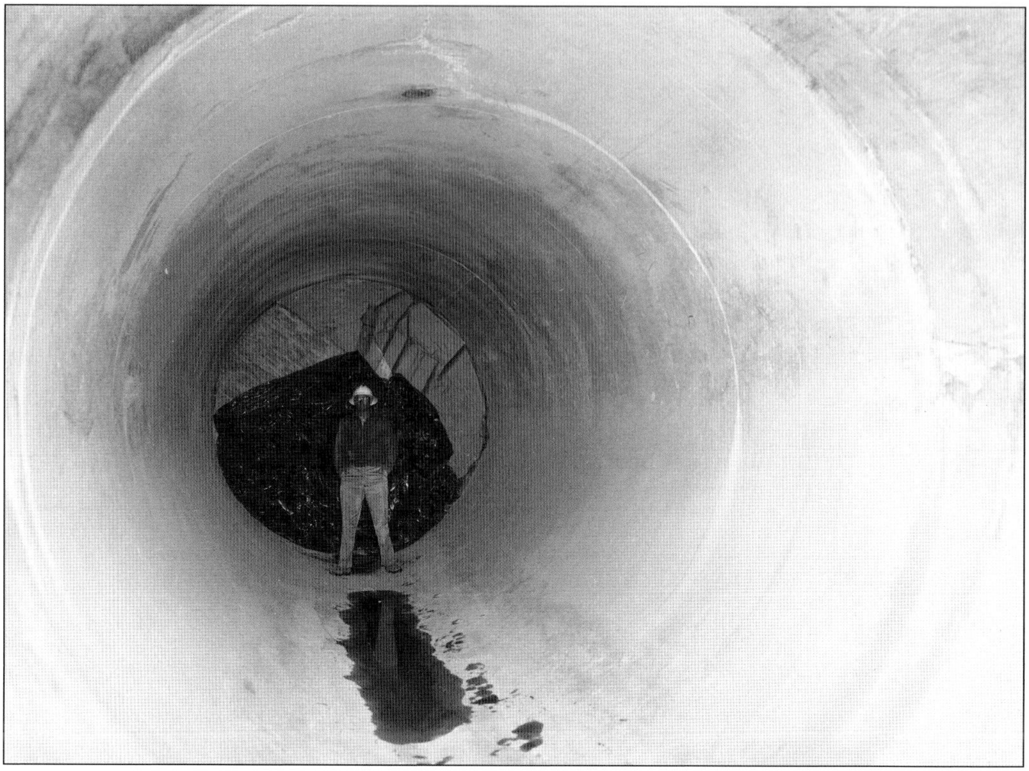

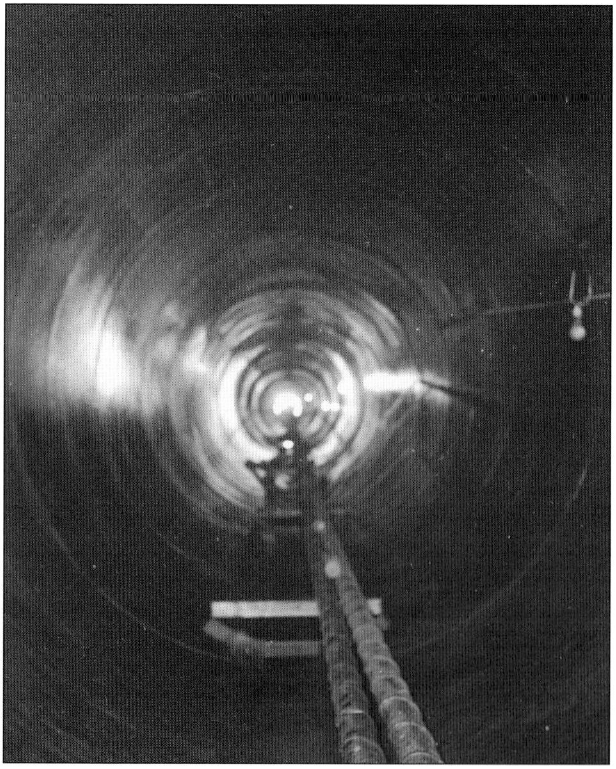

Emergency Shaft. This view at the West Portal of Roberts Tunnel was taken in November 1961.

Roberts Tunnel, West Portal. Steel lining was placed for reinforcement of the tunnel and depicted in this April 1962 photograph.

Seven

DILLON

The new Dillon does not resemble the 1950s' old Dillon—a sleepy town. The old Dillon was a town waiting for ranchers, tourists, mountaineers, and speculators to stop in and spend their money.

The new town of Dillon is big time and mountain time, with its huge and gorgeous body of water that beckons boatmen, windsurfers, and plenty of photographers, depending upon the season.

The new town of Dillon has condos and townhouses, and yes, it did keep the Dillon Community Church, some of the old houses, and the Arapahoe Café.

The new town of Dillon is a full-service community with a year-round residential population of approximately 2,800 residents. It is in a strategic location between Keystone, Breckenridge, and Vail in a beautiful place in the heart of Summit County.

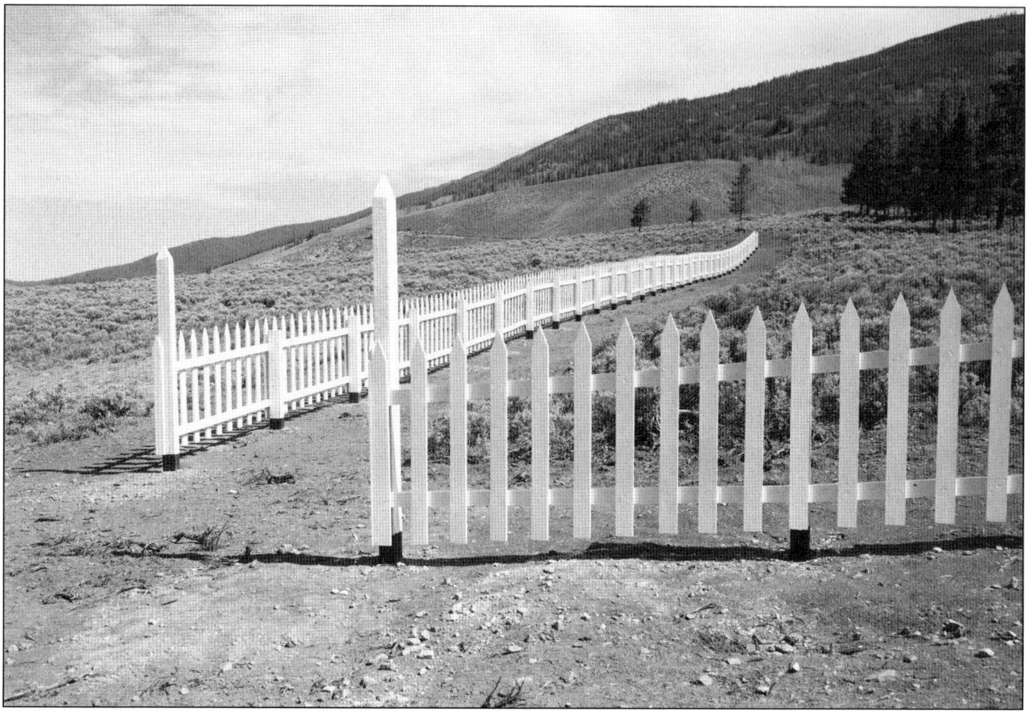

NEW DILLON CEMETERY. The entrance to the cemetery is at the southeast corner of the enclosure. The view looks northwest on June 23, 1961.

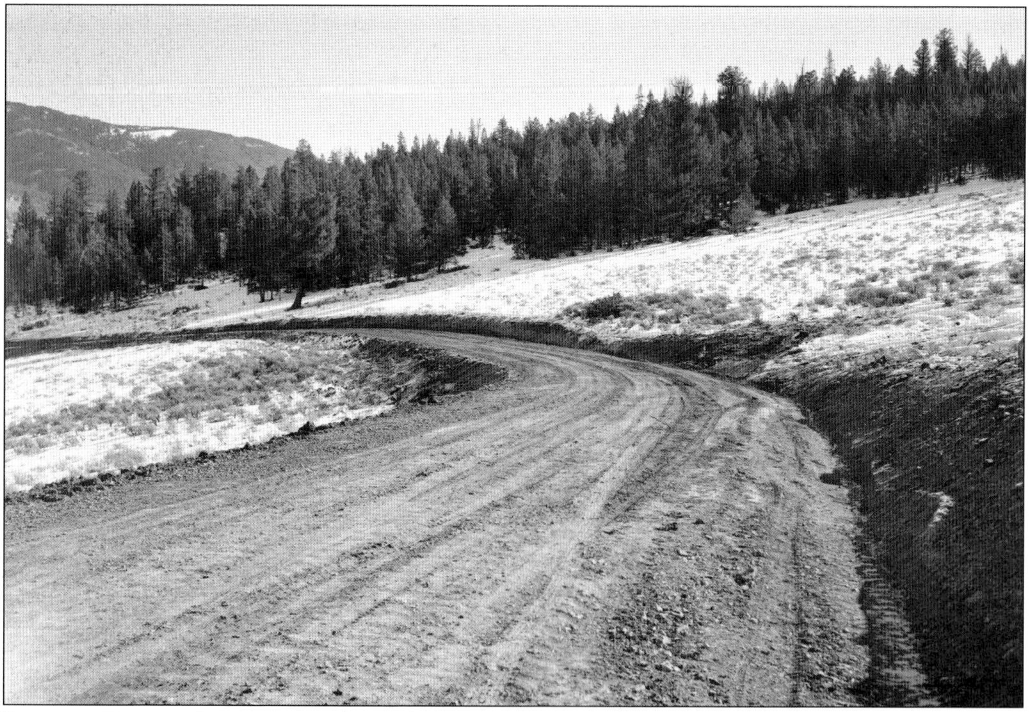

ROBERTS TUNNEL GATEHOUSE. This is the access road to the gatehouse in a view looking northwest on June 23, 1961.

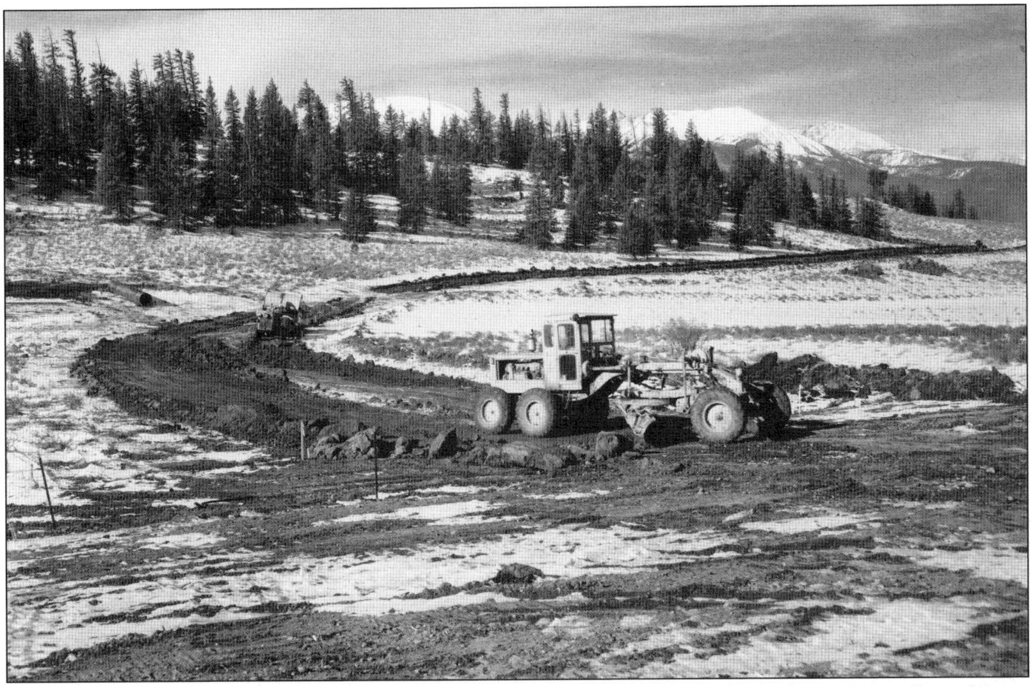

Roberts Tunnel Gatehouse Road. This view is of the entrance to the Roberts Tunnel gatehouse road. The road grading continued on to Highway 6, which had not been completed at the time of this October 1962 photograph.

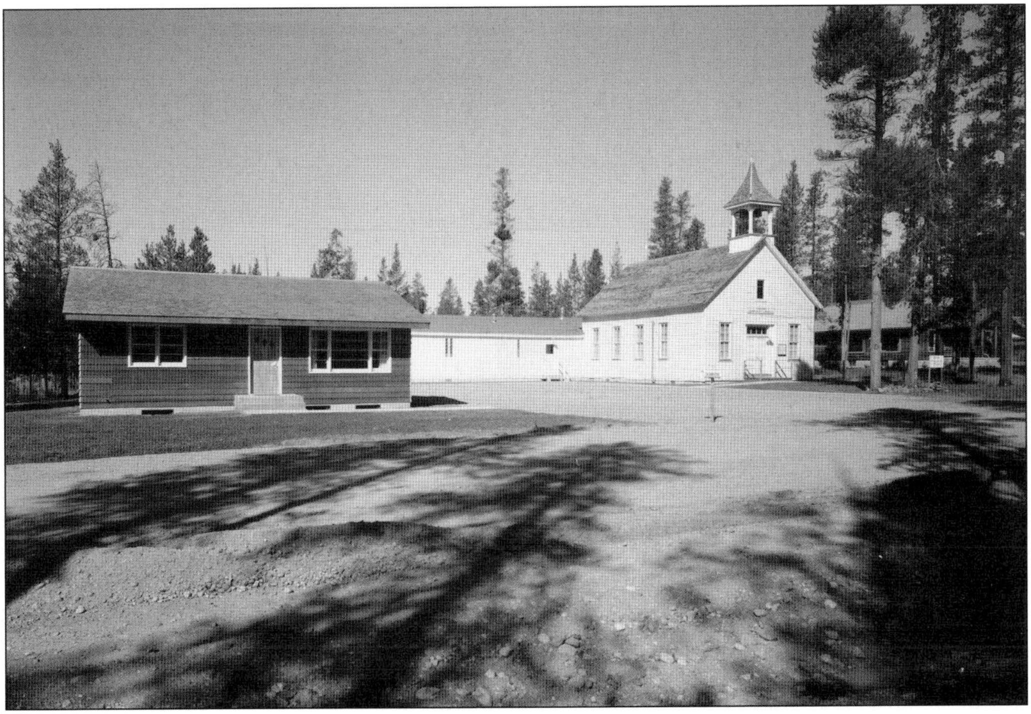

Relocated Dillon Community Church. The church is seen in this northwestern view on October 2, 1962. The parsonage is at the left.

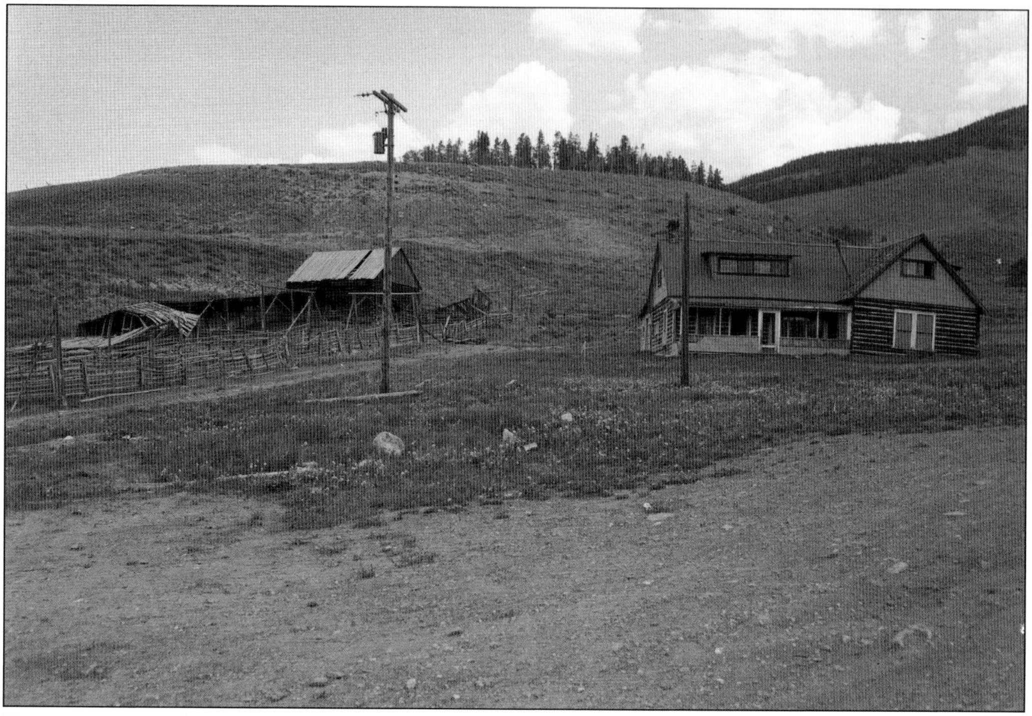

Byers Ranch. This ranch house, pictured on July 1, 1963, would in time become the headquarters of Denver Dillon Water.

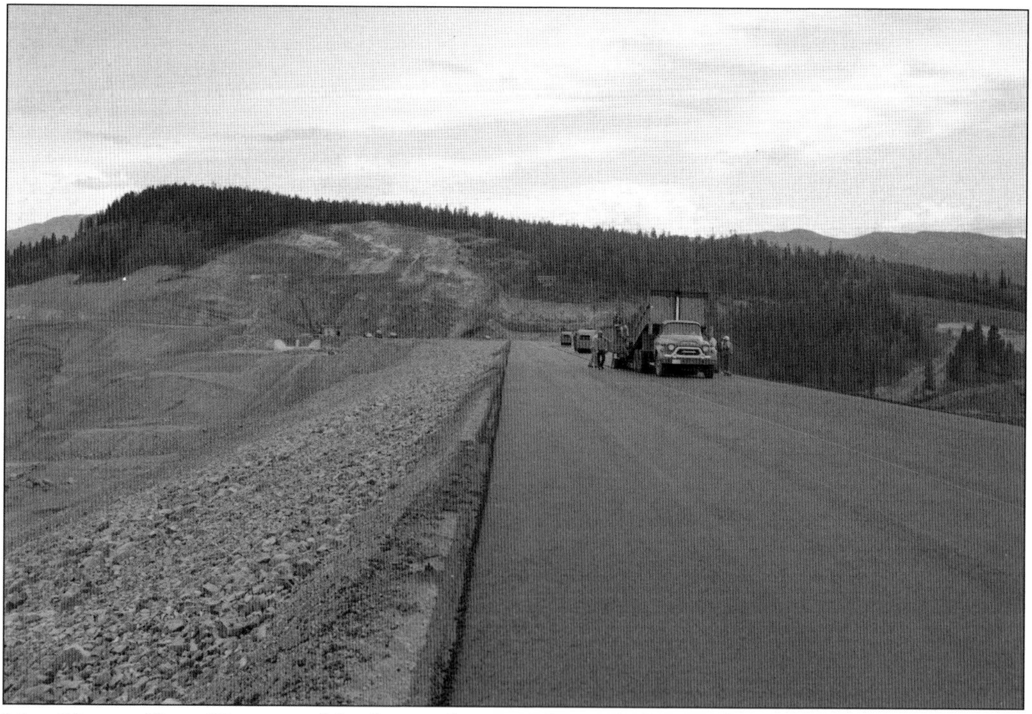

New Dillon Dam Highway. The laying down of the asphalt mat illustrates the needs of a new highway. It runs on top of the completed Dillon Dam. The photograph is dated August 8, 1963.

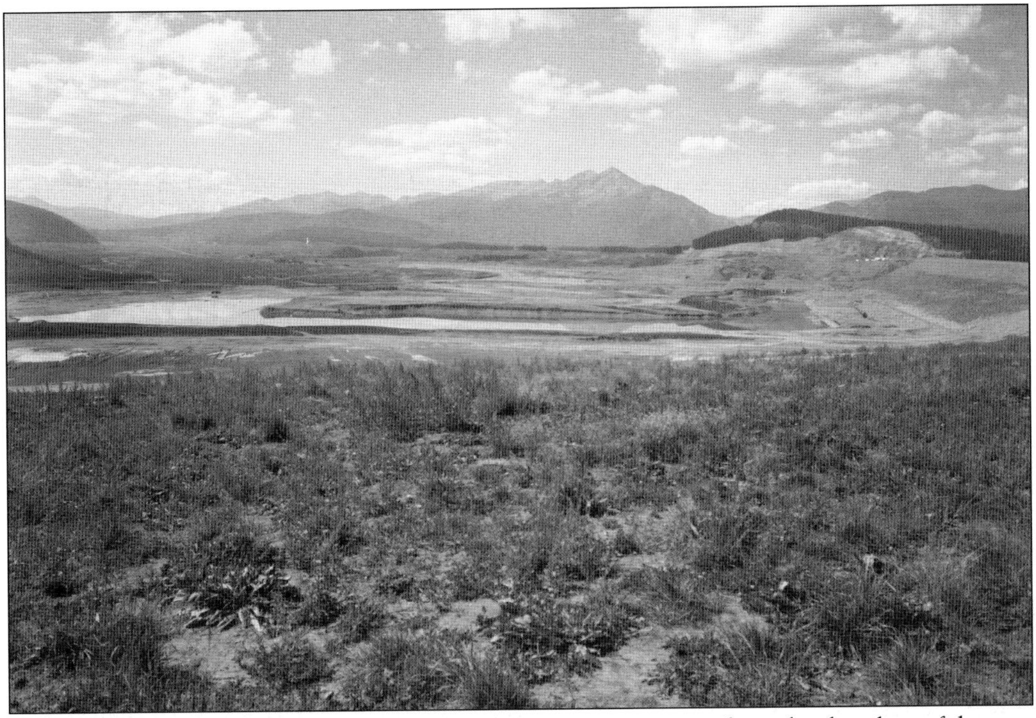

FILLING THE DAM. Dillon Dam is being filled. The vantage point is from the shoreline of the new town of Dillon. The photograph is dated September 1963.

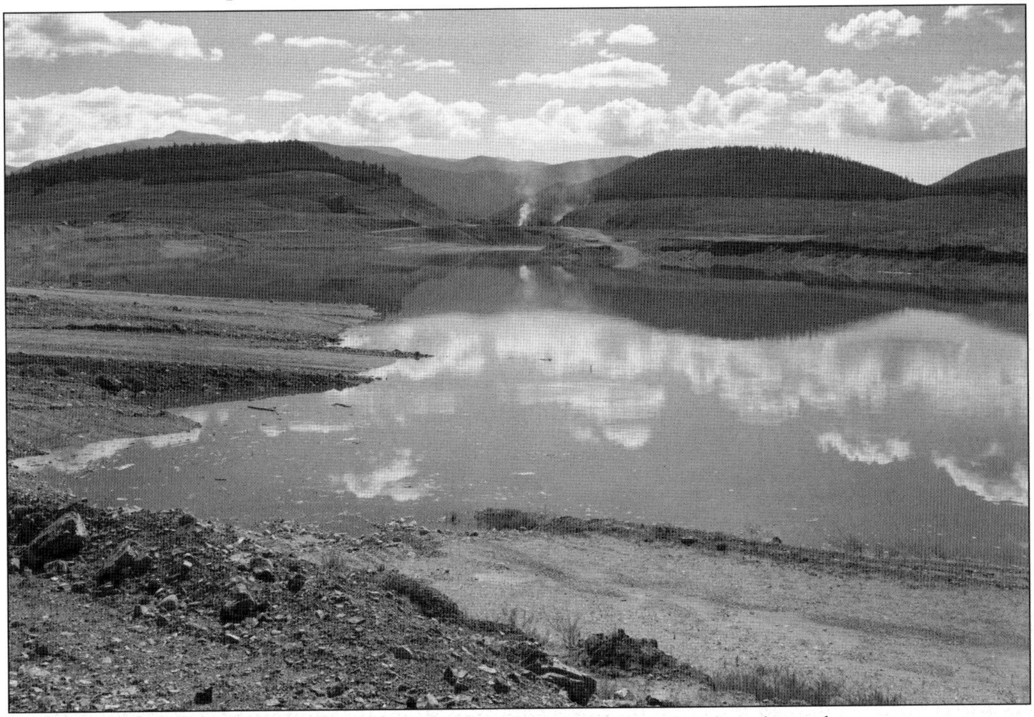

SNAKE RIVER. The Snake River is completely submerged into the dam from the canyon entrance on September 6, 1963.

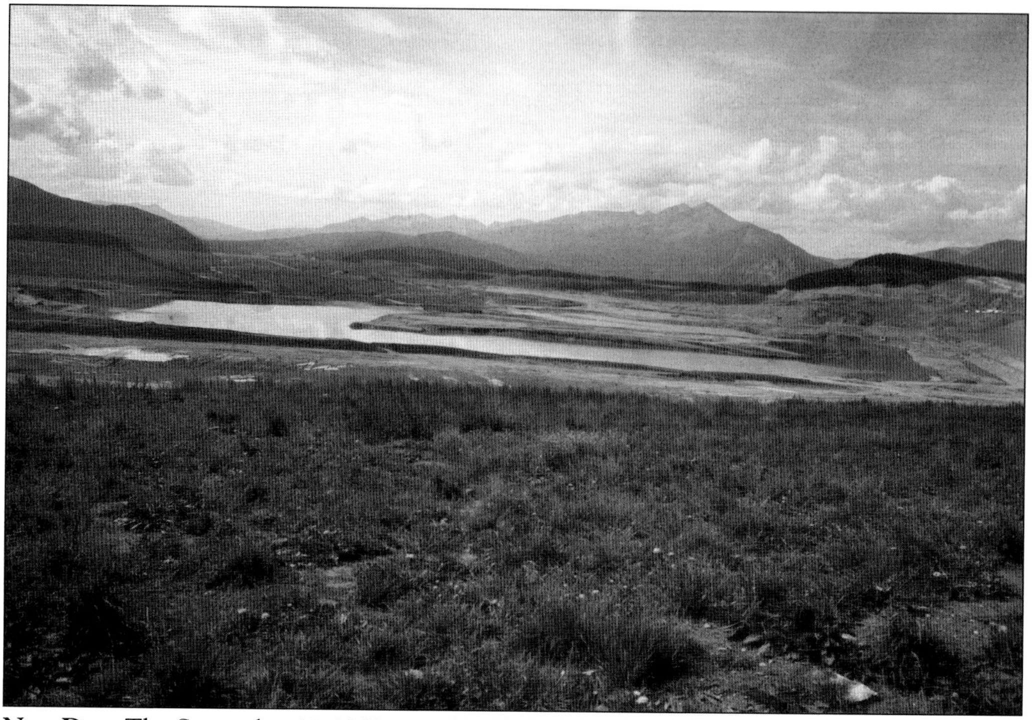

New Dam. The September 11, 1963, view here looks northeast along the new Dillon Dam from the west abutment.

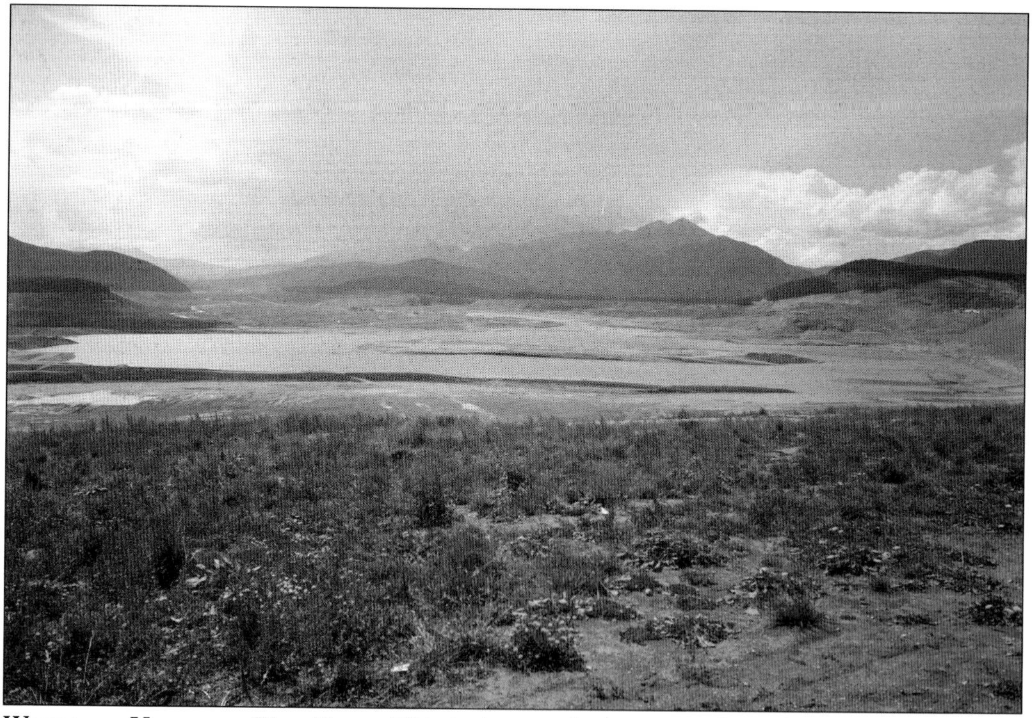

Westward View from New Town. This is the view looking west from the new town of Dillon on September 11, 1963.

Eight

SILVERTHORNE

Silverthorne is now one of the fastest growing communities in America, boasting a population of around 3,000. It became a town just 40 years ago. Highway 9 was paved through Dillon and on down the Blue River. At that time, Silverthorne was virtually an extension of Dillon. During the dam construction, it was a trailer court community for the dam construction workers and a supply depot for Denver Water. It became the town of Silverthorne when the dam was completed.

Three old buildings from old Dillon were relocated down the Blue River, and most people assumed they would continue to be called Dillon. But a town meeting resulted in the renaming of the place as Silverthorne, after a mining court judge, Judge Silverthorn, who spelled his name without an "e." The town later added an "e" to be fashionable.

The Silverthorne area has gone through several phases, from peaceful cattle ranching to placer mining to construction depot to modern mountain village. Its location on U.S. Highway 70 gives residents quick access to Cooper Mountain, Vail, Breckenridge, and Keystone for winter and summer sports.

Silverthorne today has the fashionable boutique Factory Outlet Stores, Target, national fast food chains, and a Sears outlet. Gone are the environmental hazards of the mining industry, and gone are the trailer courts that diminished the Silverthorne appearance. Financial hardship is a thing of the past. Silverthorne's focus now is enhancing its parks and trails as well as developing its town center, which opened in 2001.

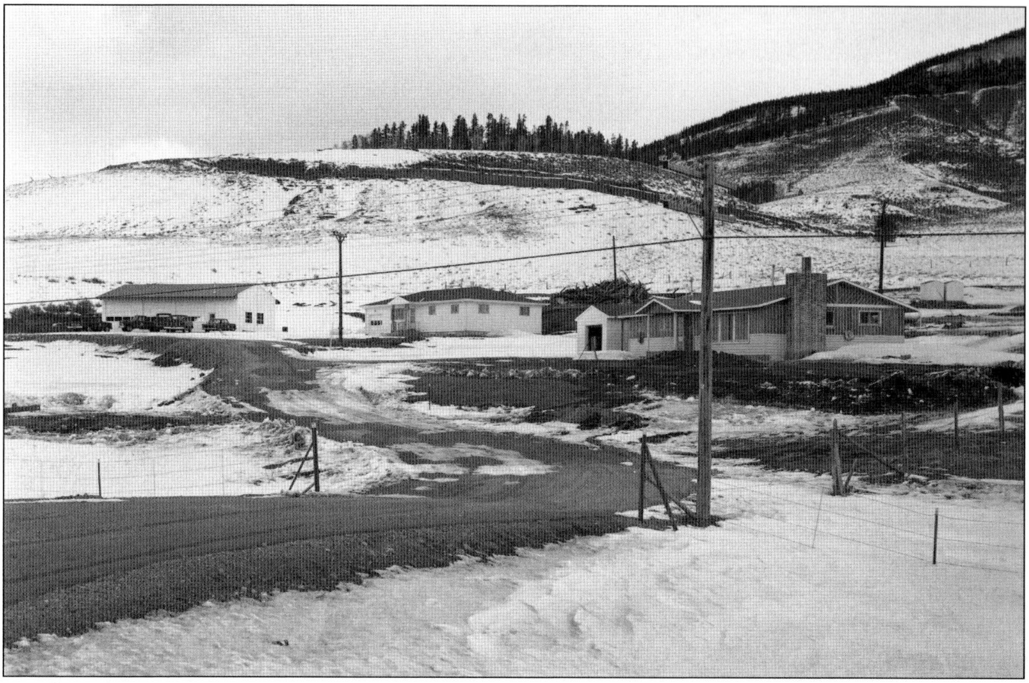

Denver Water's Dillon Headquarters. This new site was a replacement for the old Byers Ranch. The photograph faces north in March 1964.

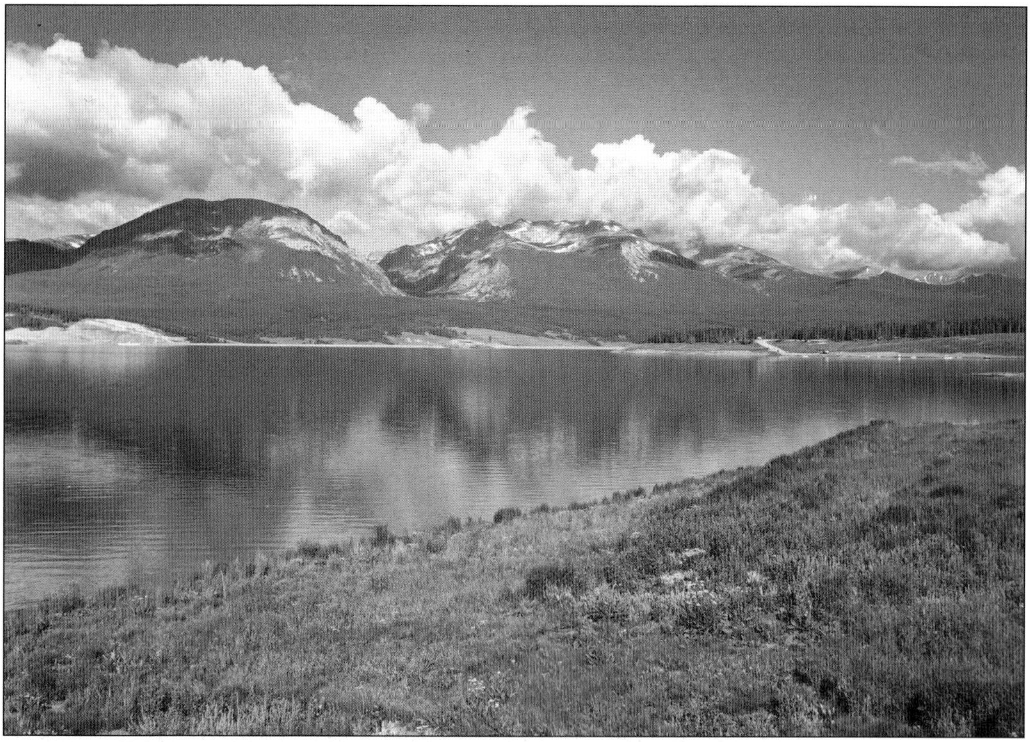

Filled to Capacity. The Dillon Dam is seen filled during the month of August 1965. The view is west, overlooking the new dam.

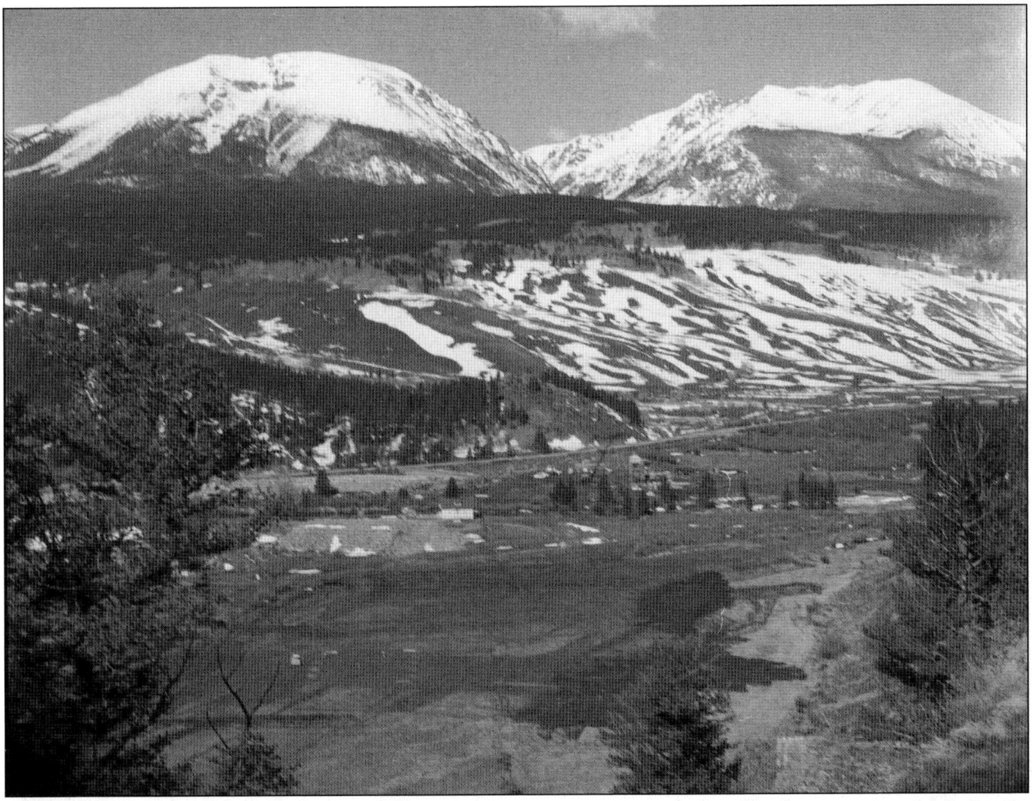

Silverthorne Overview. The new town of Silverthorne is seen in the distance on the left side of this photograph, taken on April 13, 1960. Buffalo Mountain and the beginnings of the Gore Mountain Range on the right are also visible.

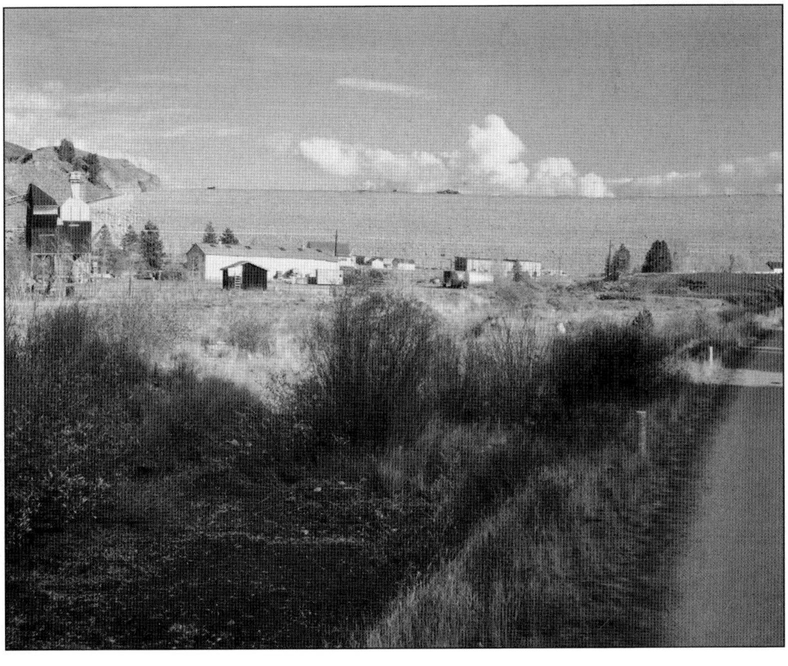

Dam Embankment, Silverthorne Side. The Dillon Dam embankment is depicted downstream from the face of the dam. The view is southeast from old Highway 9. This photograph is dated October 17, 1962.

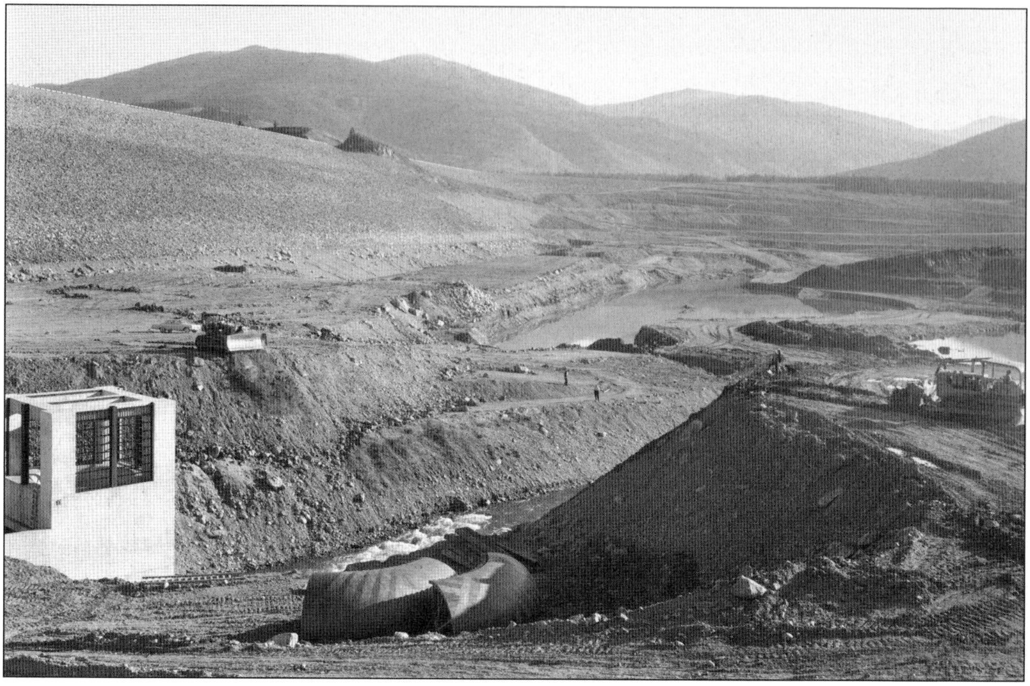

Blue River on Silverthorne Side. This location is downstream on the Blue River, looking east at the abutment. The photograph is dated May 1963.

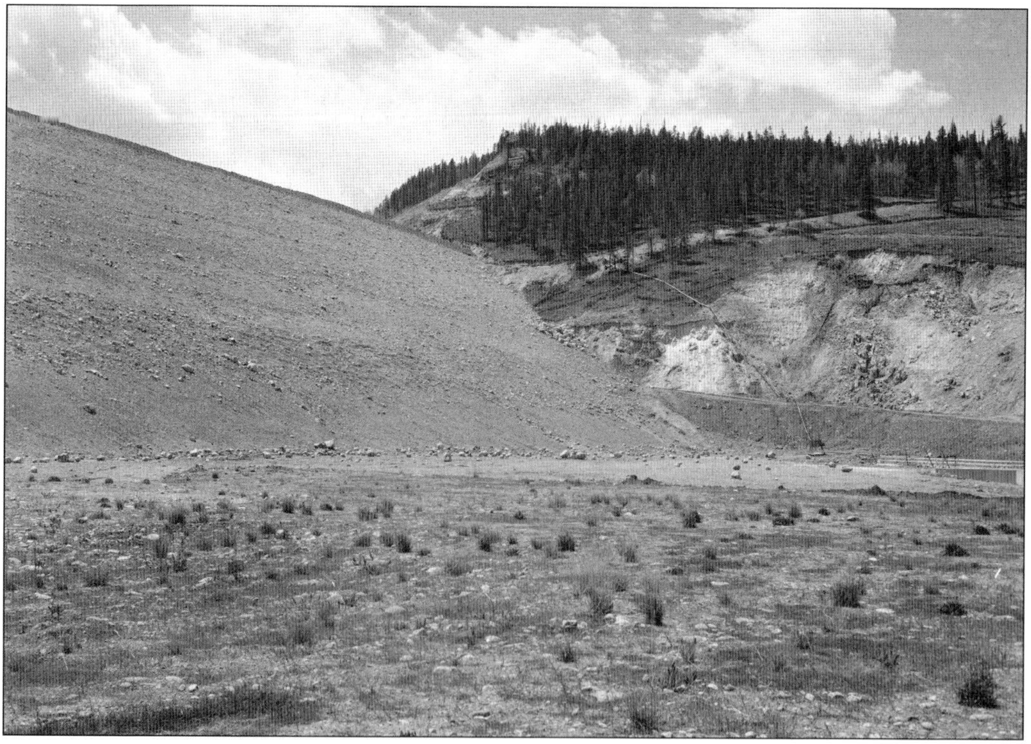

Silverthorne Embankment. The downstream face of the dam can be seen with the outlet works on the far right side, looking southwest in May 1963.

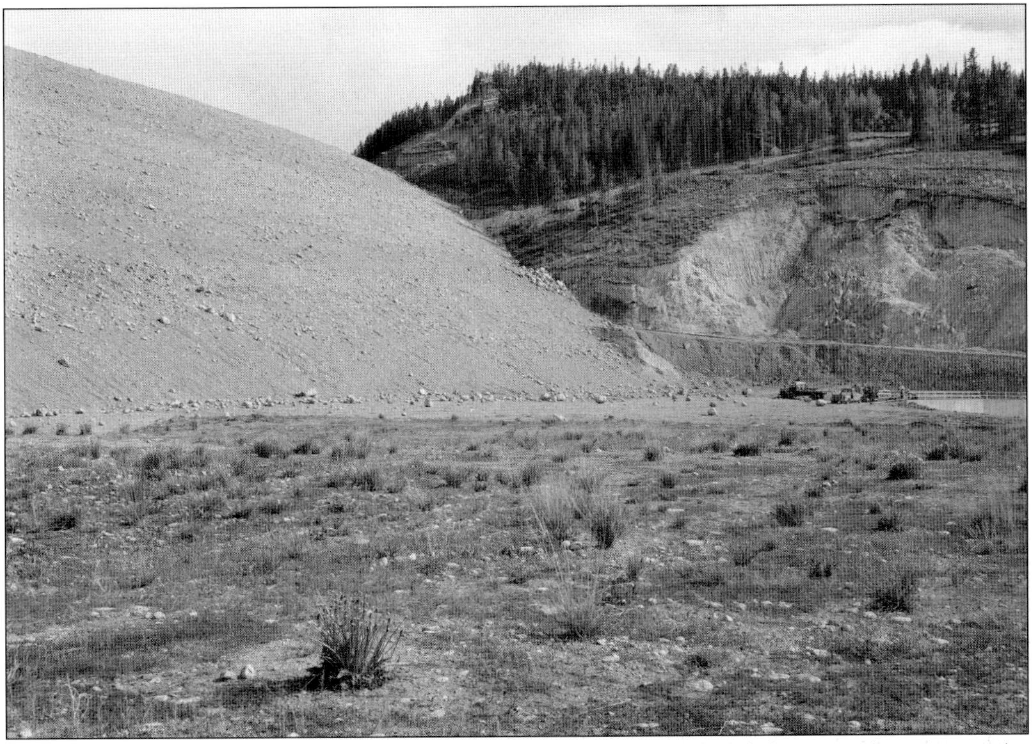

Silverthorne Face of Dam. Looking southwest, this view is toward the west abutment at the Silverthorne side of the dam. The photograph is dated June 17, 1963.

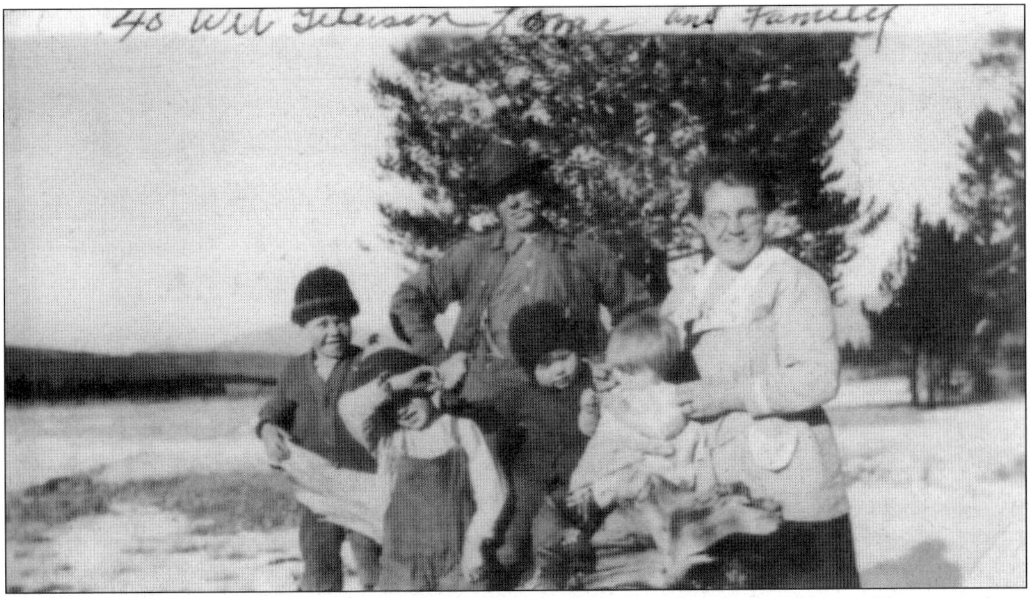

The Gibersons. Webb Giberson, Mollie Giberson, and their family are depicted here on their ranch, which was located west of Dillon and Frisco. Many of the ranches on the lower Blue River had been homesteaded. The Homestead Act was a U.S. law that gave the applicant a freehold title to 160 acres of undeveloped land for a filing fee of $10, as long as it was outside the original 13 colonies. (Courtesy of Summit Historical Society.)

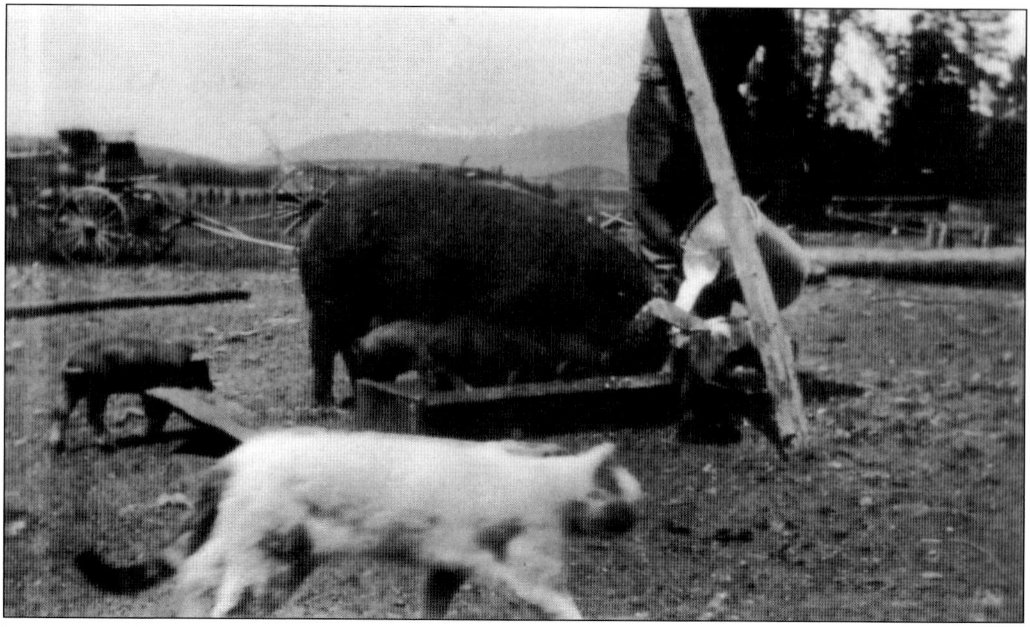

Webb Giberson Ranch and Farm Animals. A farmhand is slopping pigs in the background while a cat sneaks into the picture. (Courtesy of Summit Historical Society.)

Keener Ranch. This spread was located north of Dillon. Everyone living on a ranch had their daily assigned tasks to accomplish. The chickens, pigs, cows, and horses had to be fed daily, while planting crops and harvesting was seasonal. The photograph was taken prior to 1871. (Courtesy of Summit Historical Society.)

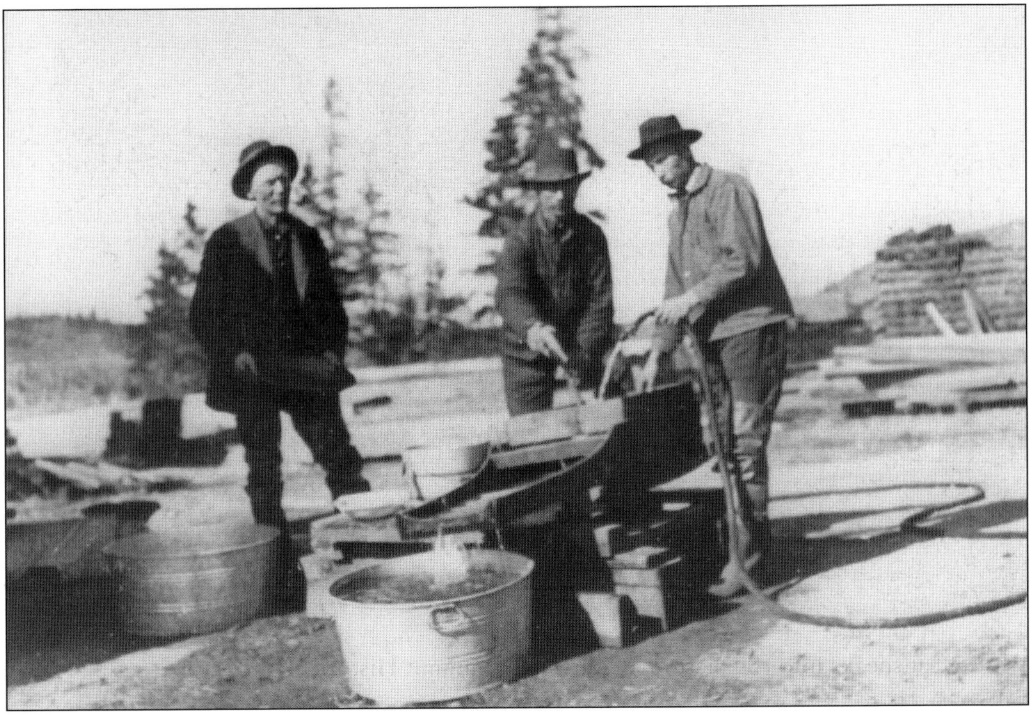

Example of Placer Mining. Placer mining, backyard style, is depicted here. Alluvial deposits of soil are washed, usually under some water pressure, and a catch bucket is used to see the mineral deposits. This photograph was taken in 1912 in the Blue River Valley ranching area. (Courtesy of Summit Historical Society.)

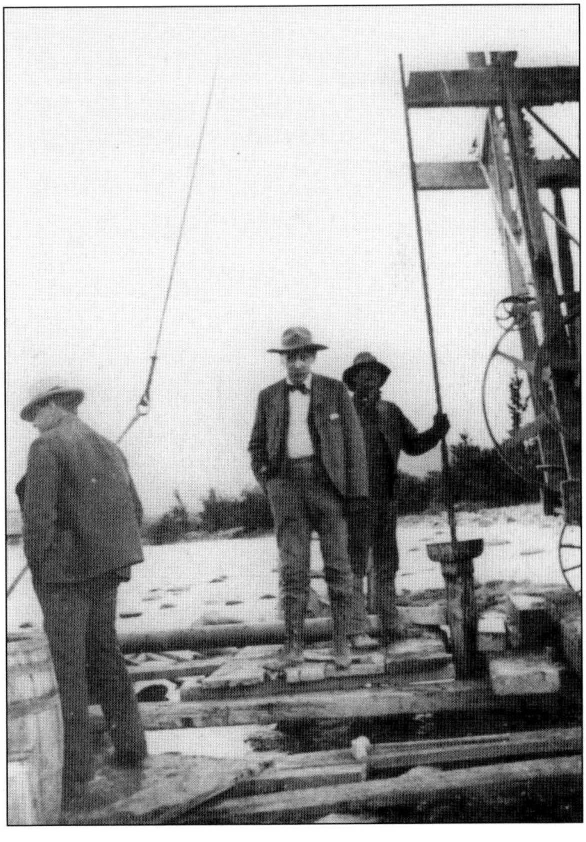

Testing for Gold. A churn drill is positioned over what is assumed to be gold-bearing gravel, and it digs a hole to confirm the deposits of gold. This photograph was taken sometime in the 1930s, in the area northeast of what is now Silverthorne on the old Fry Ranch land. (Courtesy of Summit Historical Society.)

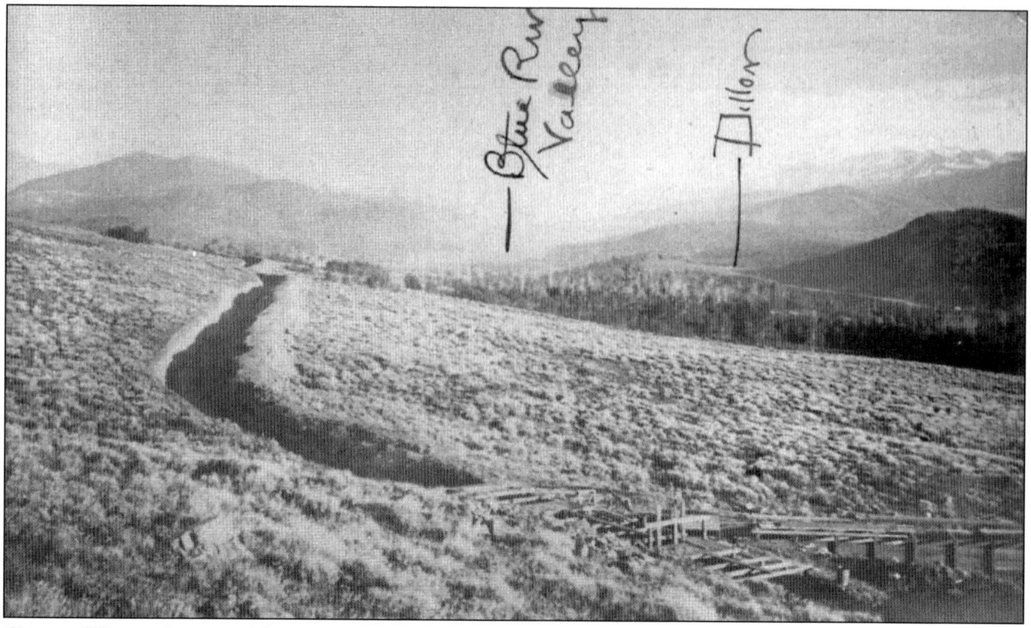

CANAL WATER SUPPLY. Placer mining, especially the hydraulic variety, required pressurized water, which is measured by PSI, or pounds per square inch. This photograph shows a canal being dug to bring water from above Keystone down to Dillon and beyond to the Blue River Valley. (Courtesy of Summit Historical Society.)

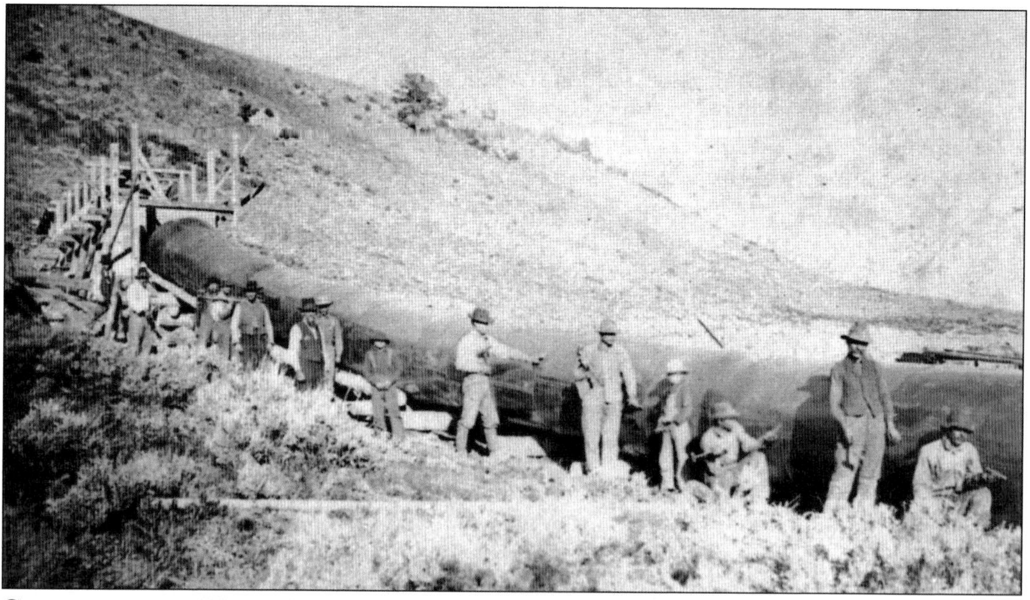

CONSTRUCTING A WATER PIPE. Under the watchful eye of company executives, men put the finishing touches on sections of a large-diameter water pipe. Water carried by the wooden flume will enter the pipe and be carried to hydraulic operations down the slope. Note the wooden bracing on the flue. A "giant" or "monitor" lies beyond the water pipe on the right. This photograph shows workmen laying the groundwork to bring this 4-foot-diameter pipe from the Keystone hills and the Snake River down to the Blue River. The bright sunlight diminished the quality of the photograph but not the content. (Courtesy of Summit Historical Society.)

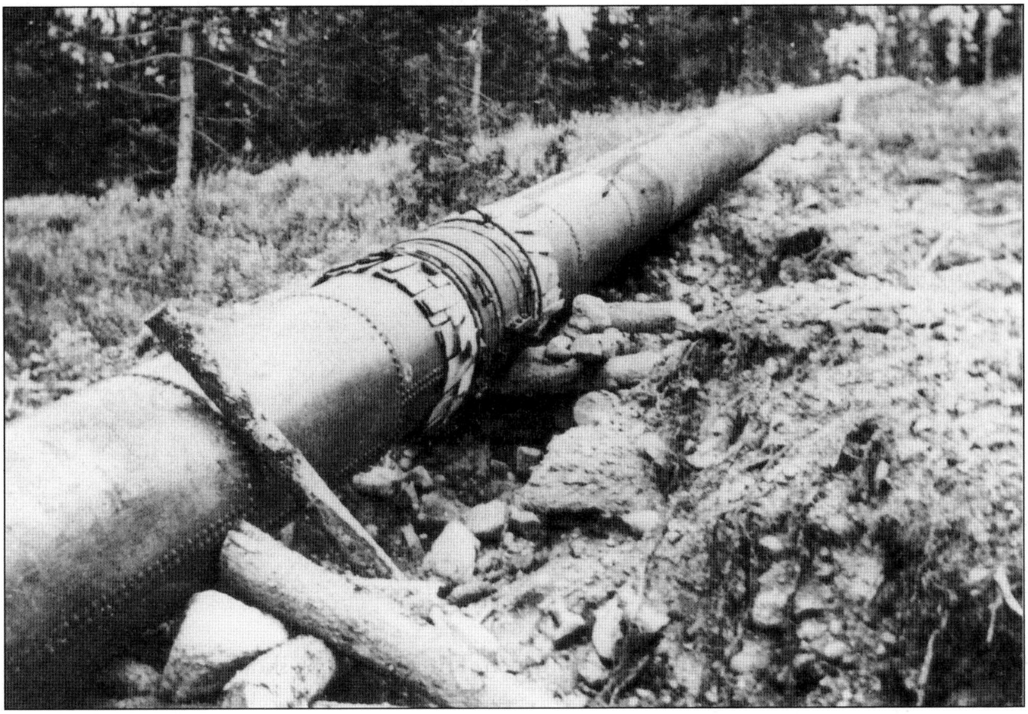

HYDRAULIC MINING. The pipeline mentioned in the photograph above was continued on down the hills to the Blue River to be used by the Oro Grande Mining Company. One of its mining operations was located on what is now Eleventh Avenue in present-day Silverthorne. The pipe came to be known as the "million-rivet pipe" because of the number of rivets put in to join the sections together. The pipe was assembled in Frisco. (Courtesy of Summit County Historical Society.)

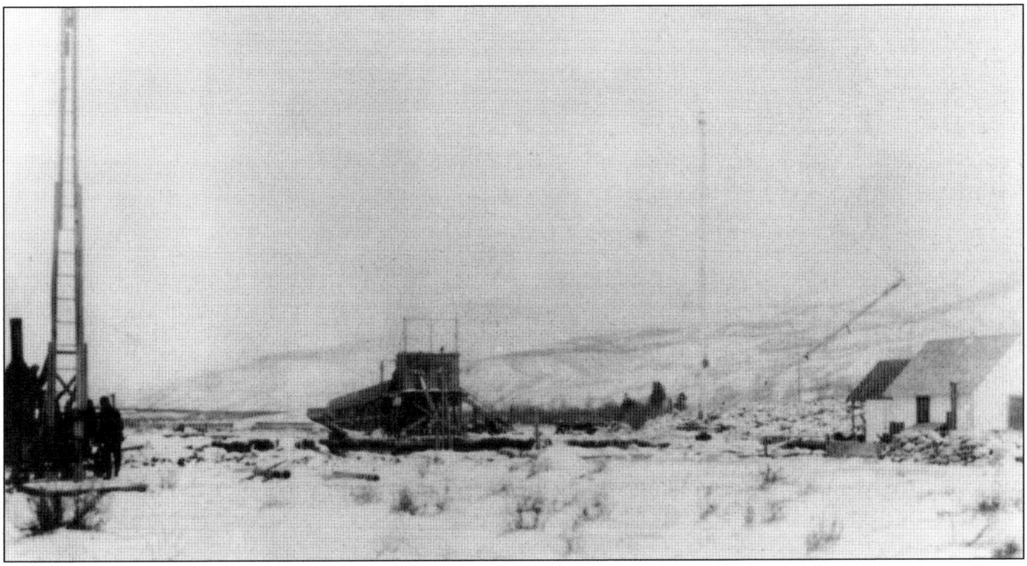

MINING WITH DREDGES. Oro Grande Company was one of the many who worked the river valleys. The piles of rock created by dredging operations surrounded the placer mining area of Blue River Valley. The photograph, dated 1910, is looking east. (Courtesy of Summit Historical Society.)

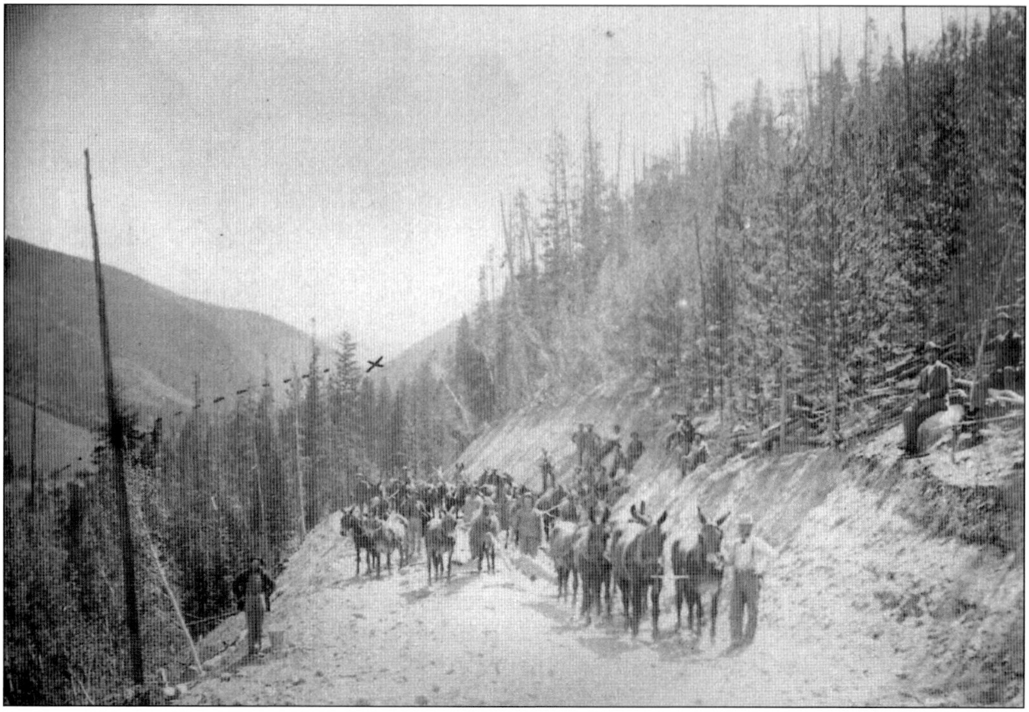

Silver and Gold Trail. This extremely rare *c.* 1900 photograph shows the initial building of the Swan Mountain Road. The mules, part-time miners, and construction workers took a second to pose for the photographer. (Courtesy of Summit Historical Society.)

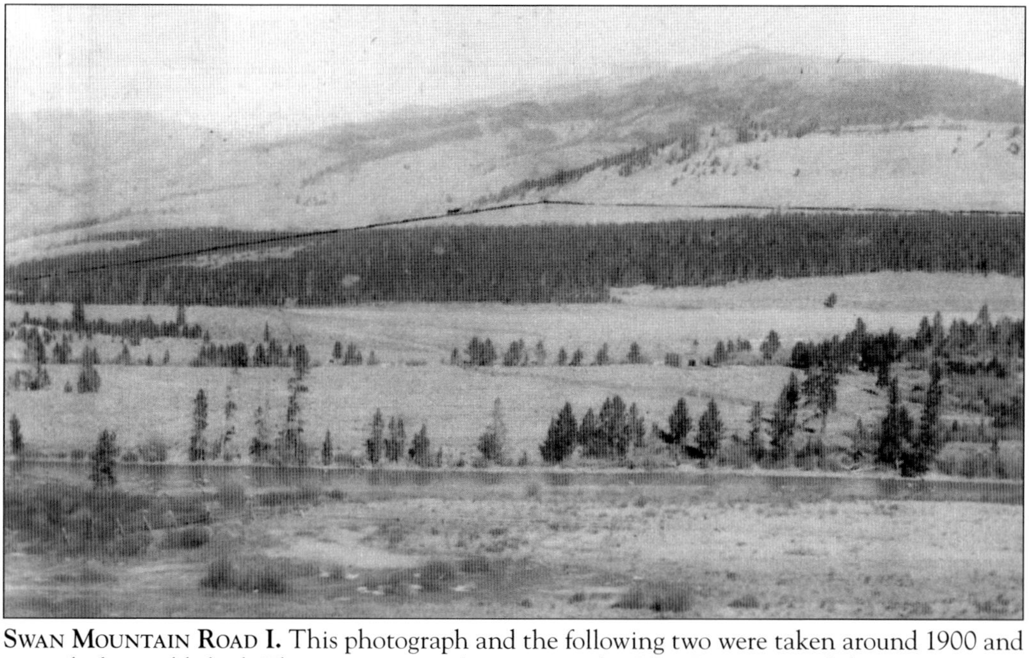

Swan Mountain Road I. This photograph and the following two were taken around 1900 and never before published. The viewpoint is from across the Blue River toward the east at Swan Mountain. The line, which is hand-drawn, shows the approximate route that the road takes. It was subsequently used by the Swan Mountain miners. (Courtesy of Summit Historical Society.)

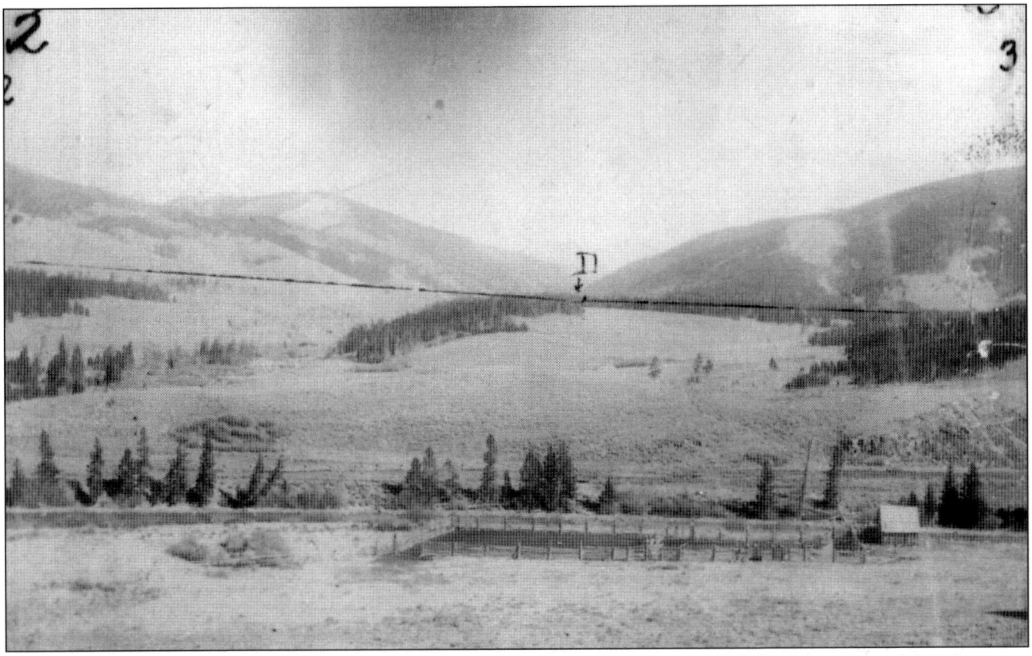

Swan Mountain Road II. The line drawn by hand is a continuation of this photograph, indicating where the Swan Mountain Road was constructed. (Courtesy of Summit Historical Society.)

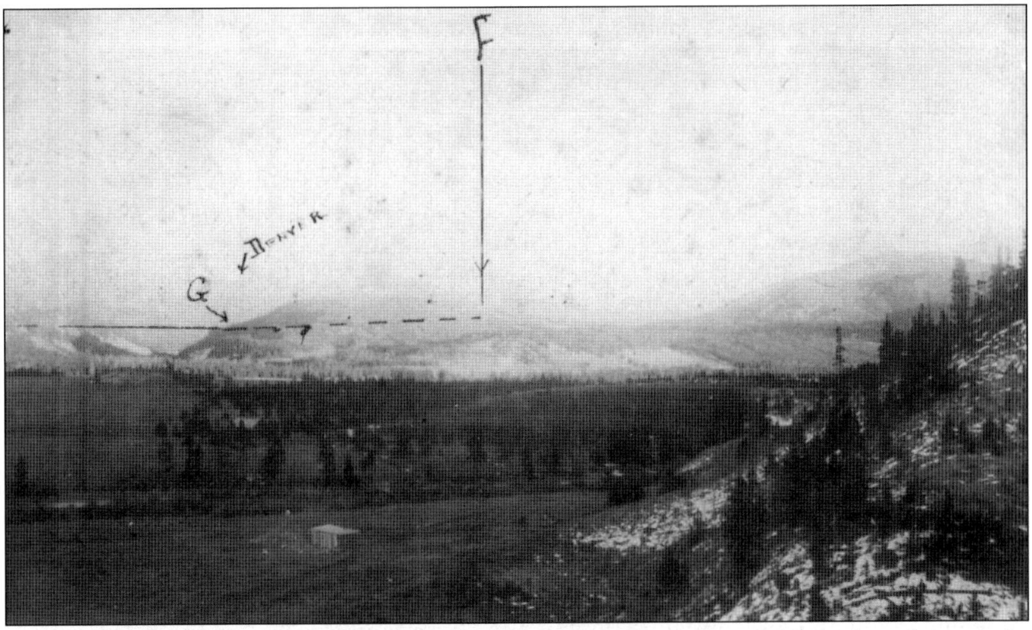

Swan Mountain Road III. This photograph depicts a continuation of the other photographs on these two pages showing the construction of Swan Mountain Road. This became the miners' gold road as they descended the side of Swan Mountain to reach the valley floor and the Blue River. From there, they had a choice of going to Breckenridge, Frisco, or Dillon. (Courtesy of Summit Historical Society.)

ACROSS AMERICA, PEOPLE ARE DISCOVERING SOMETHING WONDERFUL. *THEIR HERITAGE.*

Arcadia Publishing is the leading local history publisher in the United States. With more than 5,000 titles in print and hundreds of new titles released every year, Arcadia has extensive specialized experience chronicling the history of communities and celebrating America's hidden stories, bringing to life the people, places, and events from the past. To discover the history of other communities across the nation, please visit:

www.arcadiapublishing.com

Customized search tools allow you to find regional history books about the town where you grew up, the cities where your friends and family live, the town where your parents met, or even that retirement spot you've been dreaming about.

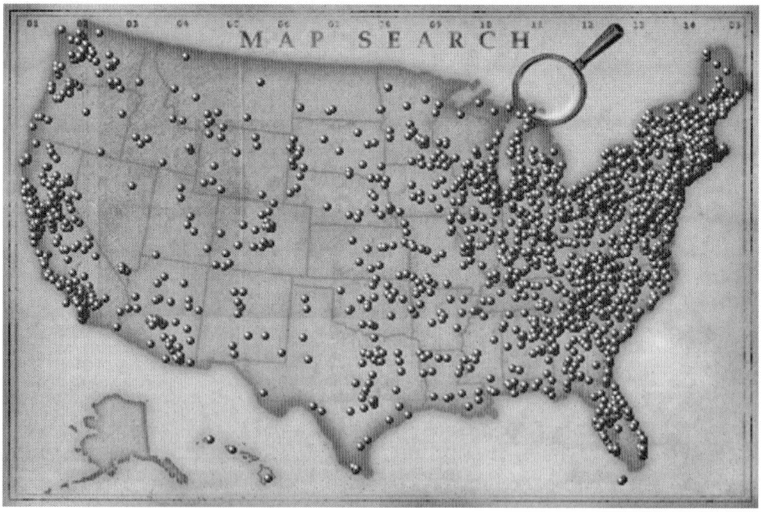